Job Analysis

A Guide to Assessing Work Activities

Sidney Gael

JOB ANALYSIS

A Guide to Assessing Work Activities

JOB ANALYSIS
A Guide to Assessing Work Activities
   by Sidney Gael

Copyright © 1983 by: Jossey-Bass Inc., Publishers
                      433 California Street
                      San Francisco, California 94104

                          &

                      Jossey-Bass Limited
                      28 Banner Street
                      London EC1Y 8QE

Library of Congress Cataloging in Publication Data

Gael, Sidney,
  Job analysis.

  Bibliography: p. 273
  Includes index.
  1. Job analysis.   I. Title.
HF5549.5.J6G33   1983   658.3′06   82-49036
ISBN 0-87589-564-6

Manufactured in the United States of America

The paper in this book meets the guidelines for
permanence and durability of the Committee on
Production Guidelines for Book Longevity of the
Council on Library Resources.

JACKET DESIGN BY WILLI BAUM

FIRST EDITION

Code 8309

A joint publication in
The Jossey-Bass Management Series
and
The Jossey-Bass
Social and Behavioral Science Series

Preface

Job analysis results can benefit practically every program of interest to human resource specialists and other practitioners whose work pertains to organization personnel. The importance and utility of job analysis in the world of work can be seen in the proliferation of job and task analysis conferences and workshops offered by universities, companies, and professional associations. In addition, current issues of professional journals in industrial/organizational psychology, human factors, ergonomics, and personnel unfailingly contain information about job analysis. Job analysis results have been used to develop job descriptions for use in other human resource programs, for instance, job evaluation; to design or redesign jobs; to devise employment and placement procedures; to establish organizational staffing requirements and spans of control; to determine training requirements; to evaluate employee job performance; and to review operations by comparing actual to desired performance within jobs and identifying overlap between jobs. Further, the federal government has mandated that new employment selection procedures be predicated on job analysis results. The goal of job analysis since its initial applications has been to enhance efficiency. In the early 1900s, job analysis techniques focused on elemental work motions and the time it took to perform them. Since then, job analysis methods have cycled through stages of loose, unsystematic examinations of global job aspects to rigorous, quantitative, systematic job studies in which large amounts of data are collected and analyzed. Still, the job analysis literature is replete with examples of confusion about job analysis in general, about definitions of key terms, and about specific applications of methods and techniques.

The job inventory approach has become one of the most popular means for analyzing jobs, probably because results obtained with a single application can be used to satisfy several objectives. This book provides comprehensive information about the job inventory approach to job analysis — how it came to be, how to plan, coordinate, and manage job inventory projects, how to derive task statements and develop and administer job inventory questionnaires to collect job task data, and how to analyze by computer the data collected and interpret the resulting quantitative information. In short, this book is a step-by-step, "how to" guide to accomplishing job analysis projects from beginning to end, with minimal use of or reliance on consultants; when job analysis consultants are employed, managers can use it to monitor their work.

To take advantage of the flexibility and power offered by job inventory analyses, a project was initiated at American Telephone and Telegraph (AT&T) in 1973 to develop a job inventory approach that would enable managers to collect and analyze detailed job content data. The result was the Work Performance Survey System (WPSS). Computer programs, essential for analyzing the kind and volume of data collected with WPSS questionnaires, were tailor-made to meet specific requirements — for example, to make it easy for managers inexperienced with interactive computer systems to use WPSS software to analyze job task data. The unique WPSS interactive computer programs and procedures that evolved through trials by fire can easily analyze large or small amounts of survey data, and the programs are available to the general public for a fee under a license agreement with AT&T, as described in Part Two of this guide. The programs, by the way, are quite versatile and can be used to analyze almost any type of questionnaire survey data.

Assiduous review of the job analysis literature may uncover some procedural guidance, but published "how to" information is indeed scarce; even less instruction can be found on the computerization and analysis of job data. This guide is intended to fill some of the void; it will help practitioners, researchers, and consultants working in business or industrial organizations, labor unions, universities, the military, or for federal, state, and local governments to help design and carry out job analysis projects. College and university faculty will also find it useful as a supplementary text for courses in industrial engineering, industrial/organizational psychology, human factors engineering, ergonomics, personnel administration, labor relations, and general management.

Each chapter in the book begins with a brief introduction and a list of objectives that the reader should be able to accomplish after studying the chapter. The material has been written and organized so that users can zero in on topics of interest. Part One contains eight chapters:

Chapter One describes the job inventory approach to job analysis and introduces readers to WPSS. Chapter Two presents a brief history of the job inventory approach, focusing on the reliability and validity of job inventory data and relative percent time spent performing tasks. Chapter Three is a detailed overview of the WPSS approach written especially for WPSS planners. Chapter Four shows how to write task statements for inclusion in a WPSS questionnaire and describes methods for analyzing and documenting job content and for observing job incumbents in order to obtain job information and derive task statements. Chapter Five describes how to plan and conduct interviews with job incumbents and supervisors to obtain job task information. Chapter Six covers the development, production, and distribution of WPSS questionnaires. Chapter Seven considers the interpretation and use of results obtained by analyzing WPSS questionnaire data. Chapter Eight discusses shortcut procedures for obtaining job task information that can be applied in small organizations and under special circumstances.

Part Two is a guide to using WPSS computer programs to enter questionnaire data in the computer, analyze the data, and obtain computer printouts that summarize the results. WPSS interactive computer printouts have been designed to enable inexperienced computer users to carry out WPSS analyses. The computer system is "user friendly" and prompts the user step-by-step throughout computer terminal sessions. All prompts and responses are in English and no special computer language is required.

Those who are concerned primarily with planning and managing job analysis projects can concentrate on Chapters One and Three; those who will actually apply the job analysis techniques and collect data should become familiar with all the procedural information. Users should understand that WPSS is a powerful tool designed to provide detailed information about jobs, and its use requires a commitment to the study of jobs and work, plus an investment of time and effort. Scaled-down WPSS procedures are also presented and can be applied when there are cost, resource, or time constraints or when there are too few job incumbents or work sites to feasibly apply the full WPSS approach. Naturally, job content information is sacrificed when a shortcut procedure is introduced.

My knowledge of and work in job analysis was nurtured by many individuals. First and foremost is H. Wayne Gustafson, my colleague at AT&T, who first proposed that the job inventory approach would be ideally suited for broad application to Bell System jobs; in fact, he had directed a couple of small applications before I arrived on the scene. I thank him for the conceptual and moral support and advice he provided.

Since both Gustafson and I worked for the U.S. Air Force (USAF), it was only natural that we borrow freely from its work on the job inventory approach. My debt of gratitude to the USAF, however, was engendered much earlier, in the late fifties, when I worked at the Aeromedical Research Laboratories, Wright-Patterson Air Force Base, Ohio, with Melvin T. Snyder, Col. Walter F. Murphy, Col. E. D. Stackfleth, and Jack D. Adams. They introduced me to, and steeped me in, task equipment analysis, qualitative personnel requirements information (another "Q" for *quantitative* was added later), personnel subsystems, human engineering, and the system's approach. It was also through an Air Force education program that I met Robert J. Wherry, Sr., who became my Ph.D. advisor. I cannot sufficiently express an appropriate degree of gratitude in this brief space for his contribution to my development—those of you who have been as fortunate as I to have so magnificent a mentor will appreciate my feeling.

My indebtedness to the USAF continued even after I started working at AT&T. We were fortunate to have Col. Howard Parris, the chief scientist at the Air Force Human Resources Laboratory, Brooks Air Force Base, Texas, and a former colleague at the Aeromedical Research Laboratories, honor my request for a meeting with Raymond E. Christal. Christal delved with us into the depths of the Comprehensive Occupational Data Analysis Programs (CODAP). Oh, how sweet it would have been if CODAP had fulfilled our software needs, but the package did not. Despite all the cooperation to help us run when we were learning to crawl, we eventually had to invent our own wheel.

I would like to single out Malcolm B. Gillette and Richard J. Campbell, both of AT&T, from among the many Bell System employees who contributed to the development of WPSS because of their strong commitment to the work through the tough developmental years. Less foresighted managers would have thrown in the towel long before the system was completed.

This book benefited significantly from a report on WPSS prepared several years ago under my direction by Applied Psychological Services, Wayne, Pennsylvania, and from a previous version I wrote for AT&T use. The WPSS computer programs and procedures, without which there would be no system, were developed under my direction by Joseph D. H. Sidley of J. D. H. Sidley Associates, Alexandria, Virginia. Luckily for me, Sidley was creative and hardly ever constrained by my rudimentary system specifications.

Every issue cannot possibly be addressed or resolved by a guide of this nature, but I hope that the pertinent ones are covered. So, although this guide is not guaranteed to turn every user into a job analysis expert, a user who follows the proposed procedures can develop objective, accurate, and complete information about a job or set of jobs.

Mendham, New Jersey   Sidney Gael
February 1983

Contents

**Part Two: User Manual
for Computerizing WPSS Data**

Figures

The Author

Sidney Gael is an industrial psychologist at the American Telephone and Telegraph Company, where for the past fifteen years he has conducted personnel research. He received his B.S. degree (1957) in psychology from Hunter College, his M.S. degree (1959) in psychology from Pennsylvania State University, and his Ph.D. degree (1966) in industrial psychology from Ohio State University. He is a member of the American Psychological Association, the Society of Industrial and Organizational Psychology, the Society of Engineering Psychologists, and the Human Factors Society. He is a certified psychologist in New York State.

Gael's research, method development, and writing have covered a broad spectrum of industrial and organizational psychology. His test validation experience includes directing a series of nationwide research projects that served as the basis for setting employment test standards for many Bell System jobs, and he has served as an expert witness before the Federal Court in equal employment opportunity litigation. He has developed a job inventory approach to job analysis, and is presently engaged in research on job analysis methods and procedures. Other current research interests include job performance evaluation and appraisal, as well as job and organization design. Gael also is developing tools and methods to help optimize the introduction of new technology while minimizing its impact on employees. He is the author of *Work Performance Survey System: A Job Analysis Procedural Guide* (1981) and is now preparing another book — *Handbook of Job Analysis.*

As a research psychologist at the Aerospace Medical Research Laboratories, Wright-Patterson Air Force Base, Ohio, Gael participated in the development of the Personnel Subsystem concept. He has been a faculty member in the Department of Psychology at the University of Bridgeport and at Hunter College.

To my wife, Eviemou, for love and steadfast faith, and to my mom and dad, Frieda and Morris, for generosity and support when they were difficult to come by.

Part One

Collecting and Analyzing Data on Job Activities

1

◳◳

Job Inventories and the Work Performance Survey System (WPSS)

◳◳

Jobs are analyzed in many organizations throughout the world in support of human resource planning and development activities. The importance and usefulness of precise job analysis results are quite apparent, given the impact of information about jobs on decisions regarding employees and organizations; in fact, most human resource programs, such as employment and training, depend to a large extent on accurate job information. One of the most frequently employed means for analyzing jobs is the job inventory approach, sometimes referred to as the task inventory approach. That job inventories are at all popular is due mainly to extensive U.S. Air Force (USAF) research and applications that have demonstrated that job inventories, if systematically developed and applied, yield reliable, useful information about jobs — a finding corroborated by work conducted in other military branches, in business and industrial organizations, in consulting firms, and in universities that use job inventories to obtain information about activities performed by job incumbents. Also contributing significantly to the popularity of the job inventory approach to job analysis are the following advantages: First, it is possible to acquire detailed information about job activities actually performed by incumbents working at a number of geographically dispersed work sites throughout an organization. Second, job inventory results can be used to address more than one objective at a time. Third, managers and analysts can carry out a job analysis project with only a modicum of job analysis training.

After completing this chapter, you should be able to:

1. Define key terms used in job inventory analysis.
2. Describe the Work Performance Survey System (WPSS).
3. Determine when to use the Work Performance Survey System.
4. List several uses for Work Performance Survey System results.

Before going any further, let us clarify the term *job inventory*. As with other terms used in job analysis, there is more than one way to think of a job inventory. Very simply, the kind of job inventory that is the focus of this guide is a comprehensive list of the tasks that are performed to accomplish a job or set of jobs — a list that is cast in the form of a questionnaire. Figure 1 shows a page from a job inventory questionnaire. Plainly, the main ingredient is the list of task statements about which questions are asked and responses are required. As you can see by the headings of the response columns in Figure 1, questionnaire respondents are being asked for information about the significance of each task that incumbents perform and the time they devote to performing each task.

The number of tasks included in a job inventory depends on the job(s) covered and can run anywhere from 100 to 500 or more tasks. The responses required are generally numbers that represent differing degrees of attributes being rated; for instance, a scale pertaining to the relative importance of job tasks may be presented as follows:

1 — Very much below average   4 — Above average
2 — Below average   5 — Slightly above average
3 — Slightly below average   6 — Above average
              7 — Very much above average

Figure 1. WPSS Questionnaire Page.

	Part B				Part C
	SIGNIFICANCE				TIME SPENT
Task List	Not Part / Minor	Substantial		Most significant	0 = No Time 1 = Very small 2 = Small 3 = Slightly less 4 = As much 5 = Slightly more 6 = More 7 = Very much more
232 Develop corrective action for substandard service.	0 1 2 3 4 5 6 7				_____
233 Examine customer records to obtain facts regarding customer complaint.	0 1 2 3 4 5 6 7				_____
234 Give advice or consent to a response on union grievance.	0 1 2 3 4 5 6 7				_____
235 Negotiate or discuss complaint (informal) with union representative.	0 1 2 3 4 5 6 7				_____
236 Notify customer or appropriate company personnel of disposition of customer complaint, claim, or inquiry.	0 1 2 3 4 5 6 7				_____
237 Obtain advice for a response to a union grievance.	0 1 2 3 4 5 6 7				_____
238 Participate in grievance meeting.	0 1 2 3 4 5 6 7				_____
239 Perform lower-level managerial or supervisory tasks temporarily.	0 1 2 3 4 5 6 7				_____
240 Provide customer records to Legal Department, court, or utility commission.	0 1 2 3 4 5 6 7				_____
241 Refer procedural question to staff for resolution.	0 1 2 3 4 5 6 7				_____
242 Resolve an office personnel, disciplinary, or dismissal issue.	0 1 2 3 4 5 6 7				_____
243 Resolve billing or listing problem with independent telephone company.	0 1 2 3 4 5 6 7				_____
244 Schedule grievance meeting.	0 1 2 3 4 5 6 7				_____
245 Testify before a court or commission regarding customer records.	0 1 2 3 4 5 6 7				_____
246 Write office procedure to resolve a problem.	0 1 2 3 4 5 6 7				_____

After you have completed all the
SIGNIFICANCE responses, turn to
Part C Instructions on the next page.

After you have completed all the
TIME SPENT responses, turn to
Part D Instructions, the last part
of this booklet.

The idea is for the respondent to read the task statement, decide how important that task is compared with all other tasks that the incumbent performs, select the appropriate code number that corresponds to the answer, and record the code number in the appropriate space on the job inventory questionnaire. There are many kinds of scales in use; in addition to those presented above and in Figure 1, others can be seen in Figures 15 through 19.

A job inventory questionnaire is structured so that job incumbents, supervisors, and other job-knowledgeable employees can be surveyed about the tasks that job incumbents perform to accomplish their work. Information can also be obtained from respondents about such personal items as their educational level, company tenure, and time in present position. Many other personal information items that are described in this book can be included in a job inventory questionnaire. It is up to the analyst to make certain that an inventory contains those questions that will provide the information needed. Information about materials, tools, and equipment used to accomplish work, working conditions, working hours, and training courses taken or needed can all be included in the background or personal information section of a questionnaire. Of course, a system will be needed to track, code, and analyze the answers obtained. The data can be tracked and coded manually, or a means can be designed so that a computer does the work. If training information is of interest, for example, one way to make it easier to computerize answers is to list a variety of the most likely training courses in the personal information section, along with associated code numbers (see Figure 22 for job title and education code numbers). Respondents then need only place checkmarks in the appropriate boxes — it is the code number that is entered into the computer. The same, of course, would hold true for materials, tools, equipment, and other items so listed.

The results obtained by analyzing questionnaire responses are primarily statistical indices or tabulations that describe task attributes, such as the significance or difficulty level of each task and the incumbents who perform the tasks. Individual task data can be combined to develop values that describe broader job activities, such as functions. Then, of course, it is up to the analyst to relate the statistical results to the objective(s) that the job analysis was supposed to achieve.

The rationale underlying the use of job inventories is that the basic source of job information is the on-the-job tasks performed by job incumbents; that job tasks can be stated and listed in a questionnaire; that as large a sample as is desired can be surveyed to obtain data about each task listed in the job inventory questionnaire; and that accurate and reliable job descriptions can be developed by systematically and thoroughly analyzing the task data collected with a job inventory. For a full-scale job inventory, computer analysis of data is an absolute necessity—the kind and volume of data collected with extensive job inventory questionnaires prohibit manual data analysis. It may be feasible to analyze job inventory data manually for a brief questionnaire administered to a very small sample, but that would be a special situation (see Chapter Eight for shortcut procedures).

Accurate and complete information can be obtained about a job with a job inventory only if the survey questionnaire is designed correctly and a respondent sample is selected appropriately. Explicit specifications regarding the information desired about a job or set of jobs and the job incumbents should be formulated when a job inventory project is initiated to make certain that the questionnaire includes those questions that will result in the desired information. Job inventory results can support a number of organizational programs because of the large amount and type of data that incumbents furnish about actual work performed. The list of tasks and their associated data is, in essence, a detailed job description. Since the data, the statistical results, the questionnaires, and the analytical procedures are stored in a computer, they are easily accessible for future use. Further, the system used to process and analyze the data provides an orderly means for disseminating a variety of job and sample details to human resource planners.

Task, Function, and Job

The job analysis literature is replete with terms—such as *job, position, module, duty, function, task, subtask,* and *element*—that are used to refer to work activities. Unfortunately, these terms do not have the same meaning for all job analysts. The reason is that different analysts associate different levels of specificity with particular terms. There is, however, an agreed-on hierarchy, ranging from the general to the specific, for the three work activity terms used throughout this guidebook, namely, *task, function,* and *job.* But is there a correct level of specificity for describing work? There are no hard-and-fast rules for deciding whether an adequate specificity level has been attained and whether all tasks are about equal in size or complexity. Task analysis, after all, is not a science. An analyst needs a general sense for the level of detail required. Will the task information obtained be useful for the purpose at hand? If the information obtained is too general, it will not be useful; if it is too specific, however, the information will be difficult to manipulate and integrate. Once a specificity level has been selected, the important thing is consistency — all work activities should be stated at the specificity level selected, should be approximately equal in size and complexity, should not overlap, and, in the aggregate, should provide a clear, complete picture of the job.

Dictionary definitions of *task* — to take the work activity term most commonly used in this guide — state that a task is an assigned piece or amount of work to be done, generally under a time limit. Synonyms presented in the dictionary are "duty," "job," "chore," "stint," and "assignment," and a check with a thesaurus yielded a few more, such as "toil," "work," "mission," and "charge." According to McCormick (1979), the USAF *Handbook for Designers of Instructional Systems* defines a task as a group of related, manual, goal-directed activities that have a definite beginning and end; it involves interaction with equipment, other people, and/or media; and when performed, it results in a meaningful product. A task, the *Handbook* continues, includes a mixture of decisions, perceptions, and/or physical activities required of one person, may be of any size or degree of complexity, and must be directed toward a specific purpose or separate portion of a total duty. In an analysis of education programs for dental auxiliary jobs, Terry and Evans (1973) reviewed a number of job analysis articles and found the following definitions of the term *task*:

- An action or sequence of actions performed closely together in time and directed toward an objective, common goal or outcome.
- A unit of work that is a consistent and significant part of a duty or is a logical and necessary step in the performance of a duty.
- An orderly, homogeneous grouping of goal-oriented human activities applied methodically to things or equipment and usually performed by one person in less than a day. Task activities have an observable start and stop and are composed of elements or simple discrete responses that are carried out in a cumulative and progressive sequence.
- A series or set of work activities needed to produce an identifiable output that can be independently consumed or used or can be used as an input in a further stage of production by the performer or someone else.

Since *task, function,* and *job* are terms used throughout this guide, the meaning of each as used in the guide is presented below. These definitions were formed from those commonly found in the job analysis literature (McCormick, 1979; Melching and Borcher, 1973):

- *Task* — a discrete organized unit of work, with a definite beginning and end, performed by an individual to accomplish the goals of a job. A task is described by a statement that starts with an action verb and includes the object of that verb. Tasks performed by job incumbents can be divided into finer and finer segments. As a general rule, tasks should be stated at a level and in a form suitable to meet the job analysis objectives at hand. Greater degrees of task specificity and detail are usually reserved for specialized technical purposes — for example, preparing training materials or maintenance manuals. Some examples of tasks are to solder leaks in a radiator, to schedule basic input for a manual data system, and to operate a paper tape punch and reader.
- *Function* — a broad subdivision of a job composed of a group of tasks that are somewhat related because of the nature of the work or the behavior involved, such as acquiring information.

There appear to be two types of functions: (1) supervisory
(organizing, planning, directing, developing, and so on) and
(2) direct work (maintaining, repairing, operating, and so on).
Functions are generally expressed with action words ending in
"ing." Examples of functions include performing preventive
maintenance, collecting data, and developing subordinates.

- *Job* — an amalgam of functions performed by individual employees. When the same group of functions is performed by a
set of employees, they are said to have the same job.

A task statement, then, is a written description of a task,
and it follows a specific, standard format. Task statements should
cover what is actually done to what. Job inventory questionnaires
are built around a list of task statements, and data are obtained
about each task statement in the list.

Functions can be formed by grouping tasks in one of several
ways, for example, intuitively or statistically. The particular type
of approach adopted and the kind of functions formed will depend
on a combination of factors, such as the analyst's orientation, the
objectives of the job analysis, and the situation that exists when
the job analysis is initiated. Functions can be formed before or
after task data are collected. Though it is not necessary to establish functions before a job inventory is administered, it is advantageous to do so. If functions are formed afterward, the opportunity to ask questions about the functions that job incumbents perform will either be lost or will have to await the administration of
another procedure designed to collect function data. After a job
inventory has been administered and task data have been obtained, certain statistical techniques, such as factor analysis or
cluster analysis, can be applied to the task data to identify work
dimensions or task clusters that can be regarded as functions. If
functions are formed beforehand, then statistically derived functions can be compared with the functions previously formed to
determine how closely they agree.

Functions can be thought of as job related, worker related,
or organization related. When job tasks are the starting point for
forming functions, as they are in the bottom-up approach described
in this guide, the end result will be either job-related or worker-

related functions. Once all the tasks that will be included in a job inventory questionnaire are available, job experts can categorize them into functions according to a guiding principle, such as the similarity of the work content, even before any task data are collected. The principle followed will determine the specific functions that will be formed: For instance, tasks may be grouped in terms of the broad job activities performed, such as negotiating with customers regardless of the reason for the negotiation; or they may be grouped less broadly in accordance with specific services provided, such as sales negotiations or bill collection negotiations. If job tasks are grouped into functions on the basis of worker behaviors, such as calculating, acquiring information, or performing clerical work, the functions formed are considered worker related. In the case of organizational functions, the organization's objectives are the starting point for determining functions — a top-down approach — and the functions that must be performed to achieve those objectives are derived without regard for or reference to jobs. Once organizational functions have been specified, function-associated inputs and outputs can be identified, and tasks that have to be performed to convert inputs into outputs can be determined. Jobs can then be designed by grouping tasks in accordance with appropriate job design principles. The top-down approach is especially useful when one is planning for and designing future jobs. The top-down and statistical approaches to determining job functions will be discussed only briefly in this book.

Job inventory questionnaires by their nature are used almost exclusively to analyze existing jobs, but it is possible to apply them in analyses of jobs that are still in the conceptual stage. The approach, of course, will have to be modified somewhat since job incumbents and supervisors are not yet available; subject matter experts will have to be relied upon to help develop the job inventories and also to serve as respondents in lieu of job incumbents and supervisors.

The term *job analysis* usually refers to a process whereby a job is dissected into its component parts and those parts are studied to decipher the nature of the work. As used in this guide, it means breaking a job down into tasks performed by job incumbents, synthesizing those tasks into job functions, and obtaining data about and studying those tasks and functions. Although this guide concentrates on a questionnaire approach to job analysis, several other techniques often used to analyze jobs are covered in detail, inasmuch as they are recommended for deriving task statements. So, even if you do not plan to use the job inventory approach, you will find information here that will help you plan job analyses and apply techniques that can be used with other kinds of job analysis approaches.

A distinction can be drawn between:

- *Information pertaining to the work itself*—the specific tasks and attributes of those tasks, such as importance, difficulty, and frequency; and
- *Information associated with, but not directly involved in, the work itself*—the skills and abilities needed to perform the work adequately, along with the characteristics of the environment in which the work is performed.

This guide is concerned almost exclusively with the first type of information. Information about the work itself is obtained directly from those employees best informed about current job content; the second type of information is obtained through follow-up work with Work Performance Survey System task information as a basic input. Results achieved with the Work Performance Survey System are invaluable for obtaining follow-up data, but a different methodology is required.

Work Performance Survey System (WPSS)

Task statements and job inventory questionnaires usually are developed and applied within a larger framework that guides the form that a job inventory questionnaire takes, the way job data are collected and analyzed, and the way results are presented. The framework that is the focus of this guidebook is the Work Performance Survey System (WPSS), a computer-aided job inventory approach developed at the American Telephone and Telegraph Company (AT&T). Tasks and functions are the units used in the WPSS process to describe and characterize jobs. From this point on, WPSS will be used in place of the term *job inventory*, except in the discussion of job inventory history.

WPSS was designed primarily to produce information that managers can use to reach effective human resource-planning and administrative decisions and, secondarily, to improve and facilitate the job inventory process — that is, deriving job tasks, obtaining quantitative data about those tasks directly from job incumbents and other job-knowledgeable employees with tailor-made WPSS questionnaires, and analyzing the data with specially developed, easy-to-use computer programs. WPSS projects have been conducted at AT&T mainly to establish the way that a given job is actually performed throughout the Bell System telephone companies, both overall and at different locations. To accomplish this, WPSS questionnaires generally have been administered to samples of job incumbents working at different job sites nationwide, and the data have been analyzed by location to identify differences and similarities in the way the work is performed. Of course, it was necessary to develop a computerized data analysis system capable of analyzing WPSS data by location (company, state, city, plant, or work group).

WPSS is ideally suited for analyzing jobs performed by many widely separated employees. Large amounts of job data can be accumulated much more economically with a WPSS questionnaire than with other job analysis methods, and the built-in uniformity allows for similar interpretations and comparisons of job data obtained at a number of different locations. When location differences are not important, job data can be collected at only a few sites (to enhance representativeness) and analyzed for the total sample.

There is no substitute for WPSS-like job analysis when hundreds or thousands of geographically separated job incumbents perform the target jobs and large samples of incumbents and supervisors are expected to provide highly specific details about job activities. Whether WPSS or a less powerful job analysis approach is appropriate can be determined by answering questions such as the following: What are the reasons for the job analysis? What kinds of results are expected or needed? Where are the target jobs performed? Is job information desired from a sample of locations? How many job incumbents are there? How many job incumbents work at each location? How large a sample of job incumbents is wanted to provide data? What kinds of data are required, for example, quantitative or qualitative? What level of specificity is needed? How will collected data be analyzed? Clearly, WPSS is the appropriate choice when the answers show that:

- Numerous employees perform the jobs to be analyzed.
- A large sample of those employees is expected to provide data about their work.
- The desired sample works at a number of different facilities.
- Quantitative job data are desired.
- A fairly high degree of specific information is desired.
- The type and volume of data anticipated will require computer analysis.

Where broad statements about a job would suffice, such as those found in the *Dictionary of Occupational Titles* (U.S. Department of Labor, 1977), WPSS may be a more powerful tool than is needed. Job descriptions used in an employment office, for instance, usually do not require the same degree of detail as do job descriptions that are needed to help establish training requirements; and if brief job descriptions for employment office use were the sole anticipated application for the job information, then another, simpler means for obtaining the information to prepare those job descriptions would be appropriate. Brief, general job descriptions, of course, can be prepared on the basis of WPSS results.

Each situation has its special circumstances that should be considered carefully. WPSS analysis might be inefficient despite conditions that favor use of the approach—for example, the need to survey a large, nationwide population of job incumbents. If it is known or assumed that job incumbents throughout an organization perform the same activities in about the same way, then observing and/or interviewing one or two job incumbents in depth and generalizing the results will be more efficient than bringing the full power of WPSS into play. The reason for the job analysis in the first place, however, is to learn how work is actually accomplished in a specific job.

WPSS Techniques. WPSS incorporates several techniques to

derive and analyze job content because no single technique will produce the specificity, objectivity, and amount of job information desired in an analysis of a job or jobs performed at a number of geographically separated worksites. Specifically, the techniques recommended for deriving task statements for target jobs and obtaining task data are as follows:

- *Observation.* Job incumbents are observed performing their work and questioned at any stage of their performance. Films and photographs may be used to study job activities. Observation is most useful with jobs composed of physically active tasks. For many jobs observation may be of limited use because all that is seen is an employee sitting at a desk, reading documents, and occasionally completing a form; or an employee may be observed working at a console, repeatedly activating a set of controls. Even in the case of jobs composed of more physically active tasks, however, observation reveals little about basic task attributes, such as task importance and task difficulty; and observation does not necessarily take in the full range of activities performed. To compensate for these limitations, it is helpful to have a job expert available for consultation during job observations, and additional methods for obtaining job information should of course be employed.
- *Content Analysis.* Materials written about a job, such as company practices, job descriptions, and training materials, can be used as sources of job task information. While content analysis of job documents can provide useful information about a job, the results should be checked, because the documents may no longer accurately describe the way incumbents actually accomplish their work. As is true of observation, content analysis by itself probably will not uncover the full range of work activities.
- *Interview.* Job incumbents, supervisors, and other job-knowledgeable employees are interviewed about actual work activities performed by job incumbents. Interviews alone might be appropriate to obtain task information when only a few employees holding the job of interest are all working at the same or nearby locations. It is not feasible, however, to rely exclusively on interviews to obtain WPSS data.

- *Questionnaire.* Job incumbents and supervisors complete specially developed WPSS questionnaires to provide information about tasks and functions actually performed by job incumbents. The use of questionnaires is most efficient when many widely dispersed employees are to be questioned about the work they perform. WPSS questionnaires are especially useful to assess similarities and differences among jobs or in the "same" job performed at numerous locations.

Practically all tasks statements listed in WPSS questionnaires are based on information obtained from interviews with job incumbents and supervisors and content analyses of written materials. Observations of incumbents performing their work play a minor role in deriving tasks statements and serve mainly to familiarize job analysts with the job environment. Altogether, the job information obtained is used to compile a list of the tasks performed by job incumbents, and the task list becomes the main part of a WPSS questionnaire. The questionnaires are administered to large samples of job incumbents to obtain data about each task listed in the questionnaire. Accurate, detailed job descriptions can then be developed by analyzing WPSS questionnaire responses with specially developed computer programs.

A variety of job analysis approaches is available, and various job analysis techniques can be combined and utilized in numerous ways. Differences in the job inventory approach alone can be found as a result of the different techniques used to derive task statements, design questionnaires, collect and analyze data, and interpret and present results. A controlling guideline during the design of WPSS was to incorporate the utmost flexibility into it, especially in the way job data are collected and analyzed. WPSS data, however, must be entered into the computer and stored and retrieved in accordance with very specific rules (Part Two of this guidebook covers WPSS data processing in detail). Moreover, WPSS computer programs are available to the public under a license agreement with AT&T as described in Part Two.

WPSS Uses. The primary users of WPSS probably will be managers who want detailed information about the way a job is performed throughout an organization, though anyone responsible for or interested in employee performance should consider WPSS as a potential tool—for example, WPSS could be the central component in a dynamic personnel management system. Results generated by applying WPSS can be used to carry out a number of personnel research, administration, and management functions. These include:

- Developing job descriptions that can be used for job evaluation, recruiting, employment, and so on.
- Designing or redesigning jobs.
- Devising employment and placement procedures that match applicant skills with job requirements.
- Establishing organizational staffing requirements and spans of control.
- Determining training requirements.
- Conducting operations reviews by comparing actual to desired performance within jobs and identifying overlapping tasks between jobs.
- Evaluating employee job performance on a comprehensive task-by-task rating form.

Once detailed task data are available, important or critical task statements can serve the uses listed above. Details associated with the procedures for using task statements identified as important will be covered later. Put briefly, however, two ways that important task statements can be used are (1) to include them in an employee job performance evaluation form and (2) to list them on a rating table or impact matrix. In the first case, employee job performance can be rated on a task-by-task basis; in the second case, the involvement matrix procedure can help bridge the gap between work actually performed and such factors of interest as skill and ability requirements, job design dimensions, and job evaluation elements. Basically, the idea is to use the involvement matrix to determine the degree to which various factors of interest are involved in the accomplishment of each important task. An involvement matrix was developed for and applied in a study of telephone company clerical jobs to determine the skills and abilities required, that is, the job qualifications. Twelve abilities and skills were used as column headings in the matrix, and immediate supervisors, after an orientation to the method, rated the degree to which each ability or skill was involved in the accomplishment of each task (row headings). The results obtained allowed an ability-skill profile to be formed for each job studied, and the profiles were compared to establish similarities, differences, and ability-based progression paths.

2

╔══╗

Development of
the Job Inventory
Approach

╚══╝

A nationwide survey of companies (Jones and DeCoths, 1969) revealed that 76 percent of the respondents used some form of job analysis and that task and duty checklists were employed by about 20 percent of the respondents. Unfortunately, it was not possible to determine from the information presented how frequently each of the different methods mentioned was employed or how many jobs were actually analyzed with each method. As a result of comparing several popular job analysis methods on a number of factors, such as the type and generalizability of the information obtained, relative cost, and utilization of results, Moore (1976) concluded that a computer-supported job inventory method had the highest potential and highest overall utility. Numerous job inventory research studies and applications have helped refine the approach to the point where accurate, quantitative descriptions of work performed in target jobs can be obtained by statistically analyzing questionnaire responses. To reach that point, however, required an investment in the job inventory approach of about a quarter of a century of diligent effort and untold resources. The Annotated Bibliography presented later is brief testimony to the work that has been devoted to researching, developing, and applying the job inventory approach to job analysis.

After completing this chapter you should be able to:

1. Describe the history of the job inventory approach to job analysis.
2. Discuss several important issues in the history of the job inventory approach.
3. Describe a few studies attesting to the value of job inventories.

A review of the job analysis literature could foster the impression that the job inventory approach had its beginnings in the early 1950s. As Terry and Evans (1973) have pointed out, however, Allen's *The Instructor, The Man, and The Job* published in 1919, described a trade analysis method that advocated forming lists (inventories) of activities performed in a trade (job). This method concentrated on securing essential facts that would be useful in preparing training courses for trades, and it was used to develop materials that helped prepare over 1,000 instructors representing thirty trades. Allen's method, as well as his work in directing and supervising instructor training centers, received national acclaim during World War I.

Comparisons of job analysis methods conducted for the USAF by Rupe (1952, 1956) and Rupe and Westen (1955a, 1955b) demonstrated that methods in current use had too many flaws. (Rupe's research, by the way, did not bode well for questionnaire surveys designed to obtain job information; in fact, however, the way that the questionnaires were used left a great deal to be desired — respondents were optimistically expected to fill in work activity statements in a free-form style.) About the time that Rupe's series of studies were concluded, the USAF initiated a search for a job analysis procedure that would satisfy a rather long list of requirements (Morsh, Madden, and Christal, 1961). The USAF wanted a job analysis method that could provide up-to-the-minute, quantified data descriptive of work performed; could be applied with small and large samples as often as deemed advisable; could be used to obtain job structure and structure change information directly from job incumbents, supervisors, and other job-knowledgeable individuals; and could provide data in a form capable of being processed electronically. Further, the job analysis should be economical to establish and maintain, amenable to changes dictated by circumstances, and subject to adequacy checks.

A search for this kind of job analysis approach was therefore launched. The search consisted of a survey of job analysis methods being used by government agencies, a review of the occupational analysis literature, and a study of the needs of USAF agencies that would use the job analysis method and results. The search team eventually concluded that some form of job inventory would best meet the specified requirements. Research and development that led to the present USAF job analysis methods was initiated in 1956 (Driskill, 1975). Although the methodology was ready for implementation in 1965, it was not until 1967 that the USAF occupational survey program got off the ground. In the meantime, three U.S. Navy (USN) researchers, Beach, Paolucci, and Milano (Kershner, 1955), had applied an equipment-oriented (as opposed to job-oriented) task inventory to establish personnel and training requirements for a particular type of equipment under study. Incumbents and supervisors working on a number of USN ships were asked to respond to a questionnaire that included questions about the level of the worker performing each task listed in the questionnaire, the level of the supervisor who oversaw the performance of each task, the degree of supervision received or given, and the frequency with which each task was performed.

Two innovations by the USAF enhanced the utility and appeal of the job inventory approach. The first was the inclusion of questions about each task listed in a job inventory for respondents to answer, in addition to having them signify with a conventional checkmark whether or not incumbents perform the tasks. Some of the questions added to task inventories pertained to task importance, task difficulty, and the time devoted to each task. The introduction of such questions, of course, raised issues about the accuracy and usefulness of the information obtained, and research was initiated to determine the utility of the new information and the worthiness of job inventory data in general. The second innovation involved computer processing and analysis of job inventory data. Probably the best known series of computer programs developed specifically to analyze job inventory data is the Comprehensive Occupational Data Analysis Programs (CODAP) developed by the USAF. CODAP is available to the general public through the National Technical Information Service, Springfield, Virginia. Other available software packages developed specifically to analyze job inventory data are AT&T's WPSS and the Task Inventory System (TIS) developed by the Center for Vocational Education, Ohio State University.

The primary computer output usually consists of a list of task statements, plus associated statistical results. One of the CODAP outputs, for instance, is in a format as follows:

Cumulative sum of average percent time spent
by all members . . . .
Average percent time spent by all members . . . .   :
Average percent time spent by   :   :
   members performing . . . .   :   :   :
Percent members performing . . . .   :   :   :   :

        Task Statement   :   :   :   :
                                            ▼   ▼   ▼   ▼
A.1   Analyze office costs and   100.00   5.00   5.00   5.00
      expenses.
A.9   Develop sales promotion   96.00   3.00   2.86   7.86
      program.
A.6   Forecast work volume.   93.50   4.60   4.25   12.11

The various columns show the percent of members who perform each task, the average percent time spent by those members, the average percent time spent by all members, and the cumulative sum of the average percent time spent by all members. Task statements usually are listed according to the percentage of respondents who perform the tasks. Note that CODAP results are percentages presented for a job or set of jobs. WPSS computer printouts (see Figure 23 for instance) also present task or function information in the rows, but the entire printout pertains to a particular attribute, such as significance; the first column of results in the printout represents the total sample, and the other columns represent various subsamples, such as location or different jobs. The cells in WPSS computer printouts contain statistics calculated for the specific task attribute.

Properties of Job Inventory Data

"GIGO" is a familiar acronym to those who work with computer data processing—Garbage In, Garbage Out. The mere capability to computer-analyze enormous volumes of data does not mean that the results will necessarily be good. The worthiness of job inventory data can be studied in a number of ways. In fact, the history of the job inventory approach is for the most part an account of investigations of the properties of job inventory data, such as their reliability and validity. Generally, the results of such investigations are represented numerically either by a correlation coefficient that indicates the degree of relationship between two data sets or by a percentage that represents the degree of the agreement or disagreement between data sets. Reliability and validity are concepts that are easy to understand, but data representing them are hard to come by.

Job Inventory Reliability. The terms *reliability, stability,* and *consistency* often are used interchangeably; evidence that a job inventory possesses sufficient reliability—that is, provides trustworthy information—usually is obtained by studying the degree of agreeement between at least two different views of the same inventory content. If a job inventory is administered twice within a short time period to the same sample, the results obtained should be essentially the same for both administrations. Inasmuch as job inventory data are subjective ratings of task attributes, the confidence placed in the responses, as well as the acceptance of the results, depends in large measure on the amount of agreement found between different raters or for the same raters at different times. Certainly, the credibility of job inventory data would be questionable if ratings of the same tasks by different respondents did not agree substantially.

McCormick (1976) stated that the logical way to assess job inventory reliability is to administer the same inventory to the same respondents not more than a week or two apart and then to compare their corresponding responses. A short time period between inventory administrations is recommended to minimize the chance that the job content will change and erroneously reduce the reliability obtained. Another method for determining job inventory reliability is to consolidate responses to questions about task attributes for an entire sample and compare the consolidated values to those obtained from another similar sample. Job inventory reliability has also been studied with a single administration of questionnaires that contain (1) sets of duplicate task statements, (2) task statements known not to be performed by respondents, and/or (3) tasks that should be performed as a unit. In each case, response veracity can be checked; task frequency responses, for example, should be the same for each task performed as a unit.

McCormick (1960), McCormick and Ammerman (1960), and McCormick and Tombrink (1960) conducted a series of studies for the USAF that produced the following results pertaining to job inventory reliability:

- Reliability coefficients were about the same for task frequency and time required to perform tasks, but they were higher than those obtained for the relative proportion of time spent on tasks and for task difficulty.
- Consistency in reporting task occurrence was not generally related to consistency in reporting other types of task information; in other words, consistency for one scale does not necessarily mean that responses for other scales will be consistent.
- "Lie detector" task statements, or tasks known not to be performed by job incumbents, and other veracity checks were responded to in a consistent way over administrations.
- Task occurrence reliability was higher when relative versus absolute scales were used in the rating process.
- A one-month administration and readministration period produced more reliable time and task difficulty responses than a six-month period, but the six-month period produced more reliable task occurrence responses than the one-month period.
- Responses to questions about task frequency, task time, mental

difficulty, and physical difficulty obtained for highly detailed and moderately detailed activity statements were about equally consistent, but more so than for broadly written activity statements. Broadly written activity statements, however, resulted in more consistent responses than moderately detailed statements when the questions pertained to qualitative features, such as the type of training received or desired; highly detailed statements fell between them but were not significantly different from either.

- Interactions among scales, recall periods, position and equipment types, and response methods were generally negligible.
- Incumbents reporting more types of information about their tasks tended to provide more reliable information than those reporting fewer types of task information.

The USAF series of studies showed that task occurrence information is at the top of the reliability list, followed by time spent on tasks, task importance, and task difficulty. The degree of reliability obtained and the absence of interactions among scales were taken to mean that job inventories were useful for collecting information over a variety of conditions and job specialities. The studies also suggest that there may be differences in the reliability of various types of data reported by incumbents in different job specialties.

In an examination of the relationship between task difficulty and task aptitude, Fugill (1973) had 343 supervisors who were working in eight USAF career ladders rate task difficulty (the time needed to learn to perform a task satsifactorily) on a 7-point difficulty scale. Correlations representing agreement between supervisors in each career field ranged from .87 to .98. Ten behavioral scientists rated the tasks on the degree of aptitude required to learn to perform the tasks, and interrater reliability ranged from .87 to .89, except for one in the .90s. Although the behavioral scientists rated a different factor and the interrater reliability did not achieve the high level obtained for the supervisors, the reliabilities certainly are acceptably high. Mead (1970a, 1970b) and Mead and Christal (1970), using the same definition of difficulty used by Fugill, found that supervisors can agree on the relative difficulty of tasks within an occupation.

Christal (1971) obtained job inventory data from almost

10,000 airmen working in thirty-five job specialties and randomly halved the data per specialty; that is, two samples were formed for each specialty. The percentages of respondents per corresponding sample performing each task were compared with the average percent time spent by the samples on each task. The median reliability coefficients obtained were in the mid to high .90s. Although reliability for individuals tended to be moderate, reliability for pooled sample data was very high. Job inventory information, Christal concluded, is very useful, and the data certainly are adequate for the statistical analyses usually carried out with job inventory data.

Let us examine some job inventory applications in other than military organizations. Terry and Evans (1973) administered a job inventory with 623 task statements to the full-time faculty in nineteen dental auxiliary educational programs and to practicing dentists who were teaching on a limited basis in those programs. The purpose of the study was to determine which tasks were taught in each program and to compare programs. Respondents provided highly stable responses to 60 duplicate task statements contained in the inventory, and agreement between faculty and dentists about whether or not tasks were taught was quite high.

In an unpublished analysis of eight telephone company Business Service Center jobs (American Telephone and Telegraph Company, 1980), the four job inventories used contained nine duplicate task statements. Although the number of veracity statements is small, they were responded to by over 1,100 employees working at sites throughout the country. Responses obtained to questions about task significance, task time, and task occurrence for the duplicated statements correlated in the high .90s across the board. Apparently, job inventory results are also reliable in nonmilitary organizations.

Job Inventory Validity. The crux of a job inventory validity investigation is to determine whether the task data correspond with "reality" or actual task involvement. Several procedures may be followed to determine job inventory validity, but the most frequently employed method is to compare incumbents' responses about job requirements with those obtained from supervisors. The most desirable way to establish job inventory validity, however, is to compare inventory responses with actual job performance data. For example, it would be ideal to compare task time ratings with clocked time for those tasks. Validity can sometimes be inferred because of a logical relationship that should exist between inventory responses and a personal item, such as job tenure — up to a point, an incumbent's capability should go hand in hand with job tenure. Reliability values may also be used to infer validity — reasonably high reliability is necessary, but not sufficient, to obtain acceptable validity — and when incumbents' responses generally agree, a form of validity (consensual) can be considered to have been obtained. Because of the difficulty associated with establishing job inventory validity, validity is often assumed if the inventory data are reliable. While reliability is not a substitute for validity, high agreement between respondents is an indication that the job inventory data are valid.

Two early studies of job inventories reported by Morsh, Madden, and Christal (1961) resulted in (1) considerable agreement between the results of incumbents' and supervisors' interviews and job inventory responses and (2) a surprising amount of agreement (a correlation of .66) between self-reported daily work records collected from bomb-navigation system mechanics over a period of four and one-half months and job inventory task frequency values — surprising because of the number of problems that cropped up during the study that usually attenuate validity. McCormick and Tombrink (1960) did not find systematic differences between job incumbents and supervisors in the consistency of information reported about the incumbents' work activities, and Moore, Sholtz, and Spilman (Moore, 1976) found moderate to high agreement in task data obtained from incumbents and supervisors working in seven job families. Carpenter, Giorgia, and McFarland (1975) found trainee and instructor daily recordings of time spent on tasks to agree to a high degree with ratings of relative time spent on tasks. Pass and Robertson (1980) pointed out, however, that when there are more than 100 tasks in an inventory, relative time spent percentages are likely to be less than 1 percent for each task and that differences averaging 1 percent per task, such as Carpenter, Giorgia, and McFarland obtained, must be considered relatively large errors.

Pass and Robertson (1980) also reviewed a study conducted by Hartley in which twelve incumbents' ratings of time spent on twenty-three work activities were compared with timed observations of those activities. Differences of 24 percent were found, and the researcher suggested that incumbents' time spent ratings are not sufficiently accurate. On-site observations were recommended as a more appropriate means for obtaining time spent values for work activities. A sample of twelve office workers, however, may not be a sufficient basis for reaching such a sweeping conclusion.

In a series of studies conducted with telephone company employees (Gael, 1977), job inventory validity was found to be sufficiently high to warrant launching the development of a standard Bell System job inventory approach. In an analysis of an engineering job, incumbents' ratings of their capability to accomplish tasks listed in a job inventory were discovered to be related to their job tenure. A gradual increase in self-appraisals was found to accompany increased job tenure. The engineers, it turned out, were not at all squeamish about rating themselves low on their capability to perform tasks, and even the most experienced engineers rated their capability to perform some tasks on the low side (certainly an indication of the veracity of their responses). In a study of four sales jobs, task statements were grouped to form broad job dimensions, such as selling and managing, and task importance responses were analyzed in terms of these dimensions. As expected, sales managers regarded managing tasks as much more important, on the average than did sales people in either of three other sales jobs, and the nonsupervisory sales job incumbents regarded selling as much more important to their jobs than did the sales managers to theirs.

The next study in the series concerned seven clerical jobs performed in Bell System telephone companies nationwide. Task importance and task difficulty averages and median task times proved to be highly correlated across locations — apparently clerks in different companies, supposedly performing the same work, agreed significantly about the importance of, difficulty of, and time spent on the tasks they performed. Task difficulty averages were low to moderate and varied within a very narrow range, leading to the initial conclusion that the low task difficulty averages were due to high experience levels among respondents. A follow-up study, however, showed that the low ability and skill levels were sufficient to accomplish the clerical work — the tasks, in general, were not difficult, and the job inventory ratings simply reflected that fact.

Relative Time Spent. One of the knottiest problems in the development of the job inventory approach to job analysis has been to come up with a means for obtaining accurate estimates of time spent by incumbents performing tasks. Many methods have been tried, some have been found more acceptable than others, and yet the issue is still an open one. Research in the early 1960s led to the use of a simple 5-point time spent rating scale that was later expanded to 7 points. Respondents were asked to rate each task on a scale ranging from 1 to 7 that represented the time spent performing a task relative to the time spent on all other tasks performed — in other words, relative time spent. The responses were converted to relative percent time spent per task by dividing each respondent's time spent rating per task by the sum of all their time spent ratings. Relative percent time spent results for a 100-task job inventory would be obtained as follows:

Task	Time Spent Rating	Relative Percent Time
1	4	1.67
2	2	0.83
3	1	0.42
.	.	.
.	.	.
.	.	.
100	3	1.25
	SUM = 240	100.00

The relative time spent value for Task 1 in the example is 1.67 percent, which was calculated by dividing the response, 4, by the sum of all the responses, 240, and multiplying by 100. The same calculation, of course, is carried out for each of the other tasks. Percentages obtained per task can be averaged across respondents to obtain averages for relative percent time spent per task. Are there problems with the method? As you may have noticed, the ratio of the largest to the smallest percentages is limited by the ratio of the largest to the smallest scale values, regardless of the actual times spent on tasks. With a 7-point scale and with the sum of task time responses 240, as in the above example, the largest percent that can be obtained is 2.92 percent and the smallest is .42 percent, a 7:1 ratio. Actual times spent on two tasks might be three hours for one and ten minutes for the other, an 18:1 ratio. Further, relative percent time spent actually is not a percent. The term is used in the WPSS process because of its wide popularity among job inventory practitioners and because the index serves a useful purpose. In the future, the values calculated may be regarded as a task-time index, not a percentage, which will facilitate dealing with the small values usually obtained at the task level.

Pass and Robertson (1980) obtained job inventory data from incumbents in four USN occupational areas and randomly split the samples to conduct stability analyses. Both the relative time spent and the percent performing values were highly stable (correlations in the .90s). When relative time spent was analyzed only for those incumbents actually performing the tasks — in other words, data for those not performing the tasks were eliminated from the analyses — stability dropped considerably (correlations in the .30s to .50s). The time and task occurrence scales were also found to provide highly redundant information, as shown by the similarity of the rank orders of tasks on each scale (correlations in the mid .90s). Pass and Robertson proposed that job inventories exclude a relative time spent question for two reasons. First, average relative time spent per task is often less than 1 percent of the total time spent, especially when there are more than 100 pertinent task statements in the inventory and integration of the information is difficult. Second, the two types of information studied appear to be redundant. Pass and Robertson suggested that meaningful task time information could probably be based on incumbents' rankings of a small number of the most time-consuming tasks. They also found that high scale stability could be attained with a sample of about forty respondents, and they proposed collecting job inventory data from much smaller samples than customarily recommended.

Despite the conceptual and methodological problems associated with task time estimates of any kind, task time information has proven to be quite useful, especially in military organizations, where the bulk of job inventory analyses have been conducted. While it is true that relative time spent percentages calculated for tasks may be too small to be useful by themselves, aggregating them into broader work activities, such as functions or duties, does make them useful. In that vein, recent analyses of jobs performed in telephone company Business Service Centers (BSCs) and Residence Service Centers (RSCs) have proved to be quite interesting because each type of organization provides similar services but to different kinds of customers. In addition, BSC and RSC jobs were analyzed about a year apart by different analysts but with very similar job inventories that included a section requesting respondents to estimate the percent of time they devote to performing each of eleven functions. Percent time averages per function, therefore, were derived in two ways — from task ratings and from function percent time estimates. Inasmuch as managers in the two types of service centers were apparently performing the same managerial work, it seemed that their respective time spent profiles should be quite similar. In fact, the degree of agreement between task-derived and function-estimated percent time averages for management jobs ranged from moderate to high (correlations from .64 to .85). Comparisons of BSC unit managers with their RSC counterparts resulted in moderate correlations for both task-derived and function-estimated percent time averages ($r = .61$ in both cases). Agreement between BSC and RSC district managers was high for function-estimated ($r = .82$) and very high for task-derived ($r = .94$) percent time averages.

The agreement obtained is reassuring, but one might wonder why task-derived averages are more highly correlated between district manager jobs than task-derived and estimated functions values are correlated within each type of district manager job. Further, if function values alone will suffice, it would be more efficient to estimate function percent time and avoid an inventory question that asks for task time ratings. As a way to enhance the possibility of obtaining more accurate function time estimates, respondents should first be required to respond to at least one, if not two, questions about each task statement so that they get the gist of the function definitions in terms of the tasks subsumed. In addition, brief narrative function definitions should be provided on the form in the job inventory where respondents record their function percent time estimates. Certainly, the issues regarding the adequacy and worthiness of task time estimates are still open to debate, but the knot is a little looser.

Recent Developments

Job inventories have been used in recent years to obtain information about tasks performed and about job incumbents that simply was not contemplated in early job inventory applications when investigators were busy concentrating on basic task attribute information. Some questions that have appeared lately in job inventories pertain to task satisfaction, interest, safety implications, and physical demands. A recent job inventory survey of the USAF ground radio operators (U.S. Air Force Occupational Measurement Center, 1981a), for instance, showed that only 51 percent of the respondents found their jobs interesting, and job satisfaction was not as high as expected even among senior supervisors and managers. As a result of a survey of incumbents in the reprographic career ladder (U.S. Air Force Occupational Measurement Center, 1981b), the USAF found that over 70 percent of graduates considered their jobs interesting and their talents and training well utilized. Siegel, Bartter, and Kopstein (1981) employed a job inventory to survey nuclear power plant maintenance mechanics about the safety implications of improper task performance and identified tasks associated with high public risk; special attention was devoted to those tasks performed infrequently, and recommendations were made for developing standards and regulations, quality assurance programs, proficiency testing, and periodic refresher training.

Gott and Alley (1980) included an innovative question about the physical demands of each task in a recently administered job inventory. The aim of the study was to establish minimum

physical requirements for various jobs. Of 87 job specialties studied, 28 fell into the highest physical demand designation, 45 into a
middle category, and 14 into a low-demand category. By studying
physical demand averages for individual tasks, 1,874 tasks were
found that required incumbents to manipulate fifty pounds or
more. Specialties with comparatively large numbers of physically
demanding tasks were identified, and indices representing the
average load on a particular group of job incumbents were calculated by relating time spent on tasks to their physical demand
values. Where physical demand is concerned, Gott and Alley
pointed out, it is important to know simply whether or not high-
demand tasks are performed even if only a small amount of time
is devoted to those tasks. The last word is not yet in on the
Physical Demands Survey, for work is continuing on both the initial assessment of overall task physical demands and on further
quantification of the specific types and levels of effort associated
with high-demand tasks.

3

⸮⸮

Planning
and Implementing
a WPSS Project

⸮⸮

The WPSS process is composed of a series of interdependent steps, each of which encompasses a set of activities and decisions, and the outcome of each step determines the direction of the next step. As can be seen in Figure 2, WPSS projects start with project planning and proceed through steps in which job task statements are developed and verified, questionnaires are prepared and distributed, data are computerized and analyzed, and results are interpreted and reported. Once detailed job descriptions and action recommendations that address the job analysis objectives have been produced, the WPSS process will slow down noticeably, but it is not over. New uses and applications of the results will arise. Inasmuch as WPSS questionnaires and data are computerized, job information can be retrieved at any time, manipulated in a variety of ways to answer additional questions about target jobs, and updated periodically at a fraction of the original cost. WPSS should be regarded as a dynamic system whose utility stretches beyond the production of an initial report about target jobs.

WPSS relies on questionnaires to obtain quantitative data about tasks performed by job incumbents and hence, about job content. After the questionnaires are developed for the jobs of

Figure 2. The WPSS Process.

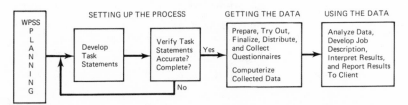

interest, they generally are administered by mail to large samples of employees working at many different sites. The major component of a WPSS questionnaire is a comprehensive list of task statements that make up a job or set of jobs, and questions are asked about each task statement, for instance: How important is each task to your job? How much time do you devote to performing each task? The responses to each question are numerical ratings structured so that they indicate whether each task is or is not performed by the job incumbent without asking that question directly.

After completing this chapter, you should be able to:

1. Determine the resources needed to carry out a WPSS project.
2. Define the functions that WPSS team members will perform.
3. Describe a WPSS project schedule.
4. List the major steps and the supporting activities in the WPSS process.

A brief description of the major steps in the WPSS process follows.

Planning a WPSS Project

The objective of a WPSS project will dictate the scope of the survey and the type of material and questions to include in the WPSS questionnaire. If the objective is to improve job design, the survey should aim at obtaining certain information. If the objective is to establish training requirements, however, the survey probably would attempt to obtain different job information. The information sought about a job may vary somewhat from project to project, but WPSS projects can be designed to satisfy several objectives simultaneously. In any case, careful definition of objectives and goals is essential to obtaining appropriate information. Typical examples of objectives that WPSS results can help achieve are:

1. Developing detailed job descriptions.
2. Identifying job entry requirements.
3. Determining training requirements.
4. Diagnosing job design deficiencies.
5. Establishing career paths.

Some objectives can be met directly with WPSS results, while others require that WPSS results be used as input to a brief follow-up data collection procedure. In any case, a WPSS project should result in the quantified information needed to achieve the objectives noted above, such as the percentage of time job incumbents devote to performing each task and function they perform, the average importance of each task to their jobs, and the average difficulty associated with performing each task.

It is not necessary to specify completely the breadth of a WPSS project during the planning process; but the more specific and complete the plan, the easier it will be to schedule the project, develop the budget, and obtain the resources required to conduct the survey and process the results. Some additional important factors that should be considered during the planning stage are the jobs to be analyzed, the number and types of locations to include in the survey, and the number of respondents that should complete the survey questionnaire.

Selecting the Jobs. A survey can be set up to analyze all jobs in an organization or in a part of an organization. An accounting department job survey, for example, could cover all accounting operations or focus on only one aspect of the work, such as disbursement. In the latter case, only the jobs involving disbursement activities would be surveyed. While the sponsoring organization should specify which jobs are to be analyzed, it is necessary to be wary of job titles — they may not be clearly defined or universal. During project planning, a good deal of lost time can be circumvented by consulting job experts and visiting or contacting several work sites to determine that the job titles supplied are, in fact, those used in the field to represent the jobs of interest. Ideally, a job title should cover one set of specific work activities carried out by all incumbents, but do not be surprised to find that local practices vary in both job titles and activities performed per job title. To carry the accounting department example a little further, the job title "processing clerk" may cover a number of different jobs in the department. In cost accounting, processing clerks may handle cost estimates and quotes; in disbursement accounting, however, they may handle expense vouchers and suppliers' invoices. In some cases, keypunch operators may be included under the title "processing clerk."

Another aspect of the job title issue that should be considered is the use of different titles in various divisions throughout a company for jobs covering the same work. Each specific situation should be checked very early in the planning stage to ensure that WPSS questionnaires will go to appropriate respondents. Careful consideration of job titles during project planning should make the course of action clear. One step that can be taken to make certain that questionnaires are distributed to the employees for whom they are intended is to prepare special instructions for field coordinators so that they will be aware of and will be able to deal with job title variations that might arise in their areas. Another means for ensuring appropriate distribution is to list the job titles of interest on the questionnaire cover page and include brief descriptions of each target job as part of the introductory information. Prospective respondents then will be able to determine for themselves whether or not they should be completing a WPSS questionnaire. A WPSS project might be designed to reach all nonmanagement jobs associated with a broad category such as payroll. Employees involved with the payroll process hold jobs with a variety of job titles—for example, "payroll allotment clerk," "computer attendant," and "processing clerk"—and the survey should be designed to zero in on the specific jobs of interest. If only a single job is of concern, all the easier.

Job level is also an issue worth considering. In some organizations, employees may have essentially the same job title except for a character that designates the level of the job—for example, "account representative-1" and "account representative-2." Will all jobs from entry level to supervisory level be included in the survey? If so, the questionnaire should include tasks performed by employees at different job levels and should be distributed to samples of employees at each level.

Determining WPSS Project Resources. In order to determine and bring together the resources needed to accomplish a WPSS project, it is necessary to have an idea of the activities that will be accomplished during the project. Examples of such activities are:

- *Deriving tasks.* Tasks performed by incumbents in target jobs are derived through interviewing job-knowledgeable employees, reviewing documents about the job or pertaining to job activities, and observing incumbents perform their work.
- *Developing questionnaires.* Task statements and other material are written in accordance with specified guidelines and processed for inclusion in WPSS questionnaires.
- *Performing clerical work.* WPSS questionnaires need to be tracked throughout the distribution and collection process. When completed questionnaires are received, they should be reviewed for completeness and certain questionnaire responses should be coded.
- *Keypunching.* Questionnaire data are keypunched for computer entry in accordance with specially developed instructions.
- *Processing data.* Questionnaire data are entered into a computer to form a WPSS data base, and WPSS computer programs are used to analyze data and obtain desired computer printouts.
- *Interpreting results.* Statistical results contained in WPSS computer printouts are interpreted in terms of job analysis objectives.
- *Reporting results.* WPSS results are presented to clients orally and in written reports.

It is possible for a few employees to become adept in several, if not all, WPSS activities; whether it is warranted to have them do so depends on the organization's philosophy, its long-range job analysis plans, and the resources available. If job analysis and data-processing specialists are available in the company, they probably will require very little indoctrination to become familiar with the WPSS process. If it is impractical for company employees to acquire the expertise needed to carry out a WPSS project, the expertise can be obtained outside the company from any of a large number of private and university-based consultants.

In lieu of a single individual who possesses all the skills and knowledge needed to apply WPSS, a WPSS project team could be formed with each member contributing to the achievement of specific parts of the project. The team should be composed of someone who can manage the project, someone who can accomplish the fieldwork, and someone who can provide technical expertise; in other words, it should have a project manager, a job analyst, and a consultant. The roles that team members should play are as follows:

- *Project manager* — a member of the client organization who is assigned full responsibility for the project. This manager should be in a position to obtain the necessary resources and cooperation, to make them available when they are needed, and to coordinate all required activities. The project manager should be able to assemble a team whose members either have or can acquire the appropriate mix of skills needed. In addition, the project manager will have to schedule, direct, and coordinate the day-to-day activities of team members, especially in regard to field coordinators through whom the team must work; field liaison is a primary responsibility of the project manager.
- *Job analyst* — a lower-level management employee who is trained to carry out all WPSS procedures and who will develop questionnaires and process data. Assuming that it would not cause a labor relations problem, nonmanagement employees who are able to carry out WPSS processes can serve as analysts.
- *Consultant* — a company employee who can become familiar with WPSS procedures and who has the expertise to provide technical guidance and participate in the interpretation of results.

Figure 3 shows the project personnel and the special services needed at each project step. The first major step, project

Figure 3. WPSS Project Resources.

WPSS PROJECT ACTIVITIES \ WPSS PROJECT RESOURCES	PROJECT PERSONNEL							SPECIAL SERVICES		
	Client	Project Manager	Consultant	Job Analyst	Job Expert	Field Coordinators	Clerical	Keypunching	Reproduction - Printing	Computer Support
PROJECT PLANNING										
Define Purpose	✓									
Select Jobs	✓				✓					
Establish Scope	✓	✓	✓							
QUESTIONNAIRE DEVELOPMENT										
Develop Statements			✓	✓	✓					
Verify Statements				✓	✓					
Prepare, Try Out, and Finalize		✓	✓	✓	✓	✓			✓	
DATA COLLECTION AND PROCESSING										
Distribute and Collect Questionnaires		✓				✓	✓		✓	
Computerize Data								✓		✓
Analyze Data				✓						✓
RESULTS										
Interpret			✓	✓						
Report to Client		✓		✓					✓	

planning, should be a cooperative venture between the sponsoring or client organization's staff, including its project manager, and a job analysis consultant. The project manager will be involved to some extent in all major project steps. The consultant and the job analyst figure most prominently during questionnaire development and when results are interpreted and reported. A job expert, who may be an immediate supervisor of target job incumbents, is needed primarily to clarify job information at various points in the process and to ascertain that task statements are accurately stated in the incumbents' jargon. Field coordinators are most prominent when questionnaires are tried out initially and when they are broadly distributed to the entire survey sample. Reproduction, keypunching and computer services are needed to print questionnaires and reproduce reports, to transfer questionnaire data into computer-readable form, and to process and analyze WPSS data.

Subsequent chapters in both Part One and Part Two explain in detail what needs to be done to accomplish a WPSS project, and they provide guidance for carrying out the activities. This book, therefore, can be used both as a procedural guide and as a training manual. Careful reading of this book, repeated references to it, and some practice in WPSS procedures should enable most users to perform their WPSS roles successfully.

WPSS Project Scheduling. The time that should be allowed to accomplish a WPSS project depends on several factors, such as the scope of the survey, the complexity of the job or jobs to be surveyed, the structure of the organization in which the jobs to be surveyed are located, and the availability of job information and resources. Despite the potential variation in schedules that these factors can cause, it is possible to offer some scheduling guidance. Figure 4 illustrates a hypothetical WPSS time-activity chart for a typical application of WPSS for a single job.

A significant part of WPSS planning can be accomplished in a single meeting between representatives from the sponsoring organization, including the project manager, and the consultant. Additional planning, such as that with field coordinators, should be arranged by the project manager as needed. The sponsoring organization should designate field coordinators shortly after the

Figure 4. Hypothetical WPSS Project Schedule.

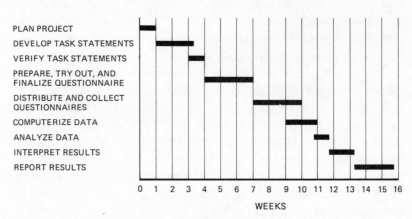

PLAN PROJECT
DEVELOP TASK STATEMENTS
VERIFY TASK STATEMENTS
PREPARE, TRY OUT, AND
FINALIZE QUESTIONNAIRE
DISTRIBUTE AND COLLECT
QUESTIONNAIRES
COMPUTERIZE DATA
ANALYZE DATA
INTERPRET RESULTS
REPORT RESULTS

0 1 2 3 4 5 6 7 8 9 10 11 12 13 14 15 16
WEEKS

first planning meeting, and the project manager should be able to communicate with field managers exclusively by telephone and mail. In other words, the project manager should not have to meet with each field coordinator personally to accomplish a WPSS project.

The amount of time ascribed to a step in Figure 4 does not necessarily reflect the intensity of the effort expended nor the WPSS team commitment. Developing and verifying task statements require highly intensive project personnel involvement within a relatively short time period. Conversely, at least half of the time required for one of the longest steps in the process — to prepare, tryout, and finalize the questionnaire — is consumed by the printing process. Similarly, questionnaire distribution and collection extend over several weeks, but very little time is expended by the WPSS team on this step.

Time economies may be realized in several ways. One is to analyze more than one job at a time, especially when the jobs are related to each other organizationally or because of their locations, the type of work performed, and the way they interface. Another way to cut the time required is to streamline the WPSS process. Special questionnaire answer sheets, for instance, can be used that allow answers to be read directly into the computer instead of keypunching them first. Questionnaires can be reproduced by a means that is much faster than having them printed, and the types of written reports desired also affect the time schedule. A full technical report will require at least a week or more of preparation time than an executive summary or an oral report. Other shortcuts will be discussed in Chapter Seven; the thing to bear in mind is that the introduction of shortcuts usually is accomplished at the expense of something else.

Developing a WPSS Questionnaire

The first big step that has to be taken to develop a WPSS questionnaire is to compile an accurate and complete list of task statements that represent the work performed by job incumbents in the target jobs. The WPSS process for deriving tasks and developing the task list includes:

- *Content analysis.* Examples of documents that should be analyzed, assuming that they are available, include job descriptions, training materials, job aids, position practices, and maintenance manuals. Not only do the documents serve as source materials for task statements, but they also help prepare for the later interviews with job incumbents and supervisors. Content analysis of job-related documents should focus on information that describes actual job responsibilities and tasks.
- *Observation.* Work-site observations of job incumbents are also sources of task statements, and they too help prepare for the interviews. They also help clarify information already obtained and provide a deeper understanding of the way a job is accomplished in its environment. Observations should concentrate on interactions of incumbents with other employees and on work flows — the inputs that generate work, the work products, and the disposition of those products.
- *Interviews.* Interviews with job incumbents and supervisors are conducted to determine the activities that job incumbents actually perform, as opposed to activities they are supposed to perform. In addition to being a rich source of task statements, interviews can help clarify aspects of a job that may have been misunderstood. Interviews with two or three employees per job at no more than three locations should be sufficient. The number of locations visited for interviews should depend on the differences found in the way the job is performed at the

first and second interview locations. Normally, two widely separated locations are sufficient. If significant differences do show up — for example, if new tasks are obtained at the second location at a rate over 10 percent — interviews at still another site should be considered. But interviewees at the first location site should be contacted to make sure that a work function was not inadvertently overlooked before going ahead with interviews at a third location.

Three types of interviews are recommended for deriving task statements:

- *Initial interviews* — the first interview conducted at each location. This interview yields the most information from which task statements will be extracted.
- *Verification interviews* — the remaining interviews conducted at each location to clarify, check, and modify job information already obtained. They are conducted in the same way as the initial interview but with different employees.
- *Follow-up interviews* — a second round of interviews conducted with small groups of two to four employees to check the accuracy and completeness of a draft of the final task list.

The resulting task statement list should be reviewed with job experts. When the WPSS team is reasonably certain that the task list is accurate and complete, it can begin to structure a WPSS questionnaire. The list of job tasks is the core of a WPSS questionnaire, and a variety of questions can be asked about each task statement, for example: Do you perform each task? How important is each task to your job? How difficult is each task? How much time do you spend performing each task? How well do you perform each task?

The number of questions that can be asked about each task statement is limited only by the ingenuity of the analyst. To avoid overburdening respondents, several versions of a WPSS questionnaire can be prepared; in other words, the same task list is used but with different questions, and different versions of the questionnaire can be administered to subsets of job incumbents.

Another important part of a WPSS questionnaire is the instructions that inform respondents how to respond (see Figures 15 through 19). WPSS questionnaires are designed to obtain quantitative answers to questions about tasks; and since the questionnaires are self-administered, it is imperative that questionnaire completion instructions be expressed very simply and clearly. Respondents should be able to complete questionnaires with little or no help—a major advantage of WPSS. WPSS questionnaire instructions should present easily understood definitions of the numerical ratings that are the required responses to questions about each task and should guide respondents through the questionnaire from beginning to end.

WPSS questionnaires should also contain questions about the respondent—for example, job location, company tenure, time in present job, educational background, and work experience (see Figure 21). The personal information identifies the respondents so that they can be reached again if further contact is necessary, and it is also a source of valuable information that should be analyzed to obtain respondent and sample profiles.

Drafts of WPSS questionnaires should be prepared and tried out with a few job incumbents before the questionnaire is administered to the entire sample. The questionnaire, in other words, should be administered exactly as it will be administered on a larger scale in the future. Tryout results should indicate where revisions are needed. When the final questionnaire is produced, it should be an easily understood document that contains a comprehensive, accurate list of task statements that describes a job or set of jobs, plus instructions for completing the questionnaire.

Collecting and Processing WPSS Data

The next phase of a WPSS project is to get the questionnaires into the hands of appropriate respondents—those performing or supervising target jobs—and to have the completed questionnaires returned for computerization and data analysis. Field coordinators generally are assigned the responsibility for distributing the questionnaires and any additional instructions for other managers and supervisors. The questionnaires designated for

each area are mailed to the responsible coordinators, who, in turn, package and send the material to appropriate field managers. The field managers distribute the questionnaires they receive to supervisors in accordance with instructions, and the supervisors give the questionnaires to appropriate job incumbents, who complete and return them for analysis. It would be possible to reach every job incumbent performing a particular job with a WPSS questionnaire; generally, however, it is more economical and practical to sample job incumbents. The sample should be chosen so that the locations and respondents represent the range of work activities performed in the jobs. The number of distribution layers will vary in accordance with the size of the management hierarchy, but distribution problems can be minimized considerably by transmitting distribution instructions to all employees in the distribution process.

WPSS data-processing requirements involve transferring data from questionnaires to the computer. Data storage, processing, and analysis can then be accomplished by activating WPSS computer programs. WPSS computerized data can be analyzed in many ways and the results presented in a variety of reports or computer printouts generated with the WPSS computer system. The number of types of reports generated to summarize WPSS data will depend on three factors—the survey objectives, the number of task attribute questions contained in the survey questionnaire, and the number of jobs covered by the survey. Figure 5 illustrates some of the types of reports that can be generated by using WPSS computer programs. The dotted part of the figure represents task attribute reports not specifically mentioned in the figure, such as task frequency, task significance, and task percent time, a report derived from task time ratings. Figures 23 through 26 contain samples taken from WPSS computer reports, and reference to them in conjunction with the discussion below will provide an initial understanding of the nature and types of reports that can be generated with WPSS computer programs; a more detailed explanation of computer-generated WPSS reports is presented in Chapter Seven.

Statistical summary reports can be generated for only one task attribute at a time. If a questionnaire, for example, contains

Figure 5. Printouts Obtainable with WPSS Computer Programs.

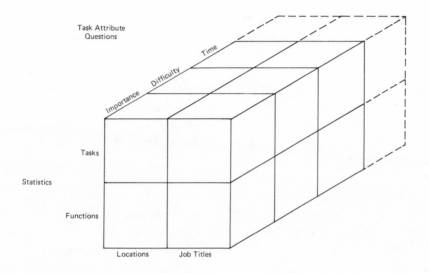

questions about task significance and task time, each has to be
reported separately (see Figure 23 for a task significance report
sample); separate reports also have to be generated for functions.
Within each type of task and function report, data can be presented by location or by job. When locations, such as company,
state or city, are of interest, the row headings will be task statements or functions, the column headings will be locations, and the
report will pertain to a specific task attribute. If more than one job
is covered by a survey, a task attribute by location report can be
generated for all jobs at once and then separate reports can be
generated for each job. If jobs instead of locations are the focus of
the report, column headings will be job titles. Again, the row
headings are either task statements or functions. Whether locations or job titles are used as column headings, the leftmost results
column is always reserved for total sample results. As previously
mentioned, questionnaire responses can also be analyzed to obtain
job information not specifically requested; this can be done, for
example, by calculating percent task time from task ratings and
by combining task results for function information. Task percent

time (% Time) reports can be produced only if a question asking respondents to rate the time they devote to performing each task is included in the questionnaire.

The values contained in each cell, or row and column juncture, of WPSS task or function statistical summary reports are:

- The average response, for example, average task importance.
- The standard deviation, that is, an index pertaining to the spread of individual responses around the average response.
- The proportion of sample responses contributing to the cell statistics.

Statistical summaries can also be obtained for personal information items by location or job title; for personal information, however, the more conventional outputs are cross tabluations with frequencies and percentages recorded in the cells (see Figures 25 and 26).

Interpreting and Reporting Results

The statistical indices contained in WPSS reports have very specific applications, and they should be interpreted with those applications in mind. Since this procedural guide cannot treat each type of application, some of the more typical applications of the indices are presented as follows:

- Averages are used to establish the most important, time-consuming, and difficult tasks.
- Standard deviations are used to identify tasks that have wider variation in responses than do others.
- Proportions are used to determine the number of incumbents actually performing each task and to compare both task overlap between jobs and task differences for the supposedly same job performed at different locations.
- Percentages are used to show the part of the total job that each task and function represent and to develop sample profiles on the basis of personal information.

Computer reports that summarize responses to each task attribute question are in effect very detailed job descriptions. Such job descriptions generally will serve as the basis for meeting various needs and objectives. Tabular computer reports, for instance, can help prepare narrative job descriptions. For applications that require more detailed information than is contained in WPSS computer reports, such as the preparation of training materials, the reports can be used to help specify the details needed.

WPSS results can be disseminated in a variety of ways, but dissemination is, of course, up to the sponsoring organization; it must decide whether the availability of WPSS results should be announced and to whom reports should be distributed. The approach recommended for presenting WPSS results combines several forms of reports. One is an oral report that should be made by the project manager to those who sponsor the job analysis. This report should be presented in a conference setting and focus on the main issues that prompted the job analysis in the first place. Next, a brief executive summary that covers significant results should be prepared and distributed to those who will attend the conference. The executive summary serves not only to inform the conferees but also to help stimulate questions about the target jobs. In fact, conference participants should be requested to come to the presentation prepared with questions about the target jobs and how the job analysis results might be used to answer questions that arise subsequent to the conference. Questions obtained prior to the conference should be answered during the presentation, and questions asked during the presentation can be answered at that time or at a later date after additional data analysis — WPSS is a dynamic system. Finally, a technical supplement should be prepared and made available to back up the oral presentation and the executive summary. The technical supplement should document the WPSS procedures followed, the specific results achieved, and other significant particulars. Inasmuch as the technical supplement will be very detailed, the sponsor probably should make it available only to those who stand to benefit from the information contained in it. A centrally located computer printout file can be maintained for reference purposes. Management should be encouraged to ask questions about the target jobs, to review the printouts for possible answers, and to access and manipulate the data stored in the computer for answers to questions that cannot be answered by analyses already conducted.

An interesting WPSS feature is that the questionnaires and the corresponding data obtained about each task and respondent can be stored in a computer and are easily accessible for further use. Moreover, periodic updates can be accomplished at a fraction of the original job analysis cost.

By way of review, then, WPSS involves: (1) deriving task statements pertaining to a job or set of jobs, (2) developing and distributing specially designed questionnaires that contain questions about job tasks and the respondents, and (3) computerizing and analyzing questionnaire data with easy-to-use computer programs. What distinguishes WPSS from other job inventory approaches are the emphasis placed on interviewing job-knowledgeable employees to identify tasks actually performed, instead of relying on written material about tasks that are supposed to be performed, and the special computer programs used to analyze task and respondent data.

4

Writing
Job Task
Statements

It is easy to compose well-written task statements, and the knack for writing them can be acquired with just a little study and practice. All that is required is that you understand and follow the simple rules presented below. Accumulating the information from which task statements can be extracted or derived requires the application of a few well-chosen techniques. This chapter describes how statements about tasks performed by incumbents holding a particular job or group of jobs should be structured, presents guidelines for writing effective, easily understood task statements, and describes two techniques for accumulating a base of job information from which task statements can be obtained.

Why is the way that task statements are written so important? As previously mentioned, the task statement is the basic ingredient of the WPSS process, and task statements constitute the basis for the results that will be obtained from WPSS questionnaire respondents. Accurate and complete WPSS job descriptions, therefore, depend heavily on the way task statements are prepared. Figure 1 contains a page taken from a WPSS questionnaire used in a survey of a middle-management job; inasmuch as the page is the last one in the questionnaire on which task statements are listed, you can see that the questionnaire contains 246 task statements. Figure 6 shows a page from another WPSS questionnaire, this time from a survey of employees working in a group of related nonmanagement telephone company jobs; it contains 280 task statements. Note the similarity of format in both cases and the different response modes that incumbents were asked to use to record their responses to the two questions asked about each task statement. (The first question, indicated by the heading of the first response field, pertains to the significance of the tasks to the job, while the second question, indicated by the heading of the second response field, pertains to the time devoted to performing the tasks). Different response modes were employed to make it easier for respondents to change their set when responding to the second question and to keep them actively involved in the response process. Task significance ratings were obtained by having respondents circle numbers printed on the questionnaire, and task time ratings were obtained by having respondents write numbers in appropriate spaces alongside task statements. if optical scanning or "mark-sense" techniques are used to computerize responses, then yet another response mode will be required, one similar to penciling in answer spaces on an IBM answer sheet.

Although one type of response mode may be easier for respondents to use than another, it is mainly the way task statements are written and presented that enables respondents to rate each task appropriately. In the two WPSS questionnaires from which the examples presented in Figures 1 and 6 were taken, task statements are listed alphabetically, and, as can be seen in Figure 6, under broad activity headings such as "Completing Forms." Level of detail was taken into account when preparing the task statements, and the level used in each example seems about the same.

WPSS relies on job documentation and job incumbents and their supervisors as sources for establishing a job information base from which task statements will be derived. The techniques recommended for making the most of these sources of information are (1) content analysis of documents written about target jobs, (2) observation of job incumbents at their work sites, and (3) inter-

Figure 6. A Page from the Service Representative WPSS Questionnaire.

	Part B	Part C
	SIGNIFICANCE	TIME SPENT

	0 = No time
	1 = Very small
	2 = Small
	3 = Slightly less
	4 = As much
	5 = Slightly more
	6 = More
	7 = Very much more

Significance scale columns: Not Part / Minor — Substantial — Most significant

Task List	Significance	Time Spent
A. Completing Forms		
001 Authorize refund of deposit to customer.	0 1 2 3 4 5 6 7	_____
002 Change treatment history or treatment class.	0 1 2 3 4 5 6 7	_____
003 Note treatment and follow-up action.	0 1 2 3 4 5 6 7	_____
004 Phone service order in English to order writer.	0 1 2 3 4 5 6 7	_____
005 Prepare a contact memo on an incoming business sales call.	0 1 2 3 4 5 6 7	_____
006 Prepare adjustment voucher to adjust a billing error or to reconcile records.	0 1 2 3 4 5 6 7	_____
007 Prepare and send form to AT&T Long Lines on overseas calls appearing to be billed in error.	0 1 2 3 4 5 6 7	_____
008 Prepare and send to customer a Transfer of Service (Billing Responsibility) Agreement form.	0 1 2 3 4 5 6 7	_____
009 Prepare change of address record, worksheet, or order.	0 1 2 3 4 5 6 7	_____
010 Prepare contact memo on intracompany or intercompany contact.	0 1 2 3 4 5 6 7	_____
011 Prepare final account write-off voucher.	0 1 2 3 4 5 6 7	_____
012 Prepare form to order office supplies, machine supplies, or forms.	0 1 2 3 4 5 6 7	_____
013 Prepare form to transfer money or debit between accounts.	0 1 2 3 4 5 6 7	_____
014 Prepare Full Station Detail form.	0 1 2 3 4 5 6 7	_____
015 Prepare Key System diagram (worksheet or graphic).	0 1 2 3 4 5 6 7	_____
016 Prepare note to inform others of changes of phone numbers, people, or locations called within the company.	0 1 2 3 4 5 6 7	_____
017 Prepare programming sheets for CENTREX or other programmable equipment.	0 1 2 3 4 5 6 7	_____

views with job incumbents and their supervisors. Each technique should focus on tasks actually performed by incumbents in the target jobs.

When you have completed this chapter, you should be able to:

1. Specify the components and structure of well-written task statements.
2. Describe guidelines for preparing well-written task statements.
3. Describe how to plan for and record observations of job incumbents performing their work.
4. Specify the documents that should be sought and reviewed for job information from which task statements will be extracted.
5. Describe a method for studying job documents to identify the activities that are performed by job incumbents.

Writing Task Statements

WPSS analysts will be writing task statements almost from the inception of a WPSS project. Before we discuss the techniques for deriving job tasks, therefore, you should become very familiar with the structure of and guidelines for writing task statements. Let us keep in mind that a task:

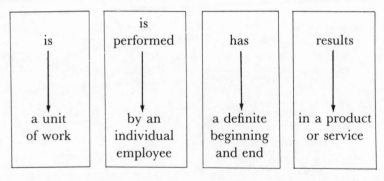

is	is performed	has	results
↓	↓	↓	↓
a unit of work	by an individual employee	a definite beginning and end	in a product or service

Given this definition, the likelihood is that tasks will be accomplished in a relatively short period of time. As a work activity comes to require more and more time, the possibility increases that the activity is a work unit larger than a task. Further, if a product or service cannot be identified, the activity is not considered a task. "Request information from another department" is not considered a task because the description of the actual work is too vague and does not sufficiently identify the output of the activity—what information from what department? In contrast, "Request customer billing information from Accounting to verify receipt of customer payment" identified specifically what was accomplished and why it was accomplished. Even in the second case, however, the task statement probably would be stated more specifiically in practice by naming the particular billing information form or the type of billing information desired and perhaps by giving the job title of the accounting department clerk contacted.

Components of a Task Statement. Task statements should be written in a manner that clearly distinguishes them from other work activity descriptions, such as descriptions of functions and subtasks. The standard grammatical form for writing task statements is the simple sentence with a subject, a verb, and an immediate object. The subject of each task statement is "I" understood and is omitted from the task statement. The verb is an action verb, and the object of the task statement is, of course, the object of the verb. A practice that seems to have evolved is to omit articles from task statements, thereby making the statements somewhat choppy, as well as shorter and less well-structured than complete sentences.

Task statements can be written rather routinely as long as the question of what is done to what is covered. Some qualifying information almost always is included in task statements to make them more complete and meaningful; for instance, a task statement might include information about the purpose that the task is supposed to serve—in other words, why it is performed. In the task statement mentioned earlier, for instance, billing information was requested from the accounting department to verify that a customer made a payment. How a task is performed is usually not included in a task statement being prepared for a WPSS questionnaire unless it is important to do so, as when a task can be accomplished in several ways. The task of digging trenches, for instance, might be accomplished with hand tools or with heavy equipment depending on the situation, and the appropriate method should be made absolutely clear in the task statement. Brevity is the watchword. A customer contact task can be written so that the "how" is contained in the action verb — for instance, "Call customers to..." or "Write customers to...." If the means used to contact customers is not important, the task statement could be written "Notify customers of...." When writing task statements, then, you should (1) begin with an appropriate action verb in the present tense — what is done; (2) include the object of that verb — what is being acted upon; and (3) include qualifying information as needed.

The chart below shows four task statements subdivided among the three components of a task statement.

What Is Done (Action)	To What (Object)	Qualifier (When Necessary)
Send	purchase requests	to the Purchasing Dept.
Type	legal affidavits	
Call	customers	to extend installation date.
Transmit	data	to other offices using data phone.

Qualifying information is needed to round out task statements under the following conditions:

HOW

For tasks that can be accomplished in more than one way.

Example: Identify component failure patterns *using automatic trouble analysis reports.*

WHY

For tasks that can have multiple purposes.

Example: Call repair service to *expedite an order.*

WHERE OR WHEN

For tasks that have multiple situations or conditions.
Example: Send erroneous service order *back to origi-nator.*

Set automatic trouble analysis equipment to day configuration *at start of shift.*

HOW MUCH OF

For tasks in which the range of what is acted upon is involved.
Example: Determine charges *for complex service orders.*

The main objective in writing task statements for WPSS questionnaires is to write them so that respondents will be able to understand them and provide appropriate responses. Guidelines based on experience and research have been developed to assist job analysts in writing task statements, and the application of the guidelines should enable you to write task statements that are easier to understand, more meaningful, and more useful than would otherwise be the case. The guidelines are as follows:

- *Specific verbs and nouns.* Task statements should be sufficiently specific so that the work accomplished is clearly defined and the task statement is concise and unambiguous. Explicit action verbs should be used to specify each task performed. Passive verbs or verbs that describe processes — for example, "assure," "determine," "evaluate," "indicate," "ensure," "supervise," and "verify" — should not be used to express task statements. The task statement "Ensure that customer service requests are accomplished on a timely basis" does not really specify a particular activity accomplished by the job incumbent; verbs that describe processes are open ended and subject to various interpretations. Nouns used in task statements should also be as specific as possible. The task statement "Repair fuel system components" could be made more specific by naming the particular fuel system component that is to be repaired — for example, "Repair fuel pumps." Likewise, the task statement "Clean work area" may be too general for use in a WPSS questionnaire.

- *One action, one object.* As a rule, tasks can be performed independently of other tasks, and only one action and one object should be included in a task statement. If a description of work covers more than one independent activity, it is not a single task. The task statement "Review and prepare cost estimates" should be separated into two tasks, "Review cost estimates" and "Prepare cost estimates." In the same way, the statement "Review files, reports, and correspondence" should be separated into three task statements, since three separate activities are covered. An incumbent might perform only one of the activities and not the others and therefore would not be able to answer questions about the tasks appropriately. In some cases, however, actions or objects may be so closely related that they form a unit of work or a single work activity. A couple of examples of such task statements and how they should be written are "Locate and repair short in wiring" and "Address letters and packages."
- *Stand-alone content.* Each tast statement should be intelligible when standing apart from other task statements. "Perform other kinds of equipment checks" is not a well-written task statement, but it might make sense if it followed a series of task statements concerning specific equipment checks.
- *Familiar words.* Task statements should be expressed in jargon that is familiar to job incumbents. If employees at different locations are known to use different terminology for the same procedure, form, equipment, or other item, alternate words should be included in those task statements—for example, "Call up (fetch) pending order on processing screen." In some environments the preferred verb was "call-up" and in others it was "fetch," so both were included in the task statement to avoid misunderstanding. Only the most common abbreviations and acronyms should be used. Acronyms can be reviewed with a job expert or checked against an operations plan to determine whether they are accepted company wide or are local terms. The first time an acronym appears in a task statement it should be spelled out—for example, "Forward payment-received notices to the Revenue Accounting Office (RAO);" in later statements the acronym can stand alone.

- *Consistent use of words.* The same actions or objects should be described by the same verbs or nouns to avoid confusion. Synonyms should not be interchanged—for instance, copy and transcribe or complete and prepare. A list of action verbs frequently used in writing task statements is contained in Figure 7. The list of verbs is only a small sample of the multitude of action verbs that can be used to write task statements—you may want to use other verbs that are more appropriate for the specific situation.
- *Compatibility with rating scales.* A task statement should be written in a manner that enables respondents to answer questions about task attributes, such as "How important is each task to your job?" "How difficult is each task?" "How much time do you spend performing each task?" It is relatively simple to test whether a task statement is compatible with the various rating scales planned for the questionnaire. Just ask yourself whether respondents will be able to rate how much time they devote to performing the task and how frequently they perform the task. If it does not appear feasible for the respondent to answer those questions in regard to a task statement, or if the answer would not make sense, then the task statement probably could stand some improvement.

If the few guidelines presented above for writing task statements are followed and the standard task statement structure is kept in mind, you will find that it is comparatively easy to write good task statements. There are, however, several types of information that should *not* serve as the basis for a task statement, and you should familiarize yourself with them. Some items to avoid when writing task statements are:

- Worker or job qualifications, such as intelligence, aptitudes, knowledge, or experience—for example, "Requires knowledge of computer operations and three months of experience to advise Marketing of customer needs."
- Participation in nonproductive activities, such as attending training courses and receiving instructions—for example, "Attend clerical skills training."

Figure 7. Action Verb List.

Accumulate	Code	Enter	Join	Place	Rewire
Adjust	Collect	Erect	Judge	Plan	Rework
Advise	Compare	Estimate		Post	Route
Aid	Complete	Evaluate	List	Prepare	
Align	Compute	Examine	Loan	Prescribe	Scan
Amend	Conduct	Explain	Locate	Probe	Schedule
Analyze	Connect	Extract	Log	Process	Secure
Approve	Contact		Lubricate	Program	Select
Arrange	Control	Fabricate			Set
Assemble	Coordinate	Figure	Maintain	Qualify	Set-up
Assign	Copy	File	Measure	Quote	Signal
Audit	Correct	Formulate	Modify		Solder
Authorize	Count	Gather	Monitor	Ready	Sort
Balance		Give		Reassemble	Store
Batch	Date	Group	Name	Recall	Survey
Buy	Deliver	Guard	Notify	Receive	
	Demonstrate	Guide		Recondition	Tabulate
Calculate	Describe		Observe	Record	Test
Calibrate	Design	Help	Obtain	Refer	Trace
Cancel	Diagnose	Hold	Open	Regulate	Transcribe
Certify	Direct		Operate	Reject	Transmit
Change	Disconnect	Identify	Order	Relay	Troubleshoot
Charge	Dispatch	Inform	Organize	Remove	Tune
Check	Dispose	Initiate	Overhaul	Repair	Type
Choose	Divide	Insert		Replace	
Cite	Document	Inspect	Paint	Reproduce	Verify
Classify		Install	Patch	Request	
Clean	Edit	Instruct	Phone	Review	Weigh
Clear	Encode	Interview	Pick	Revise	Write

- Organization policies, responsibilities, and practices — for example, "Observe safety procedures," "Treat customers courteously," or "Wear hardhat in the shop area."
- Working conditions — for example, "Work in a well-lighted room with ample room for movement."
- Imprecise or ambiguous terms, such as and/or and etc. — for example, "Call Accounting for billing adjustment information, etc."

Level of Task Statement Detail. A controversial issue confronting job analysts pertains to the amount of information to include in each task statement. Task statements can be written very narrowly or very broadly and at varying levels of detail or specificity. Before beginning preparation of task statements, analysts should determine the level of detail that will be expressed in task statements to describe the work accomplished in target jobs. The main point to keep in mind is that WPSS questionnaires need to be understood by respondents and that respondents can deal very well with the type of brief task statement developed in accordance with the guidelines already described. Some analysts, however, prefer to employ very detailed task statements at the expense of lengthening the questionnaire and increasing the time respondents must devote to responding to it. Consider the following two sets of activity statements:

1a. Update computerized customer records using a computer terminal.

1b. Update computerized customer records by entering customer name and phone number with a keyboard and cathode ray tube (CRT) and by entering instructions to the customer records information data base.

2a. Complete daily route work log to close out day's assigned route.

2b. Complete daily route work log by computing mileage driven on route (subtract mileage-out from mileage-in shown on tachograph at end of day), posting mileage information and work accomplished per stop, and presenting completed route work log with key to supervisor in order to close out day's assigned route.

Essentially, the same work is represented by the two statements within each set. But the second statement in each set is more detailed than the first and could have been made even more detailed; for instance, statement 1b could have included a computer logon procedure. If every minute detail involved in performing tasks were to be recorded in describing a job, however, several volumes would be needed to describe the activities accomplished in the simplest of jobs. Level of detail, by the way, can pertain either to individual task statements or to the number of task statements used to describe a particular work activity. If a large number of statements are used to describe a work activity, survey results usually will have to be combined and summarized to represent broader work activities; otherwise, the information will not be meaningful, since it is difficult to concentrate on and interpret data obtained for each of several hundred tasks and to develop meaningful conclusions about a job from so much data. The same is true if too few general statements are used to describe job activities—for most purposes it will not be possible to draw meaningful conclusions. It is, of course, better to obtain a large number of task statements and then deal with the problem of extracting useful information than to obtain too little information.

A distinction should be drawn at this point between tasks and subtasks, since it may not be possible to tell them apart when they are viewed out of context. We know what a task is. A subtask is simply a step performed to accomplish a task. Subtasks do not have a purpose or output distinct from the purpose or output of the task, and they cannot stand by themselves, whereas adequately written task statements can stand alone and be interpreted. Steps that are performed as part of a task need not be included in a task statement as they are in activity statements 1b and 2b above. The guidelines for writing task statements already presented are aimed at helping write task statements at approximately the same level of detail.

The Task List

The bulk of a WPSS questionnaire is composed of a list of task statements. Several techniques can be used in various combinations to obtain the job information from which task statements will be derived. The WPSS approach recommends reviews of existing job documents, observation of job performance, and interviews with job incumbents and supervisors to accumulate the information base from which individual tasks statements will be derived and task lists that completely and accurately describe a job can be prepared. As you will see later, the techniques are not equally useful; but each, in its own way, contributes to the improvement of the quality of the task list. Let us now briefly consider the way that task statements are compiled into a task list.

You need not wait until all techniques for gathering job information have been applied to begin developing a task list. In fact, once document reviews and job observations have been completed, the available job information base can be used as an aid for conducting the forthcoming series of interviews. The extent to which a preliminary task statement list approximates a serviceable description of a target job and interview aid depends on the availability and quality of existing job documentation, the usefulness of the job performance observations, and the analyst's skill in translating the available job information into task statements. The interviews should provide many task statements that are not on the list and confirm those already listed. The prescribed series of interviews will help modify some of the task statements already written and will identify those that should be rewritten or eliminated. When the interviews have been completed and the preliminary task statement list has been revised, all the information needed to compile the task list that will be included in the WPSS questionnaire should be available. If for some reason a preliminary task list cannot be generated before the interviews are conducted, interview results will provide almost all the task statements that will be used in a WPSS questionnaire.

In WPSS questionnaires, task statements are organized alphabetically by function. As defined earlier, a function is a broad subdivision of a job composed of related tasks. The tasks are related either because of the nature of the work or the behavior required; in other words, they have a particular feature of work in common. If negotiating with customers is a function performed by incumbents in the target job, then all tasks that pertain to negotiations with customers should be subsumed by, and listed alphabetically under, that function. Task statements are listed alphabetically so that tasks will not be placed in an order or performance sequence that would enable respondents to answer questions about them almost without reading each task statement. The idea is to have respondents read and respond to questions about each task statement individually. Ordering tasks alphabetically also shortens respondents' reading time and helps them recall tasks not contained on the list. All tasks beginning with the same verb are listed together; this arrangement makes it very easy for respondents to scan the task list and make certain that all tasks of each kind are included. A further benefit of an alphabetized task list is that analysts can easily spot and eliminate duplicate task statements before the list is finalized.

Function Identification

A number of methods ranging from highly statistical to relatively simple ones can be employed to identify functions. One of the simplest is used in the WPSS process; for want of a better term, it might be called the "eyeball" method. Previous work has shown that content analysis by the eyeball method yields functions that are about the same as those obtained with factor analysis, one of the more commonly used statistical means for analyzing job data to establish groups of items that have a common ground. Actually, the proposed eyeball method is a factor identification technique without the statistics. The idea is to identify the dimensions of work (functions) underlying the job simply by examining task statements.

The steps that can be employed to identify job functions by content analysis of tasks are as follows:

1. Write each task statement on a separate slip of paper or card.
2. Sort task statements into piles or clusters according to a rule aimed at grouping tasks that have something in common. All tasks involving the same broad work activity, such as negotiating with customers, maintaining equipment, distributing supplies, and so on, should be placed in the same cluster. You may find it necessary to further subdivide some of the task clusters; for instance, maintaining equipment may be subdivided into preventive maintenance and corrective maintenance. At least two analysts working independently, but under the same guiding rule, should sort the task statements.
3. Compare the clusters of task statements developed by each analyst to determine where they agree and disagree.
4. Bring analysts together to discuss their task clusters, the rationale they used to assign tasks to clusters, and the reasons for disagreements in the number and types of clusters formed and assignments of tasks to clusters.

5. Refine task clusters by moving task statements between clusters or developing new clusters in accordance with the discussion. Consensus is the goal; if the analysts cannot agree, however, another sort by a third analyst is warranted. The third sort does not necessarily have to start from scratch. The results from all three sorts should be compared as above and a consensus reached.
6. Name each cluster in accordance with the type of work represented. The cluster name is the name of the function.

Now that the structure and characteristics of task statements, the way they should be written and compiled into a task list, and the way functions can be identified have been reviewed in some detail, we can proceed to techniques recommended for gathering the job information from which task statements will be derived, namely, content analysis of job documents, observations of job performance, and interviews with job incumbents and their supervisors.

Developing a Job Information Base

After WPSS project planning has been accomplished, job information seeking can begin. The objective of this stage is to amass as much information about the work performed by incumbents in the target jobs as can be found and to use that information to prepare a complete and accurate list of task statements representing the work that incumbents carry out.

The order in which the three techniques recommended for acquiring job information should be applied is not straightforward. The techniques are covered herein more in the order in which they might be accomplished than in the order of their contribution to the preparation of task statements. If job documents, for instance, are handy, they probably will serve as the first source of job information. There is a bit of a "Catch-22" here because studying job documentation enhances the value of observation, observation of job performance at a work site helps in an understanding of job documentation, and interviews with job incumbents and other job-knowledgeable employees further an understanding of both job documentation and observations. Some analysts find it advantageous to intersperse the different techniques; for instance, job performance can be observed at different points during the job information-seeking stage, perhaps before and after documents about the target jobs are reviewed. An initial observation of a job performed at the work site may simply serve as a means for becoming familiar with the environment and the general features of a job, whereas a later observation may focus more on specific details associated with the way that the work is performed. In any case, information obtained with one technique aids in the understanding of information obtained with another. Observation and interviews also help verify information obtained by reviewing job documents and add firsthand knowledge of how tasks are actually performed.

Document Review. Documents about jobs can impart a good deal of information about the general nature and scope of a job and job functions and tasks, but documents alone cannot provide all the information needed to develop a complete and accurate task list. Content analysis of job documents should be supplemented by interviews and observations of job performance. The most probable sources of documented job information are:

- Job descriptions
- Company practices
- Position practices or guides
- Operations plans

- Training materials
- Work flows
- Maintenance manuals
- Previous task lists

A systematic approach should be employed to study job documents so that appropriate and useful information about work activities can be identified and extracted. Some steps that you can take to obtain the greatest payoff from your study of job documents are:

- Obtain as many documents about the target jobs as are available.
- Use a systematic method for marking documents to highlight tasks and functions, such as the method described in Figure 8.

Figure 8. Method for Marking Documents.

ITEM	ACTION
Function	Underline with color pencil. Write F1, F2, F3, etc.,in the margin.
Task	Underline with another color pencil. Write T1a, T1b, T2a, T2b, etc., in accordance with the appropriate functions.
Questions	Write ? in the margin. Write the question on a question list.
References	Underline with another color pencil. Write REF in the margin. Write the reference on a reference list.

• Identify other potentially useful documents referenced in the available documentation.
• Concentrate on activities performed by people, not by machines.
• Review tables of contents because documents about jobs or job-associated information may be organized by work activities.
• Study figures because they may contain task information.
• List tasks as they are identified.
• List issues, questions, and incomplete information to pursue elsewhere.

Job descriptions are excellent sources of task information, providing, of course, that they are not too old. Usually, job descriptions cover major tasks and functions, and frequently the activities are enumerated in the same form desired for an initial or preliminary task list. Figure 9 presents excerpts from the job description of a service center district manager in which tasks and functions are easily identified. A word of caution, however, is in order regarding the use of job descriptions as a source of task information in that they describe expected, not necessarily actual, job activities, and they may use language that is unfamiliar to job incumbents.

Figure 9. Excerpts from a Hypothetical Job Description.

JOB DESCRIPTION

SERVICE CENTER MANAGER

JOB SUMMARY

This position is responsible for the administration of a Service Center (SC) serving 15,000 to 20,000 accounts. Supervises 3 to 4 assistant managers, 18 to 24 supervisors, and approximately 180 to 200 nonmanagement employees who sell equipment and service products, collect company revenue, service equipment, handle billing problems, and format and type service orders. Performs personnel and administrative duties associated with the above responsibilities

Job Duties and Responsibilities

% Of Time
Involved

45%
A. Administers a Service Center serving accounts in a defined geographical area usually including both urban and suburban locations.

   1. Participates in the establishment of performance objectives for all measurements in the same Service Center. Jointly sets individual assistant manager objectives and oversees achievement of same.

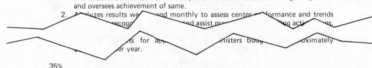

35%
B. Deals with customers and other departments to resolve problems and provide customer service.

   1. Acts as appeal point for customers' problems and complaints.

      a. Handles escalated problems for dissatisfied customers including executive complaints.

20%
C. Performs personnel and administrative duties associated with the above responsibilities.

   1. Prepares annual appraisal of assistant managers and uses the results for further development. Works with assistant managers on career paths and makes recommendations for additional development and educational programs.

   2. Handles all Union grievances appealed to District level. Furnishes briefs and

But these problems are minor and easily remedied by reviewing tasks and functions extracted from the job descriptions with job experts. Certainly by the time that job incumbents have been interviewed, job task information and terminology should be accurate, complete, and stated in the incumbents' jargon.

Documents other than job descriptions can yield many task statements, and they should be obtained and studied. Excerpts from a circuit pack-handling and maintenance practice, on which tasks have been underlined and marked, are shown in Figure 10.

Figure 10. Example of a Marked Work Practice.

When the circuit pack practice was marked, it was too early to differentiate between functions and tasks, so all activities were identified as tasks, for example, shipping (T1) and handling (T8). In addition to marked work activities, Figure 10 contains written notes about other documents that should be obtained and reviewed and questions that should be answered. Inasmuch as documents such as company practices, position practices, operations plans, training manuals, and so forth do not necessarily present information in job task form, task information probably will not be readily recognizable. Therefore, when reviewing documents to identify task information, you should keep in mind exactly what kind of information is desired. In summary, identifying and extracting task information from documents mean looking for statements that pertain to or describe activities performed by job incumbents.

Job Observation. The kind of job observation recommended for WPSS projects is a systematic procedure, not a casual visit to, or walk-through at, a work site. Job observations can vary along several dimensions; for example, they can be direct or indirect, obtrusive or unobtrusive, and structured or unstructured. Thus, incumbents can be observed at their work sites as they carry out their tasks (direct), or they can be observed on film or videotape (indirect). Direct observation should be accomplished by observing several employees performing their tasks for a period of several hours. The observer should sit alongside the incumbent and "listen in" at every step of the way. As needed, the observer should question incumbents about their activities as those activities are being performed.

Information about each action performed, the work environment, and the work flow should be recorded systematically on forms designed not only to aid in later recall of work accomplished but also to help in the preparation of task statements. It is invaluable to observe a job being performed in conjunction with a job expert who can clarify actions and work situations. If a job expert is unavailable to help with job observations, work activities not understood should be described as fully as possible and clarification obtained later when a job expert, job incumbent, or job documents can be consulted. Later descriptions of work will be aided to the extent that job activities and the means used to accomplish them are recorded exactly as they are observed — equipment and forms used should be identified and how they are used should be noted. Tasks carried out sequentially should be recorded in sequence so that, if necessary, a future user of the information can take the sequence into account. The result of job observation should be specific information recorded about the job context, the tasks performed, and the products of the work.

Obtrusive or unobtrusive observation is a matter of whether or not the observation process itself somehow interacts with the accomplishment of the work; for instance, if incumbents know that they are being observed, this knowledge might affect the way they perform. Unobtrusive, direct observation is limited to observing overt behavior and by itself is not recommended. If a job consists of few physically observable tasks, unobtrusive observation will yield very little task information unless a job expert is present for consultation. But if unobtrusive, direct job observation is desired for some reason, it will be advantageous to review job documentation prior to conducting the job observation, in addition to having a job expert at hand.

The term *structure* refers to the procedure employed to carry out a job observation and to record job information. Unstructured observations are conducted simply by visiting the workplace, observing job incumbents perform their work, and recording information about the job context and work activities in any way that is convenient and with which the observer feels comfortable. In contrast, analysts conducting structured job observations carefully select a group of representative job incumbents to observe and systematically record information about the stimuli (inputs) that generate work, the products or outputs of an individual employee's work, and the employee activity that "converts" inputs into outputs. The analyst should also record information about the environment in which the work is accomplished, interactions between the incumbent and other employees, and the materials, tools, and equipment used to carry out the work.

The nature of the job should dictate the degree of structure to use for recording job information. An elaborate observation-recording technique is unwarranted when employees who work at a desk, console, or typewriter most of the time are being observed.

Figure 11. Job Observation Recording Sheet.

JOB TITLE _____

WORK SITE LOCATION _____

WORK CONDITIONS _____

DATE _____

ACTIVITY:

Start Time: _____   Stop Time: _____   Elapsed Time: _____

INPUT that initiates activity:

PRODUCT produced (output):

EQUIPMENT, TOOLS, REFERENCE MATERIALS USED:

WHEN is activity accomplished?

How FREQUENTLY is activity performed?

Employee Comments:

Observations of craftworkers whose tasks are readily observable can prove to be a productive source of task information and thus warrant a more structured approach. Job observation forms, such as the one shown in Figure 11, can be used to help systematically record work activities, along with contextual job information, and to facilitate later formulation of task statements. Forms recommended for recording interview results, such as those shown in Figures 12 and 13, may also be useful for recording information obtained by observing job incumbents perform their work.

It will be necessary to arrange for observations through field coordinators, because the cooperation of a number of employees is needed to adequately observe job incumbents at their work sites. Each field coordinator who helps accomplish a work-site observation should be notified of the observation requirements — for example, the kinds and number of incumbents desired for the observation and how long the observation is expected to last. With knowledge of the observation requirements, field coordinators should be able to select the most appropriate observation sites and arrange to have a job expert on hand if the need for one is anticipated. Certainly, the incumbents to be observed should be representative of employees in the target jobs and have sufficient experience. Observers should be prepared to answer questions about the observation and the forthcoming survey because field supervisors may want more information than local management has provided them.

Observations of the work being accomplished, along with content analyses of documents about the target jobs, should not only familiarize the analysts with the target jobs but should also enable them to compile an initial list of task statements that will improve the focus and efficiency of the interviews to follow.

5

𐂀𐂀𐂀𐂀𐂀𐂀𐂀𐂀𐂀𐂀𐂀𐂀𐂀𐂀𐂀𐂀𐂀𐂀𐂀𐂀𐂀𐂀𐂀𐂀𐂀𐂀𐂀𐂀𐂀𐂀𐂀𐂀𐂀𐂀𐂀𐂀𐂀

Interviewing
to Obtain Job Task
Information

𐂀𐂀𐂀𐂀𐂀𐂀𐂀𐂀𐂀𐂀𐂀𐂀𐂀𐂀𐂀𐂀𐂀𐂀𐂀𐂀𐂀𐂀𐂀𐂀𐂀𐂀𐂀𐂀𐂀𐂀𐂀𐂀𐂀𐂀𐂀𐂀𐂀

A series of interviews has proved to be a most powerful
method for compiling an accurate and complete job task list for
WPSS questionnaires. Essentially, three types of interviews—
initial, verification, and follow-up—are recommended to obtain
and refine information about tasks performed by job incumbents:

- *Initial interview*—the first interview at each location. This provides a large part of the job information from which task statements will be extracted, especially when job documentation
  is scarce. If some task statements extracted from other sources
  have already been prepared, the interviewer can use them as a
  guide in conducting the initial interview.
- *Verification interview*—subsequent interviews at each location
  that serve mainly to check and modify job information obtained during the initial interview and from other sources
  and to uncover job information that may have been overlooked previously. (In a sense, all WPSS interviews are verification interviews.)

- *Follow-up interview* — interviews conducted with a small group of incumbents and supervisors to review a draft of the final task list. The purpose of the interview is to review each task statement with incumbents and to modify and edit the statements so that they are expressed in language used on the job and familiar to employees, are technically correct and unambiguous, and accurately reflect work performed by incumbents. The employees interviewed may be the original interviewees, or they may be entirely new interviewees who perform the target job at different work sites. They should, of course, be representative of the job incumbents to be surveyed.

Initial and verification interviews should be carried out in at least two locations. Normally, interviews conducted in two locations will reveal variations in job practices, terminology, and so on and reduce the possibility of biasing a questionnaire with task statements that reflect practices peculiar to a single location or company. If the number of new task statements derived at the second location is less than 10 percent of the number of task statements already available for a job, the interview phase for that job can be terminated. But if new additions to the task list are generated at a rate of 10 percent or more, it may be necessary to conduct interviews at a third location. Before doing that, however, it is advisable to check with employees at the first location to determine if some aspect of the job was inadvertently overlooked. Should that be the case, then the interview phase can be terminated; otherwise, another location is indicated. Naturally, the significance of the additional task statements should be considered in light of the cost of interviewing at a third location. Additions of new tasks at a rate of 20 percent or more indicate that interviews at a third location are definitely in order. Marked variation found in tasks performed at a third location indicate that a job expert should be consulted. It is essential to determine why so much variation is being encountered in jobs that are supposed to be the same and to decide whether interviews should be conducted at a fourth location.

After a draft task list is prepared, interviewers can initiate follow-up interviews. WPSS field coordinators should select interview sites where the target jobs are being performed in accordance with general company practices. Other factors that coordinators should consider are the nature of the area served, the degree of mechanization or electronic data-processing support, and the kind of equipment used or worked on. All these may affect the way that a job is performed. The extent to which the task statement list is modified as a result of a follow-up interview, as already discussed for the initial and verification interviews, should indicate when to conclude the follow-up interview process.

Interviewees should be experienced job incumbents and supervisors who have current knowledge of the target job. Interviews with supervisors generally yield about the same information as interviews with incumbents, but supervisors probably will (1) feel less threatened by the interview, (2) have a better perspective on job responsibilities, especially in relation to other jobs, and (3) know how the job should be performed. Differences between supervisors' views and incumbents' views of the work should be probed, but care must be exercised so that neither the supervisors nor the incumbents feel that the veracity of their information is being challenged. Verification questions can be phrased: "Did I get this right?" or "I wonder if this is correct?"

Interviews with two job incumbents and a supervisor for each job at each location should yield enough information to develop a complete task list. If information obtained during the first two interviews varies more or less than anticipated, the interviewer may decide to interview another employee or to cut the number originally scheduled. Interviews may be conducted at different locations either simultaneously or successively. If interviews are conducted successively, the interview procedure can duplicate that used at other locations or can be modified through use of information obtained in previous interviews. If a tentative task list is not available as an interview guide at successive locations, notes should be taken as in previous interviews.

After completing this chapter, you should be able to:

1.   Describe three kinds of interviews conducted in the WPSS process.
2.   List guidelines for conducting WPSS interviews.

3. Describe how to prepare to conduct WPSS interviews and record information efficiently.
4. Describe interviewing techniques that should be used to interview job incumbents and supervisors to obtain job information.

Preparing for Interviews

Interviewing requires the ability to listen and to put people at ease while directing the conversation, probing for answers, and remembering or systematically recording pertinent job information. Interviewers should not go into an interview "cold" and unprepared! Rather, all information obtained from prior efforts — observations or reviews of job documents — should be assembled and organized. The interviewer can determine what additional information is needed, what needs to be clarified and verified, and so forth. The goal of the interview is to obtain information about job performance; and just as the interviews themselves need to be planned and scheduled, so do the questions or matters to be explored within the interview.

An approach that has been found helpful is for the interviewer to formulate a list of task statements on the basis of preliminary study of the job for use as an interview guide. During the course of the interview, interviewees are asked to review each task statement on the list, correct errors, refine general work activity statements, and add tasks not included. The interviewer simply guides the interviewee through the task list.

A fresh copy of the task list should be used for each interview, but the task list may be modified to reflect information obtained in previous interviews. The task list should (1) resemble a working draft to encourage interviewees to consider it critically; (2) contain sufficient space to fill in alternate wording, additional tasks, and other information; and (3) be organized by functions, with the tasks listed alphabetically or sequentially under function headings.

Interviews can be conducted without the aid of a preliminary task statement list, but the interview will then take longer and there is a greater chance that some of the interviewee's remarks will not be understood. In the unlikely case that job documentation is unavailable, that the job does not lend itself to observation, or that the time available is too short, the interviewer should at least discuss the job with job experts to get an idea of the functions and terminology involved. One approach trained interviewers have found helpful is to be "backed up" by a job expert. During the interview, the job expert "sits in" as an observer who, if necessary, can clarify a description or otherwise fill in gaps. This procedure combines the benefits of having a trained interviewer obtain information in a useful form and a job expert contribute to completeness and clarity.

The quantity and quality of the information obtained during interviews depend to a great extent on how well the job incumbents are informed about the interview. Supervisors should inform them in advance about the reason for the interview, its location, time, and expected length, and the work-related materials to bring to the interview. Examples of such materials are forms and records received and/or dispatched, as well as documents such as blueprints, sketches, major references, job practices, and performance aids. The materials will serve to generate discussion of items that initiate work activities and of accomplishments.

Interviews should be held in a quiet room that affords privacy and where the interview process will not be disturbed. The room should be conveniently located for the interviewees and contain sufficient facilities—chairs, a table to spread out job-related materials, and electrical outlets, if needed.

A number of methods can be used to record interview information; some interviewers prefer taking a great many notes, while others rely almost exclusively on tape recordings that are transcribed after the interview is completed. While tape recordings are all-inclusive and allow several analysts to listen to interviews as many times as desired, they do have some drawbacks. Tape-recording equipment can malfunction; lengthy recordings cannot be reviewed prior to the conclusion of an interview to determine whether any salient points have been overlooked; task information cannot easily be extracted for use in immediately following interviews.

Interviewers should use any information-recording technique with which they feel comfortable, that facilitates capturing all the pertinent information, and that does not impede the progress of the interview. Basically, an interviewer should be prepared to systematically record the information in a way that makes recall and derivation of task statements easy. Printed interview-recording forms, such as those in Figures 12 and 13, have been found useful by interviewers. The left column in Figure 12 is for noting forms and other inputs that stimulate action on the part of the job incumbent, the middle column is for recording information about actions performed, and the right column is for recording the outputs or results of the actions. Figure 13 is a more elaborate form for recording and organizing information about work, and it can also be used as an interview guide to obtain as complete a picture of a job as possible. Many copies of such forms will be used during the course of an interview to record information about work activities.

Conducting Initial and Verification Interviews

General guidelines are presented below for conducting WPSS interviews and obtaining detailed information about work activities performed by job incumbents. WPSS initial and verification interviews can be subdivided into three parts: the opening or introduction; the body of the interview, in which job activities are discussed; and the closing.

Opening the Interview. Most employees enjoy talking about their jobs, but the interviewer must get them started. The course of the interview will be influenced to a great extent by the interviewer's opening remarks. It is essential, therefore, to put interviewees at ease at the very beginning of the interview. If they are suspicious about the purpose of the interview, or if an interviewer adversely affects an interviewee, for example, by appearing judgmental or too friendly, interviewees may not cooperate and may not describe their work accurately. A few simple steps that can help create a comfortable, relaxed atmosphere and reassure interviewees are to:

• Begin with an informal introduction.
• Find out how the interviewee prefers to be addressed.

Figure 12. Interview-Recording Form.

Interviewer _____ W. Smith _____ Date _____ 10-25-79 _____

Interviewee _____ R.J. Elson _____ Job Title _____ SCC Clerk _____

Bell System Experience _____ 10 _____ (years) _____ 4 _____ (months)

Experience on Present Job _____ 1 _____ (years) _____ 2 _____ (months)

Work Location _____ White Plains , N.Y _____ Telephone Number _____

Input	Action	Output
1. Accounting and time summaries	1. Enter total and post actual R work hours.	1. SCC monthly forecast and performance reports.
	2. Enter total and post actual M work hours	
	3. Calculate and post performance index ...	
2. Vendor bills Employee vouchers ... etc.	1. Investigate legitimacy of bills. Prepare payment authorization Log voucher or bill on control log. etc.	Payment authorization Payment authorization control log entry ... etc.

Figure 13. Detailed Interview Record Form.

Function Name: _____

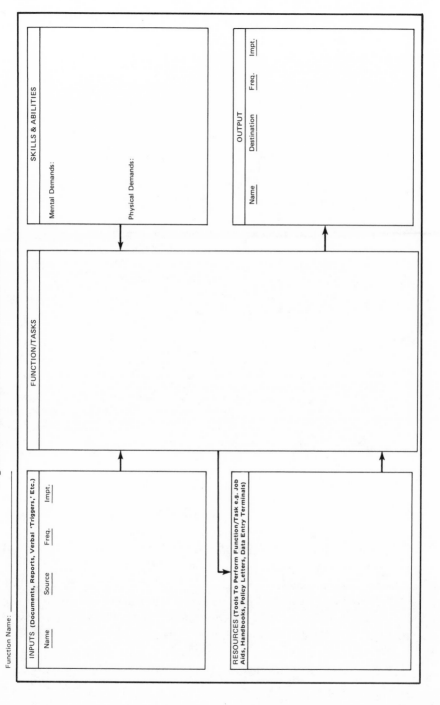

- Give the interviewee a chance to get acclimated, that is, begin with comments that promote a friendly atmosphere.
- Anticipate questions about the interview process and the use to be made of the information obtained.

A standard introduction such as the following may be used with each interviewee:

> "Hello. My name is _____,
> and I work in the ____(organization name)____ As your
> supervisor told you, we are planning to conduct a survey to
> determine the kinds of activities performed by (job name).
> We will be asking a number of people like you to describe
> their work, and we will combine the information to come
> up with a complete list of tasks performed by (job name).
> The list of tasks will be used in a questionnaire that will be
> mailed to a large number of _(job name)_."

The interviewer should describe the interview procedure and inform interviewees at the beginning of the interview that they will be asked to describe a typical workday from start to finish, to discuss and review all the work materials they brought to the interview, and to discuss each work activity mentioned in detail to get to the task level so that task statements can be extracted from the interview results. The fact that their supervisors are familiar with the purpose of the interview and what is expected to take place should be mentioned. Interviewees should also be told that neither their supervisors nor anyone else in their company will see the results of the interviews.

Initial and verification interviews may be conducted either with or without the aid of a task list. When a task list is not available, the success of the interview will depend to a large extent on the interviewee's recall and verbal ability and on skillful probing by the interviewer. When an interview is conducted with the aid of a task list, the interview procedure should also be reviewed with the interviewee. First, the interviewee should be informed that the list of task statements was derived from documents about the job and from observations of employees at work. Then, he should be told that the interview procedure will review, discuss, and critique each task statement with the objective of improving it. Interviewees should be informed that some tasks probably are stated inaccurately and that the list may contain some tasks that they do not perform. Task statements, however, should not be eliminated from the task list during the interview simply because the interviewee does not perform them. It is better to include more task statements in the list than to omit tasks that employees in the target jobs perform. The review of a preliminary task list during the interview should be aimed at answering questions such as:

- Is each task statement accurate and clear?
- Has appropriate terminology been used throughout the task list?
- Is the task list complete or have tasks been omitted?
- Have any broad areas of work been overlooked?
- Are there any inconsistencies between task statements?
- Are some task statements covered by other task statements?

Interviewees should be informed that notes will be taken throughout the interview. Notes can be taped, written on specially prepared forms, or written directly on a task list. Questions should be encouraged and answered factually; they should never be evaded, nor should any attempt be made to deceive the interviewee.

Body of the Interview. The interviewer's primary concern is to obtain accurate and complete information about the work performed by target job incumbents. If all tasks performed by job incumbents are not identified, WPSS questionnaires will be incomplete, and the survey cannot possibly provide a total picture of a job. If task statements contained in a WPSS questionnaire are inaccurate—if, for example, they contain improper terminology—respondents will not be able to answer questions sensibly.

One approach to conducting a WPSS interview, especially when a task list is not available, is to first cover very general information and slowly move on to more specific details. A convenient starting point or "icebreaker" is discussion of the interrelationships between the department in which the target job is located and other departments in the company. Another general area worth considering early in the interview is relationships between the target job and other jobs, either within or outside the department. A topic usually discussed very readily by interviewees is the work environment; for instance, how the office or plant is arranged and how many employees perform the same work at the work site. As the interview progresses, it should become more and more specific, focusing on input- and output-related activities. The interviewee should be questioned about what is done with inputs and outputs until all facets of the job appear to have been covered. The tools, equipment, and job aids used in performing the work, as well as the work load and pace, should also be discussed. This line of questioning will help establish both general and specific interfaces, work flows, and responsibilities.

When a task list is not available, the specific aspects of a job might be addressed with the following statement:

> "Think about a typical day on your job. Tell me
> the first thing you do when you come in."

When that information has been recorded, the interview can continue as follows:

> "What is the next thing you do?"

The interviewer can continue to focus on inputs (for example, forms, telephone calls, and service orders), as well as on actions taken by the employee in regard to these inputs (writing letters, filing reports, repairing equipment, and so on).

Each input and output can be discussed to determine the specific nature of each stimulus to which the job incumbent responds. Questions such as these can be asked:

- What activity should be performed when a particular input is received?
- Where do job incumbents get the information needed to perform required activities?
- What does the information look like?
- What are the outputs of the work?
- Where are the outputs sent?
- What time requirements exist?

After the first one or two inputs and outputs are discussed in this way, interviewees usually understand what is wanted, and only an occasional question will be needed to completely cover all inputs and outputs.

The existence of a task list alters the procedure somewhat. Inputs and outputs are still important but are covered in conjunction with a discussion of task statements on the list. A discussion of specific aspects of a job might be initiated as follows:

> "As I mentioned before, we want to put together a list of activities performed by ___job name___ . Here is a list of activities we developed by studying various documents, such as training materials, that are supposed to be performed by ___job name___ ."

As the interviewee looks over the initial task list, the interviewer continues:

> "We don't know if the information we used is up-to-date or accurate. Let's go over the list item by item and see what you think. We want to improve those items that are not right, to find out which activities you do that are not on the list, and to see which should be taken off."

The interviewer proceeds by reviewing each task statement with the interviewee and noting any possible modifications. The interviewer should be alert for gaps in the list that ought to be closed. One way to make certain that the task information is complete is to cover all work materials brought to the interview in conjunction with the task statement review, that is, to determine the association between each item and the tasks listed.

The interview sequences discussed above produce information from which routine tasks can be extracted. Information about exceptional tasks or those performed infrequently should now be sought. It is important to convey to the interviewee that even the smallest aspects of the job are of interest and that no activity, no matter how trivial it seems, should be overlooked.

Interviewing Techniques. Interviews rarely progress neatly within specified boundaries. Occasionally, interviewees discuss details when general information about the job is desired. They also tend to revert to sequences of work already discussed. It is not unusual for an interviewee to vacillate between specific details and general information, and, of course, it is up to the interviewer to cope with the information presented. It is important that the interviewer not be sidetracked. Interviewers should always keep the objective of a WPSS interview in mind—to obtain information about a job from which a complete and accurate list of tasks performed by incumbents can be prepared. Use of a few basic interviewing techniques and principles, as noted below, should help establish an interview pattern, put interviewees in an appropriate frame of mind, and aid in obtaining the desired job information rapidly and efficiently.

First, the interviewer should communicate to the interviewee, either verbally with responses such as "Yes" and "I understand" or nonverbally with head nodding, that the information being given is the kind of information sought. The interviewer's behavior can reinforce the kinds of responses being made by the interviewee, thereby increasing the likelihood that similar kinds of responses will continue to be forthcoming.

Second, should interviewees not understand what is wanted, be unable to verbalize, or simply be reluctant to talk about their work, they should be encouraged with prompts such as:

> "One activity you might perform is reviewing work logs. Do you do this? I'll write that down. Now, tell me some of the other things you do."

> "Let's take a look at some of the examples of the work materials you brought with you. What do you do with this form?"

Third, interviewers can make use of probes. A probe is a question that asks an interviewee to clarify a point. Probes become necessary during an interview when the information being presented is too general or vague or if the interviewer has a question about the information. The probe should be an "open-ended" question or one that allows for a free-ranging response rather than a simple yes or no. Probing is a skill that can be mastered with some practice. Several probing techniques are as follows:

- Asking short questions that begin with how, what, who, when, where, and which. After the statement "I provide information to the Marketing Department," a series of clarification ques-tions could be asked: "What kind of information do you pro-vide?" "How do you provide it?" "When do you provide it?"
- Using echo words that are aimed at obtaining specific infor-mation. After the statement "I work with service orders," the interviewer could attempt to obtain more specific information by echoing "Work with?" The interviewee will probably elabo-rate with "Yes, I check and file them. And I remove old ones from the files." Once again, an echo probe such as "Check them?" might encourage further elaboration.
- Expanding points inconsistent with previous information. In-consistencies may by the result of the interviewer's unfamili-arity with job details or inability to distinguish between similar situations. Interviewers can explain that they are unfamiliar with job details: "I don't understand that last sequence. I thought the outputs were mailed to Comptrollers. I guess I had it wrong. Could you please go over those activities again?"

Interviewers should always convey the idea that the interviewee is the expert and should never argue with him. If inconsistencies remain unresolved after a brief review, the questionable informa-tion should be flagged for later reexamination and cross-comparison.

The following kinds of questions and behavior *should be avoided* when probing:

- Closed-end questions or those that can be answered simply yes or no — for instance, questions that begin with "Do you . . . ?"
- Questions that begin with "why." These tend to be judgmen-tal, and interviewees may feel that they are being asked to jus-tify their activities. "Why" questions usually place interviewees on the defensive, and they can easily become uncooperative.
- Questions and behavior that inadvertently bias responses and diminish the accuracy of the information obtained. Leading questions — for example, "You process service orders, don't you?" — create the impression that the activity is expected to be

performed, and interviewees may respond accordingly, even though the work is not part of their job. Again, facial expressions that communicate approval or disapproval of information should be controlled, because interviewees may respond accordingly; they may provide additional information that they have been led to believe is desired, or they may stop responding altogether. Finally, a sudden change in note-taking consistency is important, and interviewees should be informed if a change is planned.

Fourth, interviewers should concentrate on the main issues, while maintaining a relaxed but businesslike atmosphere. Indications of overcontrol include very brief responses and lack of interest on the part of the interviewee and excessive talking by the interviewer. Control can be relaxed by refraining from interrupting the interviewee, returning to a subject with which the interviewee was comfortable, and changing facial expression and posture.

Interviews can also be undercontrolled. Generally, indications of undercontrol are overly long answers or frequent talking about extraneous subjects by the interviewee, too many interviewee questions, and a very lengthy interview. Control can be regained by summarizing relevant points and redirecting the interviewee to a topic of interest. At times, it may be best to be direct, and say, "For the sake of time, we'll have to move on to another topic."

Fifth, there are bound to be periods of silence during an interview. Silence should be expected and used to advantage. An interviewee may just need time to think or to make associations that might not surface if every gap in conversation were filled with comments or rapid-fire questions. At key points, silence can encourage the interviewee to talk. When an interviewee is reponding appropriately and then stops talking, resist the tendency to jump in with a question. The interviewee probably will resume talking about the topic at hand. If a period of silence is creating discomfort for the interviewee, the interviewer should ask a question about a previous item or bring up a new topic. Too much silence can be embarrassing and interfere with the continued conduct of the interview.

Closing the Interview. The interview has reached a concluding point when (1) all the materials that the interviewee brought to the interview have been discussed; (2) all the functions and perhaps all the tasks have been covered; and (3) each task on the task list, if a list was used, has been reviewed. Another thing to keep in mind is the time agreed upon with the interviewee's supervisor. If more than the agreed-upon time is needed, check with the supervisor before going on. Moreover, three hours at one sitting is about as much as interviewees can take without becoming bored and easily distracted.

Interviewees should be informed that the interview is about to conclude. A few minutes should be allowed when concluding an interview to:

- Ask the interviewee for questions.
- Request additional information or clarification.
- Reconfirm the purpose of the interview and the intended use of the information.
- Mention a possible future meeting to review the information collected (see follow-up interview).
- Invite interviewees to contact the WPSS team *through their supervisors* if they think of significant additional information.
- Thank interviewees for their help and cooperation.

Compiling the Final Task List

Information obtained during interviews and from written materials and observations will be in the form of notes and/or comments on the task lists used in interviews with different job incumbents at various locations. The next step is to condense and organize the information into a comprehensive list of task statements that collectively describe all the job activities. Task statements, however, cannot be mechanically generated from interview notes; for example, a five-minute description of an acitvity may be reducible to a single, brief task statement.

The development of useful task statements from the available information requires judgment and the ability to summarize detailed, often redundant information about job activities without distorting the information. This time-consuming, meticulous work requires a thorough understanding of how to construct descriptive task statements (see Chapter Four) and a thorough knowledge of job terminology and responsibilities. A job expert can be very helpful in deriving task statements from interview notes. An effective approach to constructing a task list is to:

- Establish the desired level of detail (specificity).
- Examine all task statements for consistency — level of detail, wording, clarity, and so on.
- Sort tasks into work categories on the basis of a similarity rule.
- Establish job functions (work categories).
- Alphabetize task statements within functions.
- Review task statements for duplication and combine redundant tasks.

Once a task list has been drafted, one or two job-knowledgeable employees or job experts should review and edit the list. The task list should then be checked for accuracy and completeness in a series of follow-up interviews scheduled about two weeks after the first round of interviews is completed. These interviews are conducted with small groups of job incumbents that may include employees previously interviewed. Follow-up interviews can be conducted at the same locations where previous interviews were held, but at least one should be conducted at a new location.

The follow-up interview should begin with an explanation of its purpose — to review a list of tasks performed by employees on jobs such as those held by the interviewees. Each interviewee should be given a copy of the task list, and the method used to develop the list should be described very briefly. The interviewees should be informed that they are to review each statement on the task list, and they should be urged to be critical of the statements. The interviewers should also inform the group that the task statements will be included in a questionnaire that will be used to survey incumbents of jobs like theirs and that their comments are vital to ensure that the questionnaire contains a complete and accurate task list.

One method for encouraging interviewee participation is to include one or two statements at the beginning of the task list that are somewhat inaccurate or poorly written. The body of the follow-up interview might be initiated with a statement such as:

> "Let's look at the first statement. Frankly, I'm not satisfied with the way it sounds. There is something wrong with it, but I'm not sure what it is. Do you see any-thing wrong with it?"

When an interviewee suggests an appropriate improvement, rein-force the response by saying:

> "Exactly! That's just what we need. I'll make the change you suggested. How about the second item on the list. I don't like that any better than the first."

The interviewer can draw attention to each task statement, reading each aloud while the interviewees follow along silently. The interviewer can then pause for comments and revise tasks statements accordingly. Generally, the discussion will concentrate only on the task statements listed, unless a series of omitted tasks has been revealed. When tasks needing modification are identi-fied, the interviewees should be involved in making the modifica-tions.

The review should be handled systematically, task by task, and the wording of each task statement should be examined. The follow-up interview should focus specifically on the following:

- *Specialized terms.* Are they used correctly? Spelled correctly? Familiar to all?
- *Similar task statements.* Are they really the same? If they are different, what is the nature of the difference?
- *Subordinate tasks.* Is one statement subordinate to another?
- *Wording.* Can general words be replaced by more specific words and imprecise terms by more accurate terms?

Examples of the kinds of changes that can be expected are:

Draft Form	*Revised Form*
• Ensure that arithmetic is correct on vouchers.	• Check arithmetic on vouchers and bills.

- Check that crew number is shown on labor charges.
- Maintain list of accounting codes for special studies requested.
- Write monthly tax reports.

- Total figures on monthly tax reports.

- File program folders.

- Solve problems when system is hung up.
- Clear card punch clip.

- Keep a list of restarts.

- Check bills for completeness.
- Maintain a record of charges for special studies requested.
- Compute data for monthly tax reports.
- Delete this entry (it is subsidiary to revised form of preceding statement).
- File contents of program folders.
- Analyze machine stops.

- Empty card punch clip box.
- Log reruns.

After the final follow-up interview, revise the task list according to the suggestions offered. When all revisions are finished and job experts are satisfied with the list, work can begin on developing a WPSS questionnaire according to the models and suggestions presented in Chapter Six.

6

╫╫

Developing
and Distributing
WPSS Questionnaires

╫╫

WPSS questionnaires that will produce the desired data about tasks and functions that job incumbents perform can be designed while the main component, the task list, is still under development. Initiation of questionnaire design, in other words, does not have to await the completion of the task list. While task statements are still being derived, task attribute questions appropriate to the specific purposes of the job analysis can be selected, response modes can be determined, appropriate directions can be prepared, and so on. When the task list has been finalized, the different parts of the questionnaire can be assembled and a reproducible copy prepared. The questionnaire can then be reproduced in sufficient quantity, and distributed to the desired respondent sample, which in turn completes and returns the questionnaire in accordance with the directions provided. The design and character of a WPSS questionnaire play a significant part in determining the quality of the job data that will be collected. In addition to the care and effort that should be devoted to the preparation of task statements, directions for answering questions about tasks must be carefully prepared and precisely worded: Questions that seek to elicit personal or biographical information should also be clear and to the point, and the questionnaire format should be easy to follow.

When you have completed this chapter, you should be able to:

1. List the kinds of questions about task statements and personal information that are most frequently included in WPSS questionnaires.
2. Describe the response scales, response formats, and directions used in WPSS questionnaires to facilitate obtaining appropriate responses.
3. Specify the way a WPSS questionnaire should be organized.
4. Describe the WPSS questionnaire pretest process.
5. Discuss the WPSS questionnaire distribution and data collection process.

Task Attribute Questions

The task attribute questions selected for a WPSS questionnaire should be based, to a large degree, on the purpose of the project. Usually, though, information about job content is obtained directly from job incumbents' and supervisors' responses to the same two or three questions about task statements. The questions conventionally included in WPSS questionnaires are:

*   How important or significant is each task to your job?
*   How much time do you spend on each task?
*   How frequently do you perform each task?
*   How difficult is it to perform each task?

Actually, the variety of questions that can be asked about task statements contained in WPSS questionnaires is almost unlimited. One questionnaire, for instance, asked, "How capable are you at performing each task?" Figure 14 indicates which of the more conventional questions are best suited for different purposes. In two cases, checkmarks appear in all five columns, indicating that all five questions are appropriate. The question "Do you perform this task?" is pertinent for each purpose listed in Figure 14, but it is not necessary to ask that question separately since it is answered by the response to another question. A zero response to a task statement question, for instance, means that the incumbent does not perform that task. So, there really are only four questions to consider in Figure 14.

Figure 14. Guide for Selecting Task Attribute Questions.

PURPOSE \ QUESTIONS	Do You Perform This Task?	How Significant/Important Is This Task To Your Job?	How Difficult Is This Task?	How Much Time Do You Spend Performing This Task?	How Frequently Do You Perform This Task?
Describe Jobs	√	√		√	√
Design/Redesign Jobs	√	√	√	√	√
Match Skill & Job Requirements	√		√		
Develop Staffing & Span Of Control Requirements	√			√	√
Establish Training Requirements	√	√	√	√	√
Conduct Operations Reviews Actual Vs. Desired Task Performance	√			√	
Compare Jobs Similarities & Differences	√	√		√	
Develop Task By Task Performance Evaluation	√	√			

Unless the total number of task statements in a questionnaire is less than 100, responding to four questions about each task statement would require too much time. It takes about ten to fifteen seconds to read a task statement and respond to a task attribute question. A questionnaire containing 100 task statements, therefore, will require that about seventeen to twenty-five minutes be spent in responding to one question about each task statement. In addition, time is required for filling out the personal information sheet and reading the directions. A 200-statement questionnaire with two questions about each task statement will require approximately two hours in all. From a practical standpoint, therefore, only one or two questions usually are asked about each task statement in a WPSS questionnaire.

When answers to four questions are needed to obtain the information desired about each task statement, the way to avoid overburdening respondents is to construct two versions of a WPSS questionnaire and administer each version to a different sample of job incumbents. The different versions would be identical except for the questions asked about tasks. One questionnaire could ask about task importance and difficulty and the other about task time and performance frequency. The results obtained with each questionnaire would be combined and analyzed together to form a complete picture of the job.

Questions about task statements are answered by rating each task in regard to a particular attribute. A numerical rating scale ranging from zero to 7 is recommended for rating task statements. Seven response categories other than zero are recommended because (1) fewer categories would tend to restrict the range of responses, (2) more categories would require finer discriminations than most respondents usually can make, and (3) an odd number of categories beyond zero allows respondents to choose a middle ground. Respondents rate task statements by selecting a single number that represents the degree to which they feel the attribute is associated with the task. The number selected is entered in the appropriate space on the questionnaire. A zero response, as previously stated, indicates that the respondent does not perform the task, and the responses between 1 and 7 represent the differing degrees (low to high) to which an attribute is associated with a task. The zero response answers the implied question "Do you perform the task?" Respondents are asked to provide a zero response instead of leaving a blank to indicate that the task statement was not inadvertently omitted.

Response Directions

The importance of clear, precise, yet brief questionnaire directions cannot be overemphasized. The following kinds of formats make response directions much easier to follow and understand:

- Highlighting important information with bold type, underlining, or other distinctive methods (bullets).
- Including examples and setting them off so that they will stand out from the rest of the text.
- Leaving plenty of space between lines to facilitate reading.

WPSS questionnaires direct respondents to go through the entire task list from beginning to end answering the same question about each task, for example, pertaining to the significance of each task to the job. When respondents have finished answering the first question about each task statement, they are directed to go back to the beginning of the task list and start answering the second question. Again, they work their way through the task list until the second question has been answered for all tasks. This method allows respondents to answer questions rapidly and effectively. Further, it prevents the response to the first question from interfering with the response to the second question, especially when answer spaces are alongside each other. Figures 15 through 19 contain directions used in WPSS questionnaires to help respondents answer the most commonly asked questions about task attributes (the directions, of course, can be modified to suit special circumstances):

- Figure 15 — directions for obtaining task significance responses. Task significance is defined as a combination of task importance, task frequency, and task difficulty.

- Figure 16 — directions for obtaining task importance responses. In this instance, an "Importance Guide" was printed on a three-by five-inch card that respondents could detach and refer to as they completed the questionnaire.
- Figure 17 — directions regarding a question about time spent performing each task. In this case, the question pertains to amount of time spent on one task as compared with amounts of time spent on other tasks; in other words, it asks about relative time spent. Respondents must work through the entire task list at least once before they can compare task statements appropriately.
- Figure 18 — directions for obtaining information about the frequency with which each task is performed. The definition of frequency will depend on the purpose of the survey. One WPSS survey used a frequency question to obtain information about how often job incumbents interacted with other organizations in their company. Each organization was listed as if it were a task statement, and respondents were asked to enter frequency information in the appropriate spaces.
- Figure 19 — directions for responding to a question about the difficulty of each task as compared with average difficulty. Again, respondents must have worked through the entire task list once before they can make the appropriate comparisons.

It is important to include in the questionnaire a definition of task difficulty that accords with the survey purpose because task difficulty can be defined in a number of ways. Some definitions of task difficulty that have appeared in job survey questionnaires are:

- The amount of training and experience required before a job incumbent can reasonably be expected to perform a task at a standard level.
- The amount of physical or mental effort required to perform the task.
- The difficulty of the task as compared with other tasks performed.
- The number of steps encompassed in a task sequence.
- The difficulty associated with learning the task.

If an appropriate definition of task difficulty is not provided, the results obtained may be misleading, especially when (as is often the case) most respondents are very experienced and now consider practically all tasks they perform to be at the low end of the difficulty scale; yet a number of those tasks may be considered very difficult by newly assigned job incumbents. One way to determine whether experience level affects responses to a task difficulty question is to compare the responses of incumbents with short job tenure to the responses of longtime employees.

Questionnaire Format and Organization

After task attributes and response scales have been selected and defined, the format and organization of the questionnaire are the next considerations. Both are important to collecting complete and accurate job information. "Complete" means that respondents answer every question contained in the questionnaire, and "accurate" refers to the appropriateness of the responses provided in relation to the response scales and the respondent's intent. A well-organized questionnaire with a good format will also help respondents complete the questionnaire more efficiently. WPSS questionnaires are prepared in booklet form with the following organization:

- Cover page.
- Introduction to the survey.
- Personal information sheet.
- Directions for responding to the first question about each task.
- Task list with response format.
- Directions for responding to additional questions about tasks or functions.
- Space for additional comments.
- Conclusion.

A professional-looking questionnaire will elicit greater respect and more careful attention than one with a casual appearance. The cover page, which should make clear that the job survey has corporate endorsement, should contain the title of the survey, list the target jobs, and include the name and location of the sponsoring organization.

Figure 15. Directions for Responding to a Question
About Task Significance.

Read each task statement carefully and decide whether or not the task is part of your present job. You are not expected to perform all the tasks listed, nor are all tasks performed in every Business Service Center. It is important that you think only of your present job, not previous jobs. Some tasks you perform are more significant for your job than others. Consider the following factors in judging the significance of a task to your job.:

    a. IMPORTANCE —   the contribution of the task to effective
                                 operations in your office.

    b. FREQUENCY —   how often you perform the task.

    c. DIFFICULTY —   how hard the task is to do or to learn to
                              do effectively.

Combine these factors in your mind to determine the significance of a task, and choose an appropriate rating according to the following.

---

0 = Definitely not a part of my job; I never do it.

1 = Under unusual or certain circumstances may be of a **minor** significance to my job.

2

3

4 = Of **substantial** significance to my job.

5

6

7 = Of **most significance** to my job.

Here is an example of how this is done:

TASK		SIGNIFICANCE								TIME SPENT
001	Review a completed order.	0	1	2	3	4	⑤	6	7	_____
002	Distribute incoming mail.	⓪	1	2	3	4	5	6	7	_____

— —

For Task 001 in the example, a "5" was circled indicating that reviewing completed orders is somewhat more than of substantial significance to the job.

For Task 002, a "0" was circled, indicating that distributing incoming mail is not part of the job.

Even if you have the responsibility to see that a task is performed, but you do not perform the task, the "0" should be circled. The number you select should be your best estimate of the significance of the task to your job.

Figure 16. Directions for Responding to
a Question About Task Importance.

2. Use the guide presented below to indicate your estimation of the importance of the task to your job.

    Importance Guide

    1 = Very minor
    2 = Low
    3 = Slightly below average
    4 = Average
    5 = Slightly above average
    6 = High
    7 = Extreme

3. Respond to every task statement that was not given a 0 response in the "Time Spent" column. Write your response to the importance of each task you now perform in the column headed "Importance."

4. Detach the card at the back of this booklet and keep it in front of you to help you make your task importance judgments.

5. Judge one task after another in the order they appear in the booklet—do not skip around.

6. Remember, tasks for which you have entered a 0 in the "Time Spent" column should not be judged on "Importance" because you do not perform those tasks.

Figure 17. Directions for Responding to a Question About Task Time.

Part C of this survey is about THE TIME YOU SPEND ON EACH TASK.

You have already identified the tasks that are part of your job by circling a number from 1 to 7 in the SIGNIFICANCE column. Now you should judge the amount of time you spend on each task and *WRITE your response* alongside the task in the Part C - TIME SPENT column. For this survey, "time" means the OVERALL AMOUNT OF TIME you devote to performing a task—OVER THE LONG HAUL; NOT EACH SEPARATE PER-FORMANCE of a task, nor to just the last few weeks.

Use the time guide shown below to indicate your estimate of the time you spend on each task you perform.

---

0 = I spend **no time** on this task.

1 = I spend a **very small** amount of time on this task as compared with most tasks I perform.

2 = I spend **less** time on this task than I spend on most other tasks I perform.

3 = I spend **slightly less** time on this task than I spend on most other tasks I perform.

4 = I spend **as much** time on this task as I spend on most other tasks.

5 = I spend **slightly more** time on this task than I spend on most other tasks.

6 = I spend **more** time on this task than I spend on most other tasks I perform.

7 = I spend a very **large** amount of time on this task as compared with most other tasks I perform.

The number you select should be your best estimate of the total amount of time you spend performing the task as compared with other tasks you perform. Again, the larger the number you select, the more time you feel you spend performing the task.

Here are three examples of how this is done:

TASK	SIGNIFICANCE								TIME SPENT
001 Review a completed order.	0	1	2	3	4	⑤	6	7	4
002 Distribtute incoming mail.	⓪	1	2	3	4	5	6	7	0
003 Detect machine defects	0	1	2	3	4	5	⑥	7	1

For Task 001 in the example, a "4" response indicates that as much time is spent on perform-ing the review task as is spent on most other tasks performed.

Since Task 002 is not performed, as indicated by the circled "0" in the SIGNIFICANCE column, a "0" should be entered in the TIME SPENT column. The "0" shows that the task was con-sidered again and not omitted by mistake.

Task 003 received a Time Spent rating of 1, which shows that detecting machine defects is devoted a very small amount of time as compared with most other tasks performed.

Please **TURN BACK to the beginning of the task list** and start rating the time you spend on each of the tasks you perform. Respond to every task statement—insert a "0" in the TIME SPENT column if you rated the task a "0" in the SIGNIFICANCE column.

Figure 18. Directions for Responding to a
Question About Task Frequency.

Instructions for Part B

Part B of the questionnaire is about how often you perform various tasks.

1. Read these "Instructions" carefully before going on.

2. Read each task statement carefully and decide whether or not you now perform the task--it is important that you think only of your present job, not previous jobs. If you do not perform a task, write a zero (0) alongside the task in the column headed "Frequency." If you perform a task, choose the closest number (from 1 to 7 in accordance with the guide presented below) to describe how often you perform the task. Write that number in the "Frequency" box along- side the task.

Frequency Guide

I perform this task:

    7 = about once each hour or more often
    6 = about every day or more often (not each hour)
    5 = about every other day
    4 = about once each week
    3 = about once each month
    2 = about once every six months or less
    1 = about once every year
    0 = I do not perform this task on my
        current job

The number you select should be your best estimate of your average frequency of performing the task. As you can see, the larger the number you select, the more frequently you perform the task.

Figure 19. Directions for Responding to a
Question About Task Difficulty.

LISTED BELOW ARE TASKS. RATE EACH TASK FOR DIFFICULTY BASED ON THE AMOUNT OF SKILL NEEDED TO DO THE TASK SATISFACTORILY.	DIFFICULTY
	1. Very much below average 2. Below average 3. Slightly below average 4. About average 5. Slightly above average 6. Above average 7. Very much above average
1. Assign personnel to installation or repair projects	
2. Brief personnel on unit security or safety rules	
3. Complete manhour accounting forms for work crews	
4. Conduct supervisory orientation of newly assigned personnel	

Coming immediately after the cover page, the introduction should explain the purpose of the survey and how respondents can help, describe the questionnaire briefly, and assure respondents that their answers will be treated confidentially. The introduction should also inform respondents that the survey is designed to study jobs, not individuals' performance on the job. It should also contain directions for returning completed questionnaires. Figure 20 shows a questionnaire introduction used in a survey of service center district managers.

Figure 21 contains a personal information sheet illustrative of those used in WPSS surveys. The information obtained here will be used in anticipated data analyses. The task data collected can be analyzed by subsets of the total sample in accordance with breakdowns of the personal information items, such as location, job title, job tenure level, experience level, and so on. Identification information can also be used to contact respondents should the need arise. Personal information sheets should allow sufficient space for responses, and simple and clear options should be available where a choice has to be made—for example, in giving job titles. The numbers printed on the right side of the personal information sheet shown in Figure 21 are keypunch instructions. The numbers 31–32 that appear alongside the question "Which job title best describes your supervisory responsibilities?" indicate to the keypunch operator that a two-digit code (supplied in advance) representing the job title checked should be punched in the thirty-first and thirty-second positions of the personal information record. By contrast, the question "How many previous Bell System jobs have you held?" does not require a code because the actual response will be keypunched in the thirtieth position of the personal information record.

Each section of a WPSS questionnaire contains directions designed to help respondents complete the questionnaire accurately and return the completed questionnaire to a designated address. But the directions that introduce and explain how to answer task attribute questions and use response scales require a little more attention than other directions. Response directions, to be effective, should contain a few completed examples, along with a few examples for respondents to work through before attempting to answer questions about tasks they perform. Directions for a second task attribute question should follow the task list. The format for the second set of directions should be similar to the directions for the first task attribute question, with the exception that the second set of directions refers respondents back to the beginning of the task list to start providing answers to the second task attribute question. Figure 1 contains directions to "turn to Part C instructions on the next page." Part C instructions cover a second question, and they in turn refer respondents back to the beginning of the task list (see Figure 17).

Task statements should be presented in a WPSS questionnaire in accordance with the following guidelines:

Figure 20. WPSS Questionnaire Introduction.

A Word About This Survey

This survey is being conducted by AT&T to update information about Business Service Center jobs. You are performing one of the jobs of interest, and you can help by completing this survey booklet. We need your responses to obtain meaningful information about the job you and others like yourself are performing throughout the Bell System.

The information you provide in this booklet will be seen only by those who are involved with processing and computerizing the data. No one in your company or at AT&T who is not associated with computerizing the survey data will have access to your responses, nor will they ever receive any information supplied by individual respondents. The purpose of the survey is to understand and describe the jobs being performed in Business Service Centers, and only information about jobs will be made available. The data will not be used to evaluate jobs.

There are four parts to this booklet. Please answer each part in order, beginning with Part A. When you finish Part A, go on to Part B. Do not start Part C until you have completed Part B. Complete Part D last. The parts are:

Part A — Background or personal information
Part B — Significance of the tasks you do as part of your job
Part C — Relative amount of time you spend on each task
Part D — Percent of time you spend on each function (groups
of tasks)

Please answer each item in each part. *Do not omit any items.*

What To Do With Your Completed Booklet:

When you have answered every item in the booklet, seal the booklet in the envelope provided and return it to the person who gave the booklet to you. That person will return the sealed envelopes to the data processing center at AT&T where the results will be tabulated.

THANK YOU FOR YOUR COOPERATION.

- List task statements alphabetically under job function headings in bold print.
- Number task statements consecutively. The number serves as a task identification and is especially useful for data analysis.
- List task statements on the left side of the page and place associated response spaces on the right side.
- Leave sufficient space between task statements so that respondents can easily match task statements with associated answer spaces.
- Highlight and distinguish response spaces by boxing (see Figure 19 or shading (see Figure 6).

Figure 21. WPSS Questionnaire Personal Information Sheet.

PART A

Part A requests information about you and your telephone company experience. Please complete Part A first. Then go on to Part B. Instructions for Part B follow Part A.

YOUR NAME: _____ OFFICE PHONE: ( ) _____
                                            (include area code)

COMPANY NAME: _____ 4-5

STATE: _____ 6-9   CITY: _____ 10-11

DISTRICT NAME: _____ 12-15

UNIT NAME: _____ NAME OF SECTION WITHIN UNIT: _____

How many *months* have you been in your present job? _____ MONTHS 25-27
(that is, in the same job classification, regardless of location or specialty)

How many *years* have you worked for the Bell System? _____ YEARS 28-29

How many previous Bell System jobs have you held? _____ JOBS 30
(if same job but at different locations, count as one job)

Which job title best describes your supervisory responsibilities? (check one)   31-32

☐ Manager, Business Service Center accounts only (level 2)
☐ Manager, Service Order Support (level 2)
☐ Manager, Business Accounts *and* Service Order Support (level 2)
☐ Business Office Supervisor (level 1)
☐ Service Order or Clerical Supervisor (level 1)
☐ Other (please explain): _____

What was the title of your previous Bell System job?
Last job: _____ JOB TITLE 33-34
What is the highest grade completed in your formal education? (check one)   35-36
☐ Less than high school graduate.
☐ High school graduate (or equivalent).
☐ 1 year of college.
☐ 2 years of college.
☐ 3 years of college.

Respondents should be given the opportunity to add tasks they perform that are not included in the questionnaire and to comment about the questionnaire in general. One means to do so is to provide a page requesting write-in comments about the directions, the task statements, and other parts of the questionnaire and to ask respondents to write in tasks they now perform that are not included in the questionnaire. Such write-in task statements do not lend themselves to electronic data processing; to the extent that they are provided, however, they are indicators of the completeness of the task list and should be useful for future applications of the questionnaire. Generally, though, open-ended requests for information are not likely to produce useful information.

The questionnaire should conclude by thanking respondents and reminding them how to return the completed questionnaires.

Data Reduction Considerations

WPSS questionnaire responses must be entered into a computer in order to be analyzed in any meaningful way. The first step in reducing and processing WPSS data is to keypunch them on cards, magnetic tape, or a disk. It is possible to circumvent keypunching and to computerize the data directly by employing a special "mark-sense" or optical scanning system. Before adopting an optical scanning system, however, you should study its costs and benefits because there may be a sufficient number of special requirements that make keypunching more attractive than optical scanning for your situation. The design of the questionnaire, in any case, is important to the data reduction process. Ideally, keypunch operators should be able to keypunch responses exactly as they appear on the questionnaire. It is impractical, however, to design a questionnaire to achieve that ideal. Keypunch operators probably will have to search for some data or translate a few responses in accordance with data code tables provided to them. Appropriate questionnaire design, however, will minimize such activity. To ensure accurate and efficient data entry, keypunch operators must be given comprehensive instructions, usually in the form of a data record layout that specified what should be keypunched where. A WPSS computer program automatically produces a record layout as an adjunct to the survey definition required to process and analyze the data. A computer-generated record layout is shown with the description of the survey definition process in Part Two of this guide under the QDEF procedure.

Responses to questions on a WPSS personal information sheet, which require filling in a blank space, marking a box, or circling a number, are the responses that present the biggest data reduction problems. Filling in blanks with free-form responses is a problem because respondents are not required or indeed expected to respond in exactly the same way. The company's name, for example, may be abbreviated by some respondents and spelled out by others, and the computer will interpret those responses differently. What to keypunch when responses are boxed and circled presents as much of a problem as do free-form responses if what is marked or circled cannot be keypunched exactly as it appears on the questionnaire. Some keypunch solutions in order of decreasing desirability due to expense and efficiency are to:

- Design the questionnaire so that responses can be keypunched directly from the questionnaire.
- Have an editor standardize or code questionnaire responses so that keypunching can be accomplished directly from the questionnaire.
- Provide keypunchers with a table of response-associated codes so that they can use the questionnaires as the keypunch media but perform table look-ups as needed to standardize or code some responses.
- Transcribe questionnaire data onto special keypunch data sheets that will serve as the media for keypunching.

The goal is to use the questionnaires as the keypunching media and to minimize the number of responses that require an editor or keypuncher to interpret and code responses or perform table look-ups. Figure 22 contains an example of the way response codes can be printed on a personal information sheet for keypunching purposes. The personal information sheet shown in Figure 22 is the same one shown in Figure 21, with the exception that keypunch locations have been deleted and response codes have been added. The items pertaining to present managerial responsibility and highest grade completed are keypunched as coded on the form (the small number printed to the left of each box). Months in previous job, years worked for the Bell System, and number of previous Bell System jobs held, however, are keypunched as filled in. The state in which the employee works is keypunched as the two-letter postal abbreviation. The remaining items, Company, City, and Last Job, have to be coded by an

Figure 22. WPSS Questionnaire Personal Information Sheet with Coded Items.

PART A

Part A requests information about you and your telephone company experience. Please complete Part A first. Then go on to Part B. Instructions for Part B follow Part A.

YOUR NAME:_____ OFFICE PHONE: (___) _____
                                                  (include area code)

COMPANY NAME:_____

STATE:_____ CITY:_____

DISTRICT NAME:_____

How many *months* have you been in your present job?_____ MONTHS
(that is, in the same job classification, regardless of location or specialty)

How many *years* have you worked for the Bell System?_____ YEARS

How many previous Bell System jobs have you held?_____ JOBS
(if same job but at different locations, count as one job)

Which best describes your present managerial responsibility? (check one)

10☐   District Manager, for Business accounts only

11☐   District Manager, for both Business and Residence accounts.

12☐   District Manager, not only for accounts, but also responsible for Installation and Maintenance activities.

13☐   Other (please explain):_____

What was the title of your previous Bell System job?

  Last job:_____ JOB TITLE

What is the highest grade completed in your formal education? (check one)

11☐ Less than high school graduate.

12☐ High school graduate (or equivalent).

13☐ 1 year of college.

14☐ 2 years of college.

15☐ 3 years of college.

16☐ 4 years of college (and/or bachelor degree).

editor or keypuncher in accordance with instructions provided, unless they are known in advance; they can then be listed with codes on the personal information sheet. Even previous job titles can be listed with associated codes if certain titles are of particular interest — to study career paths, for example. The list of job titles can be shortened considerably by designating an "other" category; otherwise, there probably would be too many job titles to list each of them separately on a personal information sheet.

Locations of items in a record can be printed on the form, as in Figure 21; their use is optional and of negligible value to keypunch operators if a record layout is provided. The basic WPSS data reduction problem is *what* to keypunch — *where* data should be keypunched is fixed and automatically provided by the data-processing system.

Pretesting and Producing the Questionnaire

Before a WPSS questionnaire is printed and distributed, it should be pretested with a few typical respondents. Even though the questionnaire has been constructed and reviewed carefully and in accordance with instructions, respondents may still have problems with some parts of the questionnaire. Thus, the temptation to rush into printing and distributing a WPSS questionnaire as soon as a draft becomes available should be resisted. The pretest should be arranged through the sponsoring organization. Participants and their supervisors should be informed in advance of the purpose of the pretest and the amount of time it is expected to take. Pretest respondents should be a small group of about four incumbents who are performing the target job and are representative of the intended survey respondents. A close approximation of the finished questionnaire should be used in the pretests so that both content and format can be checked, but the pretest questionnaire should be in a form that.is easy and inexpensive to reproduce and revise.

A WPSS project team member should personally administer the pretest of the questionnaire and observe respondents as they work on the questionnaire to see if they have any problems. The administrator should ask respondents to complete the questionnaires in accordance with the directions and request that they ask questions or discuss problems as they arise. Questions asked and problems raised by respondents should be recorded for further study. When the respondents complete the questionnaire, comments should be elicited from them about difficulties experienced in understanding the directions or in providing responses. The tryout respondents should also be questioned about the completeness of the task list. Pretest questionnaires should be examined for errors, omissions, and indications of other problems. Wording, directions, format, and so forth should be revised in accordance with pretest results.

If it is not feasible to observe a pretest group, questionnaires can be mailed to a small group of incumbents who are representative of prospective respondents. Such a procedure may provide information about distribution and collection methods as well as about questionnaire content and format. As a way of compensating for the lack of direct observation, an evaluation sheet that asks respondents to list any problems encountered with directions, responses, and so on should accompany each pretest questionnaire. Pretest respondents should also list any tasks they perform that are not listed in the questionnaire. Returned pretest questionnaires should be examined carefully for evidence of confusion or difficulty in answering questions. If a problem is evident but the reason for it is unclear, respondents may be contacted through their supervisors for clarification. Generally, though, the causes of problems will be obvious. Again, the questionnaire should be revised in accordance with pretest results.

After the questionnaire has been pretested and modified accordingly, it is ready to be printed for use in a job survey. To ensure the quality of the printed questionnaire, you should check the final text copy for errors and omissions and the camera-ready copy for special instructions to the printer, margins, position of the copy, page numbers, and so on. The printing order should be large enough to cover contingencies, and you should check the quality of the paper ordered, as well as the information about printed return envelopes for the questionnaire.

Distributing and Collecting WPSS Questionnaires

Detailed and careful planning is essential for the effective distribution and return of WPSS questionnaires. After the locations of participating organizations have been identified, the distribution and collection process can proceed. The steps for reaching appropriate respondents and collecting the desired data are as follows:

1. The sponsoring organization identifies WPSS field coordi-nators.
2. Coordinators are notified of survey requirements, and they help determine the number of respondents and survey sites.
3. Detailed distribution instructions and questionnaires are mailed to coordinators.
4. Coordinators package questionnaires and instructions and distribute them to target job supervisors.
5. Supervisors administer questionnaires to appropriate job incumbents.
6. Job incumbents complete questionnaires, seal them in the envelopes provided, and either mail them directly to the data-processing center or return them to their supervisors, who will forward the envelopes to the data-processing center and notify the responsible coordinator.
7. Coordinators track survey progress and report weekly to the project manager.

The data-processing center may be an outside firm hired to log in and examine questionnaires, code certain responses, and forward the questionnaires to the organization where the data will be re-duced and readied for computerization. The data-processing center, of course, may also be a company organization.

Specific details that must be attended to when planning the distribution of survey materials are:

*   Determine total and survey site sample size requirements.
*   Prepare instructions for field coordinators and supervisors.
*   Specify respondent job titles so that they will be easily recog-nized by supervisors.
*   List mailing addresses of field coordinators.
*   Include addressed return envelopes in each package.

As soon as field coordinators are designated, they should be called to inform them of the role they are expected to play in the project. Some of the items that should be discussed with field coordinators are (1) the purpose of the survey, (2) the survey method, (3) the date materials will be mailed and the completion date objective, (4) sample size and survey site requirements, (5) characteristics of respondents, (6) questionnaire administration procedures, (7) questionnaire return information, and (8) the WPSS team member to contact for guidance and problem resolution. The call should be followed by a letter that spells out specific instructions. Correspondence containing instructions is needed not only for field coordinators but also for field managers and supervisors, as well as for the employees participating in the survey (see Appendix for examples of correspondence). Each organization should have a respondent quota to meet, and it is the coordinator's responsibility to meet that quota. Instructions to the field coordinator should emphasize that the primary concern is the mainstream of work performed by target employees, not work performed by a few employees who may have target job titles but are performing special-project work; in other words, respondents should represent typical job incumbents, not special or temporary subgroups.

Sample size instructions should be stated so that the coordinators have some leeway in specifying the number of respondents per survey site. Operational circumstances often enter the picture, and the coordinator is the best one to determine specific numbers of respondents. For instance, if the requirement for a particular location is five or six respondents but the supervisor's group contains seven target job incumbents, the coordinator should have the discretion to elect to survey all incumbents in the supervisory group rather than exclude one or two. The instructions should also mention that it is *not* necessary to obtain data from every location where a target job is performed. In fact, for some coordinators, two or three locations may be sufficient.

Coordinators should be requested to notify field supervisors and managers of the cooperation expected in the forthcoming survey before mailing them packages of survey materials. Otherwise, the survey will come as a complete surprise, and questionnaire administration may not be accorded appropriate attention and care. The WPSS team should provide field coordinators with copies of all instructions that are meant to be forwarded to field managers and supervisors. Generally, these instructions should contain a brief statement about the purpose of the survey and the need for cooperation in obtaining the desired job information. The major emphasis should be on getting the questionnaires into the hands of appropriate job incumbents and on returning completed questionnaires. Supervisors should also be informed of the amount of time that each respondent will probably devote to completing the questionnaire. Finally, they should be told that the questionnaire may be completed by incumbents individually at their work stations or in small groups, whichever is more efficient, and that the information supplied by each respondent will be held in confidence.

Sample Size

Sample size affects the accuracy with which calculated values estimate the values that would have been obtained if all incumbents of a target job responded to the questionnaire. If information is needed about all possible variations in the way work is performed, then every incumbent should complete a WPSS questionnaire. Usually, however, survey objectives, even those concerning work performance variations, can be satisfied by sampling job incumbents working at widely separated locations. From a practical standpoint, it is advisable to sample job incumbents, use appropriate statistics to describe the sample, and infer properties about the job incumbent population from knowledge of the sample properties; that is, it is advisable to generalize from the sample to the population. Of course, sample data are of use only insofar as they allow reasonably accurate inferences about the population. Sampling keeps costs down (it reduces questionnaire completion time and the amount of data collected and processed) and makes it possible to avoid the practical problems associated with administering questionnaires to many hundreds or thousands of job incumbents.

There are no hard-and-fast rules regarding minimum and maximum sample sizes for WPSS projects. Pass and Robertson (1980) found that stable information could be obtained from much smaller samples than were customarily sought. The main concern is to sample job incumbents and yet obtain essentially the same information as would be obtained by surveying all target job incumbents. As sample size approaches the population size, the sample statistics approach the values that would be obtained if all target job incumbents were surveyed. If all target job incumbents are surveyed, then statistics calculated are no longer estimates but are the population values. Samples, though, are usually much smaller than the total number of job incumbents. If the total number of job incumbents is relatively small, it probably will require very little additional expenditure to acquire a larger percentage of the total, perhaps even 100 percent. A sample should be large enough so that it can be stratified in several ways and still allow meaningful statistical comparisons between subsamples.

WPSS applications have used a systematic sampling procedure, but sample size cannot be determined statistically for WPSS projects because the information needed to do so is simply not available. Further information on sample size can be obtained in introductory statistics texts that present formulas for determining the sample size needed in specific situations. A rule of thumb used for WPSS projects is to limit the size of the sample to 300 to 400 respondents. When the number of job incumbents does not exceed 300, all the job incumbents are surveyed. If the size of a sample is kept between 300 to 400 respondents, a range that should allow for a sufficient number of meaningful comparisons, the percentage of the total number of job incumbents represented by the sample will vary inversely with the total number of job incumbents, for instance:

Job Incumbent Total	Sample Size	Percent of Total
100–300	100–300	100
500	250–300	50–60
1000	300	30
2000	300–400	15–20
4000	360–400	9–10

To some extent, sample size should be based on the number of factors that will be studied to determine their effect on the way that work is perceived and performed; for instance, to study task difficulty for male and female employees by educational level and by location would require comparisons of task difficulty indices calculated for males and females at different locations and varying educational levels. Task difficulty data for such an example might be presented in a table such as this:

Task Difficulty Averages for Task Statement 125

Educational	Male					Female				
Level	NY	NJ	OHIO	COLO	CAL	NY	NJ	OHIO	COLO	CAL
High School										
High School Graduate										
College–1 year										
•										
•										
•										

This kind of table would contain sixty cells, and the values recorded in each cell would represent the interaction of sex, location, educational level, and task difficulty. The values in the margin represent various aspects of the three educational variables. Although only certain comparisons are likely to be of interest, any averages contained in the sixty cells or in the margins can be compared. As the number of variables to be compared increases, so does the size of the sample needed to make those comparisons.

A common statistical convention is to consider a sample of 30 or more observations a large sample and one of less than 30 a small sample. On the one hand, if the results presented in each cell of the table were based on data obtained from 30 respondents, a total sample of 1800 respondents would be needed. On the other hand, if cell results were based on 10 respondents, then 600 respondents would be needed to make up the sample. Had only three educational levels been of interest instead of six, the table would have had 30 cells, and the total sample sizes presented would have been halved to 900 and 300. The possible comparisons and associated sample sizes for large (30-per-cell) and small (10-per-cell) samples for the 30-cell table are as follows:

Task Difficulty Comparisons	Large Sample	Small Sample
Males vs. Females by		
Location by Educational Level	30 vs. 30	10 vs. 10
Males vs. Females by Location	90 vs. 90	30 vs. 30
Males vs. Females by		
Educational Level	150 vs. 150	50 vs. 50
Males vs. Females	450 vs. 450	150 vs. 150
Locations (5)	180/location	60/location
Educational Level (3)	300/level	100/level

The subsample sizes for the small sample results are thus quite respectable for the kinds of comparisons contemplated. Some analysts, however, prefer to obtain as large a sample as possible to support investigations of all conceivable subgroups that may exist among job incumbents.

The number of respondents requested from each organization participating in a job survey should be based to some degree on the proportion of the total number of job incumbents that work in each organization. If all company organizations in which target job incumbents work do not participate in a survey, the number of respondents requested should be adjusted accordingly. If, for example, a total of 1,000 job incumbents is evenly distributed across five company regions and a sample of 300 is desired, then each region should contribute about one fifth of the sample, or about 60 respondents. If one region does not participate in the survey, the four participating regions should make up for the non-participating region and contribute 75 respondents each so that the desired sample size is achieved.

The two important sample size values to consider then are:

1. The number (percentage) of all job incumbents desired for the survey sample.
2. The number of respondents who will be sought in each participating organization.

Information will be needed, of course, about the number of job incumbents company wide and per company organization. Company census data, if available, are very useful for specifying pre-

liminary numbers of respondents. These numbers can be discussed with each field coordinator. If company census data are
unavailable, field coordinators will have to provide the number of
job incumbents and their work locations, and the WPSS team will
use that information to determine the number of respondents that
should be surveyed in each participating organization.

Coordinators can be requested to select survey sites randomly if there are no special location requirements. A random
sample of survey sites within a company organization can be obtained simply by listing locations alphabetically and selecting
among them according to a predetermined percentage. If, for
example, a 25-percent sample of locations is desired and a list of
potential sites contains twenty locations, then every fourth location on the list could be selected as a survey site. Another way to
select survey sites is to write each location on equally sized slips of
paper, place them in a container, and draw the desired percentage
of slips. The idea is to select a sample of locations so that virtually
all major work variations due to differing local practices will be
covered by the sample. As is the case when sampling respondents,
a smaller percentage of locations should be drawn when the location list is long than when it is short. For example, if there are fifty
potential survey sites, ten randomly drawn sites probably will
cover all the major work variations. If there are only ten locations,
however, four to five survey sites should suffice, assuming, of
course, that there are enough target job incumbents at the locations selected to meet the sample quota. If not, sample sites
should be drawn until the sample quota can be met at the sites
selected.

Printing, Mailing, and Distributing Questionnaires

The number of questionnaires printed should exceed the
desired sample size by at least 20 percent to allow for various contingencies. Field coordinator addresses are needed for mailing
purposes, since it is coordinators who will distribute questionnaires
within their organizations. The printer should pack and mail
sufficient numbers of questionnaires to each coordinator, and the
remaining questionnaires should be sent to and stored by the
WPSS team.

Questionnaires should be mailed to coordinators on the agreed-upon date; but if for some reason the questionnaires will be mailed early or late, the coordinators should be notified. In addition to a sufficient number of questionnaires, packages sent to each coordinator should contain (1) a review of instructions for coordinators, (2) cover letters, (3) instructions for managers and supervisors who will distribute questionnaires to their subordinates, and (4) special answer sheets (if needed).

Questionnaire returns can be handled in several ways. Respondents can mail completed questionnaires directly to the data center in the addressed envelopes provided, or they can seal them in envelopes and return them to their supervisors, who will package and mail them either to the field coordinator or to the data center. If completed questionnaires are not funneled through the coordinators en route to the data center, supervisors should be requested to notify coordinators how many questionnaires were distributed, completed, and returned. A third alternative is to have respondents return completed questionnaires to their supervisors, who will quickly review them for completeness and then package and send them to the data center or field coordinator. This alternative is looked upon with disfavor for two reasons. First, it is contrary to the promise of confidentiality made to the respondents; and, second, some analysts feel that responses may be influenced by the fact that supervisors will examine the questionnaires. So, at the risk of receiving some incomplete or erroneously completed questionnaires, the third alternative should be disregarded.

Returned questionnaires will require some review and coding before data reduction can begin. If need be, an outside firm can handle the clerical work, especially if the survey is a large one (the clerical firm's address can be used as a return address for the questionnaires). The clerical work to be accomplished is to log in returned questionnaires, compare the number of completed questionnaires returned to the number distributed per organization, check each questionnaire for omissions or illegible responses, code responses as required in preparation for keypunching, group questionnaires by location, and inform the project manager about delayed returns and missing responses. If illegible or omitted responses need to be corrected—for example, if an item that is being used to subgroup questionnaires has been omitted—respondents can be contacted through the field coordinator and immediate supervisor so that the information can be obtained. As the clerical work is completed, questionnaires can be forwarded for keypunching.

Both the WPSS project manager and field coordinators should track survey progress. Generally, the project manager is interested in the number of questionnaires mailed to each coordinator and how each participating organization is progressing toward its survey objective. A tracking sheet should be set up so that it is easy to determine the status of the survey in each participating organization. When organizations have completed their part in the survey, letters should be sent to the field coordinators thanking them for their participation and cooperation (copies should be sent to their managers). Contact with other survey participants to express appreciation and thanks should be left to the field coordinators.

7

𝖑𝖑𝖑

Interpreting
and Using
Results

𝖑𝖑𝖑

Attainment of WPSS objectives is not automatic simply because a job survey has been accomplished. Project planning is of the utmost importance to achieving the objectives that provided the original impetus for a WPSS project. WPSS questionnaires must be designed and administered in a manner that guarantees that the job information sought is obtained; and, as Chapter Three indicated, data collected with WPSS questionnaires can be analyzed in many ways. To reiterate briefly, answers to questions about job content, such as task importance or significance and the time spent on tasks, can be summarized statistically on a task-by-task basis for an entire sample and for various subsamples — for example, by jobs or by locations for a single job. Task data can be combined to represent functions, and function information also can be summarized by job or location. In addition, a variety of statistical and cross-tabulation analyses of the responses to personal information items can be generated to portray the characteristics of a sample or subsamples.

The quality of the WPSS data and the kinds of results generated certainly are important, but more important — in fact, the crux of WPSS and job analysis approaches in general—is the way that the results are applied. The focus of this chapter is on the interpretation and use of WPSS results. Thus, after you have completed this chapter, you should be able to:

1. Describe several statistical indices and their meaning from the standpoint of WPSS analyses.
2. Describe the kinds of computer reports or printouts available through WPSS.
3. Interpret the results presented in WPSS computer reports.
4. Describe several ways that WPSS results have and can be used.

WPSS Computer Reports

There are essentially two types of WPSS reports or printouts. One type is a statistical summary report, such as the report shown in Figure 23, and the other is a cross tabulation, or joint frequency distribution, of respondents according to two or more information items, such as the reports shown in Figures 25 and 26. Either type of report can be obtained for task or personal data analyses; generally, however, statistical summary reports are generated for analyses of responses to questions about tasks, and cross tabulations are generated for analyses of responses to questions about personal information items. In either case, the report format is a multirow-multicolumn table. When tasks or functions are the focus of the analysis, row headings will be either task statements or functions, while column headings will represent the total sample and various subsamples, such as locations (survey sites) or job titles (but only if more than one job has been surveyed with the same questionnaire). Separate reports must be generated for each task attribute question included in WPSS questionnaires—for instance, a separate task significance report and a separate task time report. The situation is somewhat different for personal information items, because there is more latitude in the way cross tabulations can be generated. Cross tabulations of personal information are much smaller (fewer rows) than task attribute statistical summaries, and the row headings in cross tabulations usually contain levels for a personal information item, such as job tenure levels (see Figure 26) or educational levels. The column headings, again, may contain locations or job titles. At times, statistical summaries are wanted for personal information items — for example, to obtain average job tenure or average educational level. In these instances, the personal information item need not appear in either the row or the column headings. The table can be set up so that it is a location (rows) by job title (columns) table with the personal item averages appearing in the table cells. The interpretation of such a table for job tenure would be that respondents at a particular location, such as a division of a company, have held the job title represented in the column heading for the average number of years contained in the cell at the column and row juncture. A breakdown of job title tenure, such as the one shown in Figure 26, will not appear in the statistical summary table just discussed, but can be obtained easily with another pass at job title tenure information.

WPSS computer reports or printouts contain very few indices, as can be seen in Figures 23 through 26. The numbers that appear immediately beneath the column headings represent the total number of respondents per sample. The indices contained in WPSS statistical summary reports are proportions, arithmetic means, and standard deviations. The indices are defined as follows:

- *Proportion* — the number of responses that contribute to the cell statistics divided by the total number in the sample or subsample. Zero responses may or may not be included in the calculations, at the discretion of the user. If zero responses are not included in the calculations, the proportion represents the number of nonzero responses or the proportion of the sample that performs the task.
- *Mean* — the arithmetic mean, also known as the average. This is the sum of the numerical responses divided by the number of responses. The mean is a measure of central tendency that indicates the magnitude of the sample responses. Again, although zero responses may be included in the calculation, they usually are not.

- *Standard deviation* — an index that provides information about the dispersion or variability of individual responses around the mean value.

A proportion, mean, and standard deviation are presented in each cell of a statistical summary table so that the reports can be scanned quickly for information about (1) the proportion of incumbents in the samples who actually perform each task, (2) the magnitude of their responses, and (3) the degree to which individual responses vary around the mean value. It is very easy to use the proportion information to make several quick comparisons. Simply by scanning down a column, you can quickly identify those tasks performed by a majority of the incumbents and those performed by very few incumbents in that sample. As previously mentioned, proportions of incumbents performing tasks at different locations can be used to determine where the same job is performed differently. With job titles in the column headings, the proportion of incumbents in different jobs performing each task will be side by side, and scanning across the columns will enable you to pinpoint those tasks that are performed across jobs. Attention should be given to any overlap that is not understandable.

An examination of the means will identify those tasks that are regarded as more important, more time consuming, and more difficult that others; by checking across the columns, you can spot large differences between sample means very easily. Here, too, the proportion of incumbents performing the tasks should be considered, because more faith can be placed in an average based on a large number of responses than in an average based on a very small number. In the same vein, it is easy to compare the degree of response variation across samples. The standard deviation will be small when there is little variation around the mean. This is an indication that sample members responded similarly; and, as responses spread out more around the mean, the standard deviation becomes increasingly larger. Generally, a pattern will emerge for the size of the standard deviations so that unusual standard deviations can be detected easily. Further detail on means and standard deviations and how they may be used in statistical comparisons can be obtained by referring to most introductory statistics texts.

A table that summarizes the percentages of time incumbents spend performing tasks can be generated with WPSS programs even though the responses to a task time question are obtained on a scale ranging from one to seven. The only task attribute that has been analyzed this way up to now is task time. A percent time per task is calculated for each respondent (see Chapter Two for an explanation of the calculation for deriving percent time from task time responses), task percent time values are averaged across respondents, and the results are displayed in a task % Time table. A similar table can be generated for each task attribute question included in a questionnaire; at present, however, time spent seems to be the only attribute that can be analyzed meaningfully this way.

Perhaps a brief example will help you to understand the indices contained in WPSS statistical summary reports. Consider the following two sets of five responses to a question about task significance.

	Set 1	Set 2
	3	1
	3	1
	4	4
	5	7
	5	7
Total	20	20

The means are calculated for each set as follows:

$$\frac{\text{Sum of Responses}}{\text{Number of Responses}} = \frac{20}{5} = 4.0$$

The means are equal, but it is obvious that the values in Set 2 are spread more around the mean than in Set 1. The standard deviations are 1.0 for Set 1 and 3.0 for Set 2, a finding that confirms our inspection of the data. So, the complete picture emerges only after the standard deviations are known. The responses in the first set agree more about the significance of the task for the job than do the responses in the second set, which actually demonstrate little agreement. If everyone in a sample provides the same response, there is no variation and the standard deviation is zero — each response, in other words, equals the mean. The mean, of course, should be interpreted in terms of the scale definitions provided in the questionnaire. In accordance with the significance scale shown in Figure 15, tasks with a 4.0 mean would be considered to be of substantial significance to the target job, but a standard deviation of 3.0 should promote additional inquiry about the task represented by the second set of data.

The indices contained in cross-tabulation reports are frequencies that represent the number of respondents classified in the category represented by the cell and percentages that show that part of the sample represented by the cell frequency. Two percentages are found in each cell — one shows the percentage that the cell frequency represents of the row total frequency and the other shows the percentage it represents of the column total frequency. A simple example that illustrates the nature of a WPSS cross-tabulation table for sales personnel job tenure in two company divisions is as follows:

Job Tenure		Eastern Division	Western Division	Total
	FREQUENCY	30	20	50
Under 5 years	ROW %	60	40	100
	COL %	30	40	33
	FREQUENCY	70	30	100
Over 5 Years	ROW %	70	30	100
	COL %	70	60	67
	TOTAL	100	50	150
	ROW %	67	33	100
	COL %	100	100	100

The cross tabulation can be examined within division (column values), between division (row values), and for the total sample (marginals). The totals show that there are 150 sales personnel in all, and the column totals show that the Eastern and Western Divisions have 67 percent and 33 percent of the total, respectively. As can be seen in the row totals, there are 50 sales personnel with under and 100 with over five years of job tenure. The breakdown by division indicates that the Eastern Division has 60 percent and the Western Division has 40 percent of all those with under five years of job tenure. Of all sales personnel with over five years of job tenure, the Eastern Division has 70 percent and the Western Division has 30 percent. Within the divisions (columns), the Eastern Division has 30 percent of its sales personnel with under and 70 percent with over five years of job tenure, and the Western Division has 40 percent with under and 60 percent with over five years of tenure.

Four samples taken from WPSS computer reports are presented in Figures 23 through 26. The particular samples were selected to illustrate the variety of reports that can be generated with WPSS computer programs. The reports are all from a survey of Business Service Center district managers, a middle-management job. In this job survey, most of the respondents (101 out of 113) selected the same job category alternative to represent their jobs, so task data were analyzed only by location and not by job title.

The sample report shown in Figure 23 was taken from a task significance report, which is representative of all task attribute statistical summary reports. Had more than one job been surveyed with the same questionnaire, a similar report would have been generated with job titles instead of company names in the column headings. As you can see, some of the words in the task statements have been abbreviated or otherwise shortened to fit the space available. The first task results cell in Figure 23 contains the information that 97 percent of the total sample perform Task 1, that the mean significance level is about 3.7, which is close to the midpoint of the significance scale used in the questionnaire, and that the standard deviation is about 1.7, which is the ballpark for other standard deviations in the column. Information contained in the Task 3-C&P Telephone Company cell indicates that all five managers in the C&P sample perform Task 3, that the average response is 5.0, which is high, and that the standard devi-

Figure 23. Sample from a Task Significance Statistical Report.

```
                                    SURVEY: 1000
STATISTICS FOR SIGNIFICANCE
--------------------:----:-----------:----------:-----------:-----------:----------
                    :    COMPANY
SIGNIFICANCE        :    :   TOTAL   :C&P       :ILLINOIS   :INDIANA    :MICHIGAN
--------------------:----:-----------:----------:-----------:-----------:----------
                    : N= :    113    :    5     :    6      :    2      :    5
--------------------:----:-----------:----------:-----------:-----------:----------
   1. ANALYZE OFFICE :PROP:   0.97   :  1.00    :  0.83     :  1.00     :  1.00
COSTS/EXPENSES FOR   :MEAN:   3.673  :  3.400   :  2.800    :  5.000    :  4.400
BUDGETING PURPOSE    :STD :   1.714  :  0.894   :  1.789    :  1.414    :  2.302
--------------------:----:-----------:----------:-----------:-----------:----------
   2. ASSIGN DEVELOP-:PROP:   0.92   :  0.80    :  0.83     :  1.00     :  1.00
MENT OF LONG RANGE   :MEAN:   4.048  :  4.000   :  4.000    :  6.500    :  3.000
FORCE/TRNG REQRMNT   :STD :   1.787  :  1.155   :  1.414    :  0.707    :  2.000
--------------------:----:-----------:----------:-----------:-----------:----------
   3. DETERMINE      :PROP:   0.90   :  1.00    :  0.83     :  1.00     :  0.80
PERSONNEL NEEDS FOR  :MEAN:   3.578  :  5.000   :  2.800    :  3.500    :  3.000
A NEW PROJECT        :STD :   1.714  :  2.000   :  2.049    :  2.121    :  1.414
--------------------:----:-----------:----------:-----------:-----------:----------
   4. DETERMINE      :PROP:   0.92   :  0.60    :  0.83     :  1.00     :  0.80
WORK FLOW &          :MEAN:   3.375  :  4.333   :  3.000    :  2.500    :  3.250
OFFICE DESIGN LAYO   :STD :   1.769  :  1.528   :  2.121    :  2.121    :  1.258
--------------------:----:-----------:----------:-----------:-----------:----------
   5. DEVELOP        :PROP:   0.79   :  0.80    :  1.00     :  1.00     :  0.40
ABSENCE & TARDINESS  :MEAN:   3.382  :  3.750   :  3.000    :  4.500    :  2.000
POLICY               :STD :   1.655  :  0.500   :  2.000    :  2.121    :  1.414
--------------------:----:-----------:----------:-----------:-----------:----------
   6. DEVELOP        :PROP:   0.97   :  1.00    :  1.00     :  1.00     :  0.80
ANNUAL FORCE PROGRAM :MEAN:   4.691  :  5.600   :  3.500    :  6.500    :  4.250
                     :STD :   1.801  :  1.342   :  1.049    :  0.707    :  2.500
--------------------:----:-----------:----------:-----------:-----------:----------
   7. DEVELOP        :PROP:   0.83   :  0.60    :  1.00     :  1.00     :  0.80
DISTRICT BUDGET &    :MEAN:   4.309  :  6.333   :  2.833    :  3.500    :  4.250
EXPENSE PROGRAM      :STD :   1.878  :  1.155   :  1.941    :  3.536    :  2.062
--------------------:----:-----------:----------:-----------:-----------:----------
```

ation is 2.0. As can be seen by looking across the Task 3 row, the C&P sample seems to regard the task as more significant than do the total sample and the other company subsamples shown in the printout. Tasks 2, 6, and 7 appear to be the most significant tasks shown in the sample report, and they are each performed by a large majority of the managers.

The report shown in Figure 24 is noticeably different from either of the report categories previously described. The row headings are functions, and the column headings represent the total sample and company subsamples. The values contained in the report are percentages of total time (%TOT) devoted to functions. Function percent time (%Time) is obtained from task percent (%Time) values. First, all the individual respondent task %Time values for a function are summed, and then the function sum is divided by the sum of all task %Time values. A glance at

Figure 24. Sample from a Percent of Time Report.

%TIME		COMPANY TOTAL	:C&P	:ILLINOIS	:INDIANA	:MICHIGAN	:MOUNTAIN
	:N= :	113	5	6	2	5	2
1. ADMINISTRATIVE PLANNING	:%TOT:	13.235	12.139	12.318	18.421	10.993	14.450
2. GATHER & ANALYZE DATA	:%TOT:	16.341	14.052	14.893	15.166	16.411	14.265
3. TRAINING & DEVELOPMENT	:%TOT:	10.256	8.936	9.756	7.526	11.872	11.099
4. CUSTOMER CONTACTS	:%TOT:	6.128	6.462	4.354	5.047	5.488	4.518
5. INTERDEPT. RELATIONS	:%TOT:	8.662	7.858	6.169	7.696	9.687	10.158
7. ADMINISTERING OFFICE RECORDS & PERSONNEL	:%TOT:	12.108	12.407	15.207	12.933	11.934	7.789
8. COMMUNITY & PUBLIC RELATIONS	:%TOT:	2.882	4.557	4.322	4.266	1.728	0.811
9. PERSONNEL EVALUATION	:%TOT:	10.009	9.943	11.807	9.904	10.346	10.148
10. INTER-LEVEL COMMUNICATION	:%TOT:	11.169	12.822	11.315	9.924	12.285	15.798
11. PROBLEM HANDLING	:%TOT:	9.211	10.824	9.860	9.118	9.255	10.964

the column headed Total in Figure 24 shows that the largest percentage of time is devoted to Gathering and Analyzing Data (16 percent) and the smallest to Community and Public Relations (2.9 percent).

The cross tabulation shown in Figure 25 summarizes responses to a question about the number of months survey respondents have held their present job titles. The report presents a tabulation of results by job tenure categories (row headings). The job tenure categories should be interpreted as up to ½ Year, between ½ Year and 1 Year, between 1 Year and 2 Years, between 2 Years and 3 Years, between 3 Years and 5 Years, between 5 Years and 10 Years, and More Than 10 Years. Each cell in the report contains the number of respondents classified in that cell, as well as

Figure 25. Sample from a Job Tenure Cross-Tabulation Report.

```
                              SURVEY: 1000
---------------------:----:---------------:-------------:------------:------------:------------:
                     :    COMPANY
TITLE TENURE         :    :  TOTAL   :C&P        :ILLINOIS    :INDIANA     :MICHIGAN    :MOUNTAIN
---------------------:----:---------------:-------------:------------:------------:------------:
                     : N= :  113     :   5       :   6        :   2        :   5        :   2        :
---------------------:----:---------------:-------------:------------:------------:------------:
        *ROW  TOTAL* :FREQ:  112     :   5       :   6        :   2        :   5        :   2
                     :COL%: 100.0000% : 100.0000% : 100.0000%  : 100.0000%  : 100.0000%  : 100.0000%
                     :ROW%: 100.0000% :   4.4643% :   5.3571%  :   1.7857%  :   4.4643%  :   1.7857%
---------------------:----:---------------:-------------:------------:------------:------------:
1/2 YEAR             :FREQ:   16     :   1       :   0        :   1        :   1        :   1
                     :COL%:  14.2857% :  20.0000% :   0.0    % :  50.0000%  :  20.0000%  :  50.0000%
                     :ROW%: 100.0000% :   6.2500% :   0.0    % :   6.2500%  :   6.2500%  :   6.2500%
---------------------:----:---------------:-------------:------------:------------:------------:
1 YEAR               :FREQ:   29     :   1       :   0        :   1        :   2        :   1
                     :COL%:  25.8929% :  20.0000% :   0.0    % :  50.0000%  :  40.0000%  :  50.0000%
                     :ROW%: 100.0000% :   3.4483% :   0.0    % :   3.4483%  :   6.8966%  :   3.4483%
---------------------:----:---------------:-------------:------------:------------:------------:
2 YEARS              :FREQ:   13     :   2       :   3        :   0        :   0        :   0
                     :COL%:  11.6071% :  40.0000% :  50.0000%  :   0.0    % :   0.0    % :   0.0    % :
                     :ROW%: 100.0000% :  15.3846% :  23.0769%  :   0.0    % :   0.0    % :   0.0    % :
---------------------:----:---------------:-------------:------------:------------:------------:
3 YEARS              :FREQ:   10     :   0       :   0        :   0        :   1        :   0
                     :COL%:   8.9286% :   0.0    % :   0.0    % :   0.0    % :  20.0000%  :   0.0    %
                     :ROW%: 100.0000% :   0.0    % :   0.0    % :   0.0    % :  10.0000%  :   0.0    %
---------------------:----:---------------:-------------:------------:------------:------------:
5 YEARS              :FREQ:   14     :   0       :   1        :   0        :   0        :   0
                     :COL%:  12.5000% :   0.0    % :  16.6667%  :   0.0    % :   0.0    % :   0.0    % :
                     :ROW%: 100.0000% :   0.0    % :   7.1429%  :   0.0    % :   0.0    % :   0.0    % :
---------------------:----:---------------:-------------:------------:------------:------------:
10 YEARS             :FREQ:   15     :   0       :   1        :   0        :   0        :   0
                     :COL%:  13.3929% :   0.0    % :  16.6667%  :   0.0    % :   0.0    % :   0.0    %
                     :ROW%: 100.0000% :   0.0    % :   6.6667%  :   0.0    % :   0.0    % :   0.0    %
---------------------:----:---------------:-------------:------------:------------:------------:
MORE THAN 10         :FREQ:   15     :   1       :   1        :   0        :   1        :   0
                     :COL%:  13.3929% :  20.0000% :  16.6667%  :   0.0    % :  20.0000%  :   0.0    % :
                     :ROW%: 100.0000% :   6.6667% :   6.6667%  :   0.0    % :   6.6667%  :   0.0    % :
---------------------:----:---------------:-------------:------------:------------:------------:
```

the percentages of all respondents classified in the particular column and row that the number represents.

The Row Total-Company Total cell contains the information that 112 respondents provided job tenure information and that they represent 100 percent of the respondents classified in both the row and the column; that is, they represent the total sample. An examination of the Total column shows that 45 respondents (sum of the ½ Year and 1 Year cells) have up to 1 year of tenure in their present job titles and that they represent about 40.1 percent of the total sample. The remaining 60 percent of the sample is quite evenly distributed across the categories. The Row Total-C&P cell contains the information that the managers represented are 100 percent of the column total and about 4.5 percent of the row total; in other words, the 4 managers represent the total C&P sample and 4.5 percent of the total sample. The 2 Year-Illinois cell contains the information that 3 managers in the Illinois sample have between 1 and 2 years in the job title and that they represent 50 percent of the Illinois sample and about 23 percent of all the managers with between 1 and 2 years of tenure in the job title.

The cross tabulation shown in Figure 26 summarizes responses to a question about the length of time survey respondents have been employed by the Bell system. The report presents the results by tenure category for the total sample and company subsamples. Each cell is interpreted in the same way as those in Figure 25. Actually, there are five more tenure categories than the computer printed; since none of the respondents had less that 5 years of company tenure, however, the computer suppressed those tenure categories. The 10 Years-Total cell contains the information that 8 managers in the sample have been employed by the company for between 5 and 10 years, and those 8 managers represent about 7.1 percent of the total sample. Most of the managers, 93 percent, as can be seen in the More Than 10 Years-Total cell, have more than 10 years of company tenure. A statistical summary (not shown) provided the information that the average company tenure for the sample was about 22 years. In the C&P column, it is plain that 4 managers, or 80 percent of the C&P sample, have been with their company more than 10 years, whereas 1 manager has less than 10 years of company tenure — that one manager represents 12.5 percent of the managers in the total sample that have less that 10 years of company tenure.

Figure 26. Sample from a Company Tenure Cross-Tabulation Report.

BELL TENURE		COMPANY TOTAL	:C&P	:ILLINOIS	:INDIANA	:MICHIGAN	:MOUNTAIN
		SURVEY: 1000					
	: N= :	113	5	6	2	5	2
ROW TOTAL	:FREQ:	113	5	6	2	5	2
	:COL%:	100.0000%	100.0000%	100.0000%	100.0000%	100.0000%	100.0000%
	:ROW%:	100.0000%	4.4248%	5.3097%	1.7699%	4.4248%	1.7699%
10 YEARS	:FREQ:	8	1	0	0	1	1
	:COL%:	7.0796%	20.0000%	0.0 %	0.0 %	20.0000%	50.0000%
	:ROW%:	100.0000%	12.5000%	0.0 %	0.0 %	12.5000%	12.5000%
MORE THAN 10	:FREQ:	105	4	6	2	4	1
	:COL%:	92.9204%	80.0000%	100.0000%	100.0000%	80.0000%	50.0000%
	:ROW%:	100.0000%	3.8095%	5.7143%	1.9048%	3.8095%	0.9524%

Direct Uses for WPSS Results

WPSS results can be very useful for identifying and selecting task statements for further application. After all, the reason for breaking jobs down into tasks and studying the tasks is to be able to use the job study results in support of human resource administration and management programs. Decision criteria are needed, however, to help distinguish those tasks that will be considered further for a specific application from those that will be set aside. Task importance information, for instance, is crucial for establishing training requirements. First, however, it is necessary to distinguish the important from the unimportant tasks. Any point selected to help make this kind of distinction should be toward the high end of an importance or significance rating scale. One way to proceed is to single out tasks that attained reasonably high averages—for example, an average rating of at least 5 on a 7-point significance scale—and then concentrate on only those tasks performed by 50 percent or more of the job incumbents surveyed.

Task statements can be selected on the basis of statistical results contained in WPSS computer reports and applied directly in a number of ways. WPSS computer reports, for example, summarize responses to questions about tasks actually performed by job incumbents and, in effect, amount to highly detailed job descriptions. The computer reports can thus be used in preparing more conventional narrative job descriptions, or they can be used as they are or in a slightly rearranged form—for example, tasks can be rank ordered within function on the basis of the statistical results.

Significant or important tasks, moreover, can be the starting point for establishing formal training requirements and for developing training materials and courses. Task statements are sufficient for identifying topics that should be covered by training, but further division of tasks into subtasks and elements is necessary for development of training material. When job training is already available, training materials can be reviewed in conjunction with task statements to determine whether or not significant tasks are covered by the training. If significant tasks are not covered, new training development should be considered to cover those tasks. Less significant tasks can also be examined in light of existing training to make certain that it covers all job aspects that should be covered. Should formal training not include some of these less significant tasks, they may be incorporated into it, or they may be relegated to on-the-job training.

Significant tasks can also be used to develop rating forms on which job performance can be rated task by task. Figure 27

Figure 27. Excerpts from a Task-Oriented Rating Form.

RATING DIRECTIONS

Rate the effectiveness with which the employee being evaluated carries out each task. Think of performance effectiveness as a combination of factors that yields acceptable work under normal conditions. Consider productivity or work volume, accuracy or quality, thoroughness, and reliability when rating performance.

Read each task carefully, decide how effectively it is performed, and enter a checkmark (√) in the column that best represents the effectiveness with which the employee carries out the task. If you have not observed the task being performed, or if the task is not part of the employee's job, check the Not Observed or Not Performed column.

EXAMPLE

	Slightly	Somewhat	Rather	Quite	Decidedly	Very	Extremely	Not Observed	Not Performed
Compare Installation order change with original order to determine reason for change				√					
Determine mileage charges for customer account								√	

In the example above the task performance rating scale has seven effectiveness categories ranging from "Slightly" to "Extremely" effective. In the example, the employee was rated as "Quite" effective at performing Task 1. The supervisor has not observed the employee perform Task 2, as indicated by the check in the Not Observed column.

How effectively does the employee:	Slightly	Somewhat	Rather	Quite	Decidedly	Very	Extremely	Not Observed	Not Performed
A. Internal Contacts									
1. Call Maintenance to obtain information on an order that is overdue for completion . .									
2. Call Maintenance to expedite, cancel, or postpone an order									
3. Negotiate with Maintenance on such matters as unusual service requests and incorrect service orders									
4. Notify Maintenance of appointment changes									
B. Credit									
5. Administer credit screen for new customers									
6. Determine whether a deposit is required from customer									
7. Determine the deposit amount required for a new account.									

shows excerpts from a task-oriented rating (TOR) form that supervisors used to rate clerk job performance in a study of TORs. Significant tasks were selected to represent each function performed by the clerks and task performance effectiveness was rated at one of seven points ranging from "slightly effective" to "extremely effective." The rating form also provided supervisors with a way to indicate that they had not observed a task being performed or that a task was not part of a particular clerk's job. Task ratings and weighted function values (function weights were obtained from job supervisors) can be combined in different ways to gauge function and overall performance effectiveness, and rating results can be used in employee appraisal to feed back information about strong and weak points. Two separate TOR studies conducted with different types of telephone company jobs have shown that the properties of TORs are at least as good as, if not better than, those obtained for other kinds of job performance rating methods. Further, TOR forms are easy to develop and use, supervisors require very little orientation in the use of the forms, and only five to ten minutes are required to rate an employee. (Supervisors have been very satisfied with the TOR approach and favor its adoption.) Of course, it will be necessary to work out the details associated with applying TORs on an ongoing basis; that is, it will be necessary to settle on administrative procedures, standards and evaluation categories, and procedures for using the information in appraisal sessions.

Note also that job information can be obtained from a variety of sources and compared. One way is to compare surveyed job performance with centrally designed jobs and work methods to determine whether work is being accomplished in accordance with company practices, specifications, and training. Reasons for differences discovered between standards and actual practice can be investigated to determine whether the way jobs are being performed should be brought into line with the standards or whether the standards should be modified to accord with the way the jobs are being performed. A second, already-discussed way to use survey results in comparisons of job performance is to compare tasks performed by incumbents in the "same" job working at different sites. Differences obtained, especially in task occurrence, indicate that the job is not being performed the same way at each location.

A third way, also discussed previously, is to compare tasks performed by employees working in different jobs to identify overlap, assuming that workers in the different jobs either complete the same questionnaire or answer questions about the same task statements listed in different questionnaires. When incumbents in different jobs are surveyed with the same questionnaire, a results table can be generated in which adjacent columns contain task information for the jobs being compared; it then becomes a simple matter to identify those tasks being performed by employees in the different jobs. A fourth way is to compare supervisors' views of the tasks that should be performed with the tasks incumbents report they actually perform. When supervisors and incumbents complete the same questionnaire, their respective results also can appear side by side in a computer printout so that it will be very easy to see where they agree or disagree on task occurrence, task importance, task time, and so on.

A less immediate use for WPSS results is in future analyses of the same jobs. Since WPSS task statement text as well as results are stored in a computer, the same task statements may be retrieved, supplemented, and administered again, and updates of the computerized data base can be accomplished at a fraction of the original job analysis cost. Current data can be compared with previously obtained data to identify job changes that occurred over time.

A few conclusions based on direct applications of WPSS results obtained in several projects follow. First, immediate supervisors (first-level managers), second-level managers, and clerks were found to be devoting significant percentages of their time to performing technical analysis work that should have been performed almost exclusively by craft employees.

Second, field supervisors were still completing, and therefore duplicating, paperwork that was also being completed in an operations control center introduced to centralize various functions performed in the field. It was recommended that an orientation program be developed for field supervisors that would present, among other things, the reasons for centralizing certain formerly dispersed functions in the new control center organization, as well as the associated benefits for the field supervisors.

Third, job content for switching-equipment technicians

working in electromechanical environments was found to differ markedly from that for switching-equipment technicians working in electronic environments. Work associated with the newer, more advanced electronic equipment included more information processing, evaluation of coded information, and decision-making, and less hands-on work.

Fourth, a significant part of a highly skilled technician's job was devoted to monitoring a video screen that displayed results of automatic tests of switching equipment. Upon observing an indication of an equipment malfunction, the technician would alert the appropriate switching office and pinpoint the malfunctioning equipment so that it could be corrected very quickly. It was recommended that instead of having the technician monitor the display, an audible signal be added to the video monitor to alert a supervisor when a malfunction occurred. The supervisor, in turn, would alert the appropriate switching-equipment office.

Fifth, four sales jobs evaluated at different levels were analyzed primarily for the purpose of designing a validation study for a selection procedure (Gael, 1977). The results showed that similar work was being performed by three of the sales employees. Sales managers, however, differed considerably from the three sales employees in the importance attributed to functions performed. As expected managers considered tasks associated with managing and administration more important, whereas sales employees considered tasks related to selling and to technical features of the work more important. Job similarities and differences were taken into account in identifying selection instruments and defining performance criteria. The sales organization underwent a major reorganization shortly after the job analyses were completed, however, and the validation study was not carried out.

Finally, significant job tasks performed by supervisors of clerks who processed service orders were used as a starting point to conduct interviews with job experts in preparation for centrally developing a new training course to be used nationally to train the supervisors. The interviews were conducted at a number of locations throughout the country to make certain that variations in the way subtasks were performed would be taken into account when the training materials were developed.

Follow-Up Uses for WPSS Results

Several human resource programs require more information than can be obtained directly from WPSS questionnaire analyses; for example, information about the qualifications needed for specific jobs — knowledge, skill, and ability — is basic to designing selection test validation studies and employment procedures. To bridge the information gap, WPSS results can be used to select tasks for a brief, follow-up data collection procedure aimed at supporting a particular human resource program. The same general, follow-up data collection procedure can be designed to meet several objectives, but the specific objective will dictate which items or factors should be used in the data collection process. For example, two objectives that can be achieved with the WPSS follow-up procedure are to (1) derive job knowledge, ability, and skill requirements and (2) design or redesign jobs to correct deficiencies and to meet efficiency and motivational goals.

The steps for carrying out the WPSS follow-up procedure are as follows:

1. Establish criteria for selecting tasks to include in the follow-up procedure — for example, specify that the task have at least a 5.0 importance average and that at least 50 percent of the job incumbents perform the task.
2. Identify all tasks that meet or exceed the specified criteria.
3. Select and define all factors, such as abilities and skills, that will be used to rate each task.
4. Prepare a table in which significant tasks are the row headings and the factors of interest are the column headings. Figure 28 shows a sample taken from a table used to examine the skill and ability requirements for the voucher audit clerk job.
5. Select a method for rating the degree to which factors pertain to task statements — for example, an involvement rating scale ranging from no involvement to a large degree of involvement.
6. Specify the desired number of raters and the characteristics they should possess.
7. Select data collection sites and determine the number of raters desired per location.

Figure 28. Sample from a Follow-Up Procedure Rating Table.

VOUCHER AUDIT CLERK
TASK STATEMENTS

ABILITIES/SKILLS

Task Statement	1 COMP	2 S&W	3 MEM	4 NF	5 REAS	6 INF	7 TS	8 PER	9 SS	10 DEXT	11 PS	12 SPELL
1. Check Expense Vouchers For Incorrect Entries.												
2. Note Expenses On Expense Voucher That Require Separate Explanation.												
3. Correct Errors On Vouchers.												
4. Check Estimate Numbers Against Account Numbers.												
5. Compute Use Tax.												
6. Record Information On Summary Sheet For Keypunch.												
7. Mark And Sort Records For Attention Of Records Clerk.												
8. Identify Charges That Cannot Be Paid By Field Draft.												
9. Calculate Whether Supplier Discount Has Been Credited.												
10. Post Bills Against Accounts Or Contracts.												
11. Check For Account Codes Or Types Of Bills That Support Special Studies.												
12. Correct Errors Listed By Computer On Error Report.												
13. Check Charges To Particular Accounts And Subaccounts For Appropriate Department Authorization.												
14. Compute Percentages And Prorate Amounts On Suppliers' Bills.												
15. Discuss Errors Detected With Employees In Other Departments.												
16. Obtain Account Code Information.												

Note: The abbreviations that appear as column headings are defined on p. 141.

8.   Arrange through field coordinators to meet with small
     groups of raters at field location.
9.   Conduct rating sessions that have been designed to last no
     longer than three hours.
10. Analyze data and interpret the results.

The follow-up procedure was developed with immediate
supervisors in mind as the raters, but that is not a necessary condition. Although immediate supervisors probably are the most
knowledgeable employees from whom to obtain the desired ratings, other job experts also could serve as raters. For example,
behavioral scientists who are familiar with ability and skill definitions and rating methods can serve as raters, but they would have
to be trained in the rating process and understand each task. And
there are simply too many subtleties, even in the performance
of entry-level job tasks, to expect behavioral specialists to understand the tasks in the short time period usually available to obtain
the desired ratings. Moreover, as the number of jobs being studied
increases, the situation clearly favors using supervisors who are
job experts.

A study aimed at determining job qualifications for seven
clerical jobs from entry to top level (Gael, 1977) will be used as an
example to describe and discuss the WPSS follow-up procedure.
The seven jobs studied were service order clerk, payroll allotment
clerk, revenue reports clerk, voucher audit clerk, keypunch ope-
rater, computer operator (single stream), and computer operator
(multistream). The number of task statements in the questionnaires administered to samples of job incumbents ranged from
thirty-two to eighty, so an importance criterion was established that
would eliminate only the least important tasks from the follow-up
procedure.

The step following the selection (or elimination) of task
statements for the follow-up procedure is to identify factors that
will be used to rate each statement, such as abilities, skills, and
job design dimensions. Rating tables should be formed in which
the row headings are task statements and the column headings are
factors pertaining to the particular objective at hand. Inasmuch as

the objective of the clerical study was to determine job qualifications, the factors used to rate task statements and head the rating-table columns were abilities. Setting job qualifications is a matter of translating job knowledge and tasks into abilities and skills. Playing tennis, for example, may be said to require a high degree of perceptual-motor coordination, and editing a book to require a high degree of language ability. Under other circumstances, the column headings could have been job design dimensions, knowledge items, and so forth. If a question should arise about the applicability of a factor, it should be included, because it is better to collect the data and then determine that the factor does not apply than to omit a factor and later discover that it should have been included.

The twelve factors used in the clerical study were selected, and in some cases modified, from a list of fifty-five abilities and skills developed by E. Fleishman (Human Resources Laboratory, 1975) because of their apparent relevance for the clerical jobs under study — abilities such as explosive strength were easily eliminated. Definitions for the twelve factors are as follows:

1. Comprehension (COMP) — ability to understand the written and spoken language of others. This factor is a combination of oral comprehension and written comprehension.
2. Speaking and Writing (S&W) — ability to express oneself through written or spoken language so that others will understand. This factor is a combination of oral expression and written expression.
3. Memorization (MEM) — ability to remember information such as words, numbers, pictures, and procedures. Pieces of information may be remembered by themselves or with other pieces of information.
4. Number facility (NF) — ability to add, subtract, multiply, and divide. These can be a part of other operations such as finding percentages.
5. Reasoning (REAS) — ability to apply rules to problems and to come up with answers or to combine pieces of information to form a rule. This factor combines inductive and deductive reasoning.

6.   Information ordering (INF)—ability to follow correctly a rule or set of rules for arranging things or actions in a certain order. The rule or set of rules to be used must already be given. The things or actions to be put in order can include numbers, letters, and mathematical or logical operations.

7.   Time sharing (TS)—ability to shift back and forth between two or more sources of information.

8.   Persuasion (PER)—ability to present information in order to influence the opinions or actions of others.

9.   Social sensitivity (SS)—ability to act suitably in a social situation regardless of the exact nature of the social contact. This involves adjusting behavior to fit the occasion and depends on figuring out how other people will act.

10. Dexterity (DEXT)—ability to make skillful, coordinated movements of the fingers, hands, and arms. This factor is a combination of finger dexterity and manual dexterity.

11. Perceptual speed (PS)—ability to compare letters, numbers, pictures, or patterns both quickly and accurately. This ability also involves comparing a presented object with a remembered object.

12. Spelling (SPELL)—ability to spell words correctly.

Should a tryout of the rating process show that more time is required to rate tasks than supervisors can reasonably be expected to devote or that the process is too tedious, the rating procedure can be shortened by reducing either (1) the number of tasks to be rated or (2) the number of factors on which tasks will be rated. A task statement list can be subdivided to form two or more versions of a rating table with the same factors as the column headings. After the data are collected, they can be combined and treated as if only one table had been used. Another way to reduce the number of task statements included in a WPSS follow-up rating table is to employ stringent criteria in the task selection process. If a large number of factors are going to be used in rating tasks, the factors could be subdivided to form more than one version of a rating table. As is the case with task statements, the different versions could be administered to different sets of raters and the results combined to develop a complete picture of the job. As a last resort and at the risk of obtaining incomplete information, the burden can be reduced by having job experts rate functions instead of tasks. The tasks associated with each function should be listed beneath the function so that the raters will all have the same information regarding the work encompassed by each function.

A rating method must be selected or devised to rate the intensity of relationships between tasks and factors such as abilities. The specific meaning of each point on a rating scale—for example, a one-to-seven scale—should be defined, and raters should be trained to understand each value. A variety of methods has been used to define rating values. One of the simplest is to employ single words, such as *slightly*, *very*, and *extremely* (see Figure 27) to cover the range from low to high. Another way to define rating-scale values is to use behavior descriptions to represent different values along the rating scale. Figure 29 shows a behaviorally anchored rating scale that was developed to rate the degree of memory required to perform tasks (Human Resources Laboratory, 1975). The behaviors listed on the scale serve as a guide to help select a value that best represents the degree of memory needed. Behavior statements for each item that will be used to rate tasks are generated by a small group of subject matter experts (SMEs), who are asked to write as many high-, medium-, and low-value behaviors as they can in a five-minute period for the particular factor under consideration and then go on to the next factor. A lengthy list of behavior statements usually results, and the statements are then assigned values by the SMEs. Statistical analysis of those values helps select and place behavior statements at specific points on the rating scales. As can be seen in Figure 29, the behavioral anchors are about 5.9, 4.7, 2.5, and 1.3.

Follow-Up Procedure Rating Sessions. Data collection locations where a sufficient number of appropriate SMEs are available should be selected. Raters do not have to be job incumbents, but they must be very knowledgeable about the way the job in question is currently being performed. The number of raters should range between six and ten per rating session and at least ten per job. Field coordinators should be requested to arrange for the rating sessions. They should be asked to provide a quiet conference room with enough tables and chairs to accommodate the SMEs

Figure 29. A Behaviorally Anchored Rating Scale.

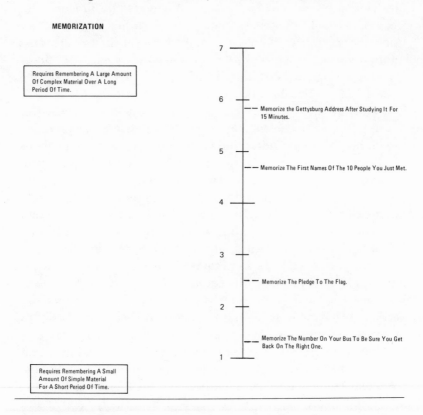

MEMORIZATION

Requires Remembering A Large Amount Of Complex Material Over A Long Period Of Time.

7

6
—— Memorize the Gettysburg Address After Studying It For 15 Minutes.

5
—— Memorize The First Names Of The 10 People You Just Met.

4

3

—— Memorize The Pledge To The Flag.

2

—— Memorize The Number On Your Bus To Be Sure You Get Back On The Right One.

1

Requires Remembering A Small Amount Of Simple Material For A Short Period Of Time.

and to make available any equipment needed, such as an easel or projector. Coffee, doughnuts, and other amenities that will help make the meeting a more pleasant experience also should be arranged through the field coordinator. The administrator should make certain to bring sufficient numbers of all forms, pencils, and other materials that SMEs will use.

The follow-up procedure rating session should proceed as follows:

1. SMEs should be told why they were selected to participate in the rating session, and the purpose of the rating session should be explained.

2. The general rating procedure, including behavior state-
    ments, words, and so on used to define rating-scale points,
    should be discussed.

3. The factors that will be used in rating task statements, such
    as abilities and skills, should be discussed thoroughly. During
    the course of the discussion, each SME should be asked to
    provide examples of behaviors, not necessarily from the job
    under study, that he or she believes requires high, moderate,
    and low degrees of a factor. It is extremely important that
    SMEs understand each factor before rating task statements.
    The discussion, therefore, should continue until the SMEs
    demonstrate with their examples that they have a good grasp
    of each factor.

4. SMEs should be given copies of factor definitions—for
    example, on three-by-five-inch cards—so that they can refer
    to them as frequently as desired during the rating session.

5. Common rating errors (see Cascio, 1978), such as tendencies
    to concentrate ratings as midscale or extreme values, should
    be identified and discussed briefly. When raters are cau-
    tioned about such errors, they tend to provide better rat-
    ings.

6. At the point when SMEs are ready to rate task statements,
    the rating tables on which they will record their factor by task
    ratings should be distributed and reviewed in conjunction
    with the rating scales. SMEs should be instructed to rate each
    task statement in the list one factor at a time to facilitate the
    rating process—the rater's set remains the same while he or
    she is rating each task statement. Again, raters tend to pro-
    vide better ratings when they are properly instructed about
    the use of the rating scales and the rating procedure. If sev-
    eral jobs are represented by the SME group, the administra-
    tor should make certain that each SME receives the correct
    rating table.

7. When each SME fully understands the rating procedure, the
    orientation should end and the rating process should be initi-
    ated. SMEs should be told that they can leave as soon as they
    have completed the rating table.

8. While SMEs are recording their ratings, the administrator should monitor the group to see that the rating tables are being completed as suggested, that is, in a downward sequence, and that SMEs are referring to the appropriate factor definition as they rate the task statements.

9. When SMEs have completed the rating procedure, they should turn in their materials and they can then leave.

The rating session thus has a large instructional component, and the administrator is, in essence, an instructor. For practically all instructional situations the instructor needs to be well prepared, and the rating session is no exception. Accordingly, the administrator should be furnished with a guide that covers in considerable detail the way the rating session should proceed. Visual aids should be provided to the extent that they will help put points across, and the administrator should practice conducting the rating session while using the guide and the visual aids.

Data Analysis. Ratings obtained with the follow-up procedure can be analyzed in several ways, and a few are suggested below. As a minimum, ratings obtained in the WPSS follow-up procedure should be analyzed to obtain (1) the degree of rater agreement, (2) job profiles and profile similarity where warranted, and (3) the degree or relative degree to which each factor of interest is involved in the work performed.

A measure of rater agreement is needed because of the subjectivity inherent in the rating process. As discussed in Chapter Two, the confidence in and acceptance of ratings depend in large measure on the agreement among ratings of the same work supplied by different raters. The ratings are not meaningful if raters do not agree substantially about the degree to which various factors are involved in jobs. In the clerical study, about ten to fifteen supervisors per clerical job completed rating tables, and analysis showed that the obtained interrater agreement was satisfactory. Ability factor averages generally were on the low side, indicating that the abilities included in the analysis are required only to a low degree to perform the clerical jobs studied.

Ability profiles were formed for each of the seven clerical jobs by using the average ability ratings as profile points. A measure of profile similarity was calculated per pair of job profiles by (1) obtaining the differences between profile points, (2) squaring the differences, (3) summing the squared differences, and (4) obtaining the square root of the sum of the squared differences. The resulting values indicated how closely pairs of profiles resemble each other — the larger the value, the less the profiles are alike. The range of theoretical profile difference values for the clerical study is zero to 20.8. In the former case, each of the pairs of profile points would have the same average value; and, at the other extreme, all differences between profile points would be at the maximum value of six (all ones and sevens — $\sqrt{12 \times 6^2}$ = $\sqrt{432}$ = 20.8). Of course, it is virtually impossible in practice to obtain the theoretical values at the extremes of the range.

Profile similarity values for the seven clerical jobs are presented in Figure 30. The smallest profile similarity value is .67 and the largest is 2.61 — both involve the payroll allotment and voucher audit clerk jobs. As a group, the seven jobs are more alike than unalike as far as abilities are concerned. Most of the profile similarity values are between 1.00 and 1.50. Values below 1.00 were obtained in comparisons between the voucher audit clerk job and the payroll allotment clerk job (.67) and between the single-stream computer operator job and the multistream computer operator job (.75). Only two profile similarity values fell between 1.50 and 2.00 — those obtained for the payroll allotment clerk and the service order clerk jobs and for the service order clerk and the multi-stream computer operator jobs. All profile comparisons with the keypunch operator job exceeded 2.00, indicating that in terms of abilities the keypunch operator job is the most different job of the seven.

The method described above is one way to obtain and use information about a variety of factors involved in jobs. Variations of the same basic approach have been applied in a number of ways (for instance, see Drauden and Peterson, 1977). The variations usually are due to the statistical analyses of the data collected, which range from simple to complex. The WPSS follow-up approach on a complexity scale falls closer to the simple than to the complex. Cornelius and Lyness (1980), for instance, used a total of thirteen skills, abilities, and job characteristic scales to

Figure 30. Profile Similarity Values for Clerical Jobs.

	VOUCHER AUDIT CLERK	PAYROLL ALLOTMENT CLERK	COMPUTER OPERATOR SING. STR.	COMPUTER OPERATOR MULT. STR	REVENUE REPORTS CLERK	KEYPUNCH OPERATOR
SERVICE ORDER CLERK	1.18	1.59	1.44	1.58	1.46	2.48
VOUCHER AUDIT CLERK	–	0.67	1.19	1.28	1.28	2.61
PAYROLL ALLOTMENT CLERK		–	1.20	1.18	1.00	2.56
COMPUTER OPERATOR –SS			–	0.75	1.06	2.01
COMPUTER OPERATOR – MS				–	1.33	2.26
REVENUE REPORTS CLERK					–	2.38

rate job tasks. The procedure adopted to produce skill, ability and job characteristic values for jobs as a whole was to use the average of the three highest task ratings rather than a sum or average across all tasks. In this way, jobs would be scaled at the highest level required to perform the work instead of at an average level.

At the other extreme, statistically elaborate methods for establishing skill and ability job requirements were applied to results of two sets of analyses conducted in support of employment selection research (Employment Research and Systems Group, 1980, 1981). In each set of job analyses, one with four jobs and the other with three, task importance or similarity data were analyzed statistically to identify broader work components or task clusters, and each work component was rated in terms of twenty-six knowledge, skill, and ability factors presented in the form of behaviorally anchored rating scales. The twenty-six scales were selected from a much longer list by eliminating those scales pertaining to clearly inappropriate abilities and skills. The results of further statistical analyses suggested that the raters were able to use the ability scales reliably and differentially with respect to scale importance for different work components. Lastly, work component ability profiles were analyzed statistically to develop scores for use in determining which tests should be included in employment test validation studies.

The relative degree to which a factor is involved in a job can be determined by averaging SME rating-table results and forming a table of averages for each specific job. The remaining steps for determining the relative involvement of each factor are to (1) sum the averages in each column to obtain column totals for each factor and (2) divide each factor column total by every other column total to obtain a relative involvement ratio for each factor.

In the unlikely event that some cells in the table of averages are blank, it would ·be more appropriate to use column averages instead of column sums to determine the relative involvement of each factor for a job. Involvement ratios can be recorded in a table such as the one shown in Figure 31, which was developed to examine the relative need for abilities to perform the voucher audit clerk job. The abilities in Figure 31 are listed in order of their column sums, so the ratios decrease from top to bottom and increase from left to right. Only the top half of the table need be completed because the bottom half simply mirrors the top. Ratios close to 1.0 indicate that the two abilities being compared are about equally involved in carrying out the work. In the analysis of the voucher audit clerk, a ratio of about 1.3 to 1.4 or greater indicates that the two ability averages being compared are required to different degrees,* and it is more than likely that the ability with the larger average is needed more than the ability with the smaller average to perform the work. The larger the ratio, the more the ability with the larger average is needed to carry out the job tasks.

If factors are rank ordered on the basis of their column sums or averages when involvement ratios are recorded, it is easier to note those factors with comparatively large or small involvement ratios. The three top-ranked abilities needed by voucher audit clerks, as can be seen in Figure 31, are comprehension, memorization, and reasoning. The relative need for comprehension and memorization is about the same; comprehension is needed slightly more than reasoning, more than most of the remaining abilities, and much more than spelling, which is the least needed of the twelve factors studied. Persuasion, number facility, social sensitivity, and dexterity are also needed, but the need for these abilities appears to be on the low side. The result for number

---

*A statistical test, the *t* test, was used to determine whether ability averages differed enough to say that one ability was required more than another. Ratios of 1.3 to 1.4 generally were obtained when comparing significantly different means. Most introductory statistics texts cover the use of *t* tests for comparing means.

Figure 31. Ability Involvement Ratios.

ABILITY	COMP	MEM	REAS	S&W	PS	TS	INF	PER	NF	SS	DEXT	SPELL
COMPREHENSION		1.10	1.35	1.53	1.64	1.77	2.09	3.29	3.29	3.29	3.83	5.75
MEMORIZATION		—	1.24	1.40	1.50	1.62	1.91	3.00	3.00	3.00	3.50	5.25
REASONING			—	1.13	1.21	1.31	1.55	2.43	2.43	2.43	2.83	4.25
SPEAKING & WRITING				—	1.07	1.15	1.36	2.14	2.14	2.14	2.50	3.75
PERCEPTUAL SPEED					—	1.08	1.27	2.00	2.00	2.00	2.33	3.50
TIME SHARING						—	1.18	1.86	1.86	1.86	2.17	3.25
INFORMATION ORDERING							—	1.57	1.57	1.57	1.83	2.75
PERSUASION								—	1.00	1.00	1.17	1.75
NUMBER FACILITY									—	1.00	1.17	1.75
SOCIAL SENSITIVITY										—	1.17	1.75
DEXTERITY											—	1.75
SPELLING												—

facility was investigated further by checking with a few SMEs. Although voucher audit clerks do deal extensively with numbers, they use electronic calculators to accomplish all calculations, which are themselves routinized. Audit clerks thus require very little number facility.

The top three rank-ordered abilities across all seven jobs were comprehension, memorization, and reasoning, with the exception of the keypunch operator job for which dexterity tied comprehension for the top rank. Certainly, the implication of such results for identifying and studying employee selection instruments is clear.

Function Identification. Job designers usually have a head start because very few functions are entirely new. Generally, functions have been performed in prototype or active operational organizations for a while, perhaps years; therefore, much of job design consists of redistributing functions and reconfiguring existing jobs. Imaginative job designers, even under the most unusual circumstances, can formulate future job activities. At one time, the activities astronauts were going to perform were entirely-new — no one had ever "flown" in outer space before. Yet, analysts at the National Aeronautics and Space Administration (NASA) were able to specify the activities that astronauts would perform during space missions, including extravehicular activities, years before the first suborbital flight was completed.

Functions performed or to be performed by an organization can be identified in a number of ways. When task information is

available, tasks can be grouped into larger, somewhat homogeneous work activities or functions by SMEs or by statistical
analysis of task data (a bottom-up approach). When organizations are in the planning stage and jobs do not yet exist, a WPSS
approach cannot be used to obtain job information directly from
incumbents and supervisors. Instead, SMEs can provide the
information desired about future jobs. With an organization's
objectives as a starting point (a top-down approach), a panel of
SMEs can identify the outputs that have to be produced to achieve
the objectives and the functions that need to be performed to produce the outputs. Then, by successively breaking functions down
into smaller work activities, SMEs can develop the tasks subsumed by each function. Note that at this point, it has not been
necessary to allude to specific jobs in order to specify, describe,
and analyze functions and tasks. The WPSS process can still be
applied in a modified fashion to obtain task data—for example,
task significance and task time. In this case, SMEs will provide
the task attribute data in rating sessions that are essentially the
same as the previously described rating session for obtaining ability and skill information. The major difference is that the focus of
the rating session is on task attributes. The top-down or system
approach in which work activities are anticipated systematically
has a long history in military system development programs, and
descriptions of the approach can be found in most human factors
engineering texts (for example, see Meister, 1971).

   Function Assignment and Job Design. Once functions have
been identified, the job design process can begin. Functions can
be listed in a function assignment table such as the one shown in
Figure 32. The activities listed in the table were identified through
the WPSS process for several jobs being performed in a relatively
new organization, and SMEs used the table to assign functions to
job types and levels in preparation for reassembling functions and
tasks into more efficient jobs. As can be seen in Figure 32, functions are the row headings, and job levels and types are the column headings. The task confronting the SMEs was to assign
functions to broad categories—management and nonmanagement jobs—and, within the nonmanagement category, to craft
and clerical jobs. Function assignments were signified by marking

Figure 32. Function Assignment Table.

Function		Management	Craft	Clerical
1.0	Perform General Processing			
1.1	Process Reports			
1.11	Process Service Reports			X
1.12	Process Monthly Forecast			X
1.13	Process Efficiency Reports			X
1.14	Process Time Reports			X
1.6	Maintain SCC Status Boards			X
1.7	Handle Work Inputs		X	X
1.71	Handle Document Work Inputs		X	X
1.72	Handle Telephone And Verbal Inputs		X	X
1.8	Develop Or Update Pricing Guide	X	X	
1.9	Perform General Administrative Duties		X	X
3.0	Perform Analysis And Equipment Control			
3.1	Perform Results Analysis	X	X	
3.2	Perform SCCs Administration	X	X	

the appropriate column(s) alongside each function. SMEs were asked to assign functions without regard for the way the jobs were currently being performed, a very difficult task because of their close association with the organization and jobs under study. Note that in some instances different aspects of the same function were assigned to different levels and job types. An additional function assignment issue that remains to be resolved is whether functions designated for management jobs should be performed at different management levels. After functions have been assigned to levels and types, attention can turn to specifying the tasks subsumed by functions and grouping the tasks and functions into tentative jobs.

Factors that should be considered when designing jobs can be thought of as system and process factors and personnel factors. Examples of factors of each kind are as follows:

System and Process Factors	*Personnel Factors*
Work flows	Abilities/skills/knowledge
Function and task sequences	Aptitudes
Equipment required	Career advancement
Materials required	Recognition/achievement

Environment   Task significance
Location   Skill variety
Function and task characteristics   Autonomy
                                             Consistent relationship

A number of job characteristics have been identified as important in attempts to enhance the motivating potential of a job. Several of the personnel factors listed above are variations or offshoots of job characteristics recommended for study both by Turner and Lawrence and by Hackman and Lawler (Aldag and Brief, 1979). Since the job characteristics recently defined by Hackman and Oldham (1980) are acknowledged to contribute to the design of jobs that employees find more meaningful and in which they will be more productive, and since the definitions of those job characteristics can be used in WPSS follow-up rating sessions, they are presented here:

- *Skill variety* — the degree to which a job requires a variety of activities that involve the use of a number of different skills and talents.
- *Task identity* — the degree to which a job requires completion of a "whole" and identifiable piece of work, that is, doing a job from beginning to end with a visible outcome.
- *Task significance* — the degree to which the job has a substantial impact on the lives of other people, whether those people are in the immediate organization or in the world at large.
- *Autonomy* — the degree to which the job provides substantial freedom, independence, and discretion to the individual in scheduling the work and determining the procedures to be used in carrying it out.
- *Job feedback* — the degree to which carrying out the work activities required by the job provides the individual with direct and clear information about the effectiveness of his or her performance.

System, process, and personnel factors should be considered in the design of jobs. Checklists covering a wide range of job design

design principles and questions about job design adequacy have been proposed to help assemble tasks into efficient, rewarding jobs (McCormick, 1979). You may find it difficult, however, to apply some of the suggested items—for instance, to design or redesign jobs so that they are sufficiently difficult to be challenging and sufficiently diverse to be interesting and also to include work cycles that are long enough so that the work is not repetitive or boring. Certainly it is advisable to follow the job design principles proposed, but job designers need, and should expect, much more specific guidance, for example, definitions of sufficiently difficult, sufficiently diverse, and optimum work cycle length. It is very easy to stipulate that a work cycle should not be too long or too short, but it is quite another matter to design a job accordingly.

Job design should be an iterative process, and the place to start is with work flows. Assuming that functions have already been identified, function work flows should be developed and reviewed to pinpoint functions that can be eliminated from the work flow, combined with other functions, or added to the work flow. Functions should be eliminated from a work flow if they either duplicate or overlap each other or do not contribute to the organization's objectives. (They may belong to another work flow, however, and should be set aside for future consideration). Functions can be added to a work flow to fill performance gaps discovered, and functions that appear to review or coordinate the work of other functions can be combined with those functions.

The basic approach to assembling functions and tasks into jobs is to selectively and successively consider the system, process, and personnel factors listed above while reviewing functions in the work flow. As the review proceeds, tentative job structures can be developed. The tentative job structures then can be scrutinized and modified in terms of other factors. The end result should be jobs that employees experience as meaningful and for whose outcomes they feel personally responsible.

The function flow itself provides the initial stimulus for subgrouping functions. A way to start subgrouping the functions in a work flow is to segment the work flow at the point where two functions have to be performed simultaneously. The series of functions in each segment is a subgroup; whether or not the sub-groups of functions will become individual jobs or several jobs depends on other factors that remain to be considered. System and process factors should be taken into account first, because of the considerable constraints they impose on work activities. Job designers obtain clues about the functions and tasks that are good candidates for being assembled into work units and jobs by con-sidering such factors as:

- Equipment — tasks associated with the same major equipment, such as a mainframe computer.
- Location — tasks performed at the same location.
- Materials — tasks that require the use of the same materials.
- Sequence — functions or tasks that have to be performed in sequence.
- Output — a task whose output becomes the input to another.
- Environment — tasks requiring a similar environment, for example, a low illumination level. Tasks requiring dissimilar environments should not be combined.

In addition to system and process factors, products and services can also serve as focal points for grouping work activities. Func-tions and tasks, in other words, can be assembled into jobs in accordance with the product lines and services provided. To go one step further, customers and clients, markets served, and geo-graphical locations may also play a part in bringing work activi-ties together to form jobs.

Tentative job structures developed in accordance with system and process factors, which are aimed at maximizing efficiency and minimizing production costs, can now be studied in terms of personnel factors that will help determine the extent to which the tentative job designs incorporate characteristics that promote employee welfare and motivation and decrease counter-productive behavior, as well as enhance efficiency and productiv-ity. The WPSS follow-up procedure can be applied to study job design in much the same way as it was applied to study ability and skill requirements. The follow-up rating-table row headings, as in the previous example, would be the important or significant tasks, while the column headings would be personnel factors or job characteristics, such as skill variety, task identity, and so on. The follow-up procedure can help identify strong and weak job design features on a task-by-task or function-by-function basis, and where indicated the design can be modified to improve job quality.

Job design principles and job dimensions were discussed to point out another application of the WPSS follow-up procedure. In fact, the procedure can be employed to study a number of job-related charcteristics. In each case, the rating-table rows are the same, but the column headings change in accordance with the topic of interest. Those who would like to pursue job design principles and procedures further can refer to the works already mentioned.

8

¶¶¶

Shortcut Procedures
for Small Organizations
and Special Situations

¶¶¶

WPSS is a powerful approach for obtaining and studying job content. There is no substitute for WPSS when, as described earlier, the objective of a job study is to determine how a job is actually being performed at a number of widely dispersed work sites and the large number of job incumbents involved precludes personal contact with each one. Should WPSS prove to be a more powerful tool than is needed — for example, when the job to be analyzed is performed in a very small organization — then a short-cut version of WPSS can be applied. An abbreviated version of WPSS might be more applicable than the full WPSS approach if (1) only a small number of incumbents perform the target job and they work at very few sites, (2) similarities and differences in job tasks performed at different work sites or by different jobs are not of concern, (3) a time constraint exists that could not possibly be met if the full WPSS approach were to be applied, or (4) the resources needed to carry out a WPSS project are not available.

The major steps in the approach are for the most part *not* eliminated in the shortcut procedure, but they are considerably abbreviated and simplified, and they are accomplished more expeditiously. WPSS questionnaires, for instance, are not produced for the shortcut procedure in the same manner as they are for a large-scale WPSS project, nor are they mailed to respondents. Nevertheless, the same type of questionnaire is used. The short-cut WPSS procedure rests on the same principles and concepts as the full WPSS appraoch. If it is substituted when the full WPSS approach is applicable, however, important job information will be traded off for expedience — job information by location will be sacrificed, the sample size will be very much smaller, making the use of task statistics questionable, and job task statements and data will not be computerized and stored as a permanent record of the job analysis that can be employed readily in future updates. There are, of course, situations that call for job analyses approaches different from the approach represented by WPSS. Consider the case where a handful of employees working at one or two locations perform a particular job. It probably would be better in that situation to observe and interview all the job incumbents to determine the activities they actually perform and how they perform them; in other words, there would be no need to develop and administer a job inventory questionnaire.

The shortcut procedure is an SME-conference approach to analyzing jobs. The shortcut procedure is similar in some respects to the WPSS follow-up interview discussed in Chapter Five and in other respects to the WPSS follow-up data collection discussed in Chapter Seven. When you have completed this chapter, you will by fully familiar with the shortcut procedure. While you may not be able to conduct a shortcut SME conference after studying this chapter, you should be able to:

1. List the steps in the shortcut procedure.
2. Distinguish differences between the full WPSS procedure and the shortcut procedure.
3. Describe the shortcut SME conference, including the preparatory steps.
4. Describe the abbreviated questionnaire scales and task data analysis used in the WPSS shortcut procedure.

Full-Scale and Shortcut WPSS Procedures Compared

Let us now consider the major steps in the full-scale WPSS approach as they are carried out in the shortcut procedure. The steps are as follows:

Planning. All project planning should occur prior to the SME conference, just as it does in a full-scale WPSS project. The main consideration in planning for the shortcut procedure is the selection of a conference leader and identification of SMEs. Other considerations include finding a place to hold the conference, setting up a schedule and an agenda, and gathering the materials that will be needed to conduct the conference, such as forms and instructional aids. Several elements normally part of WPSS projects do not have to be considered; for example, there is no need to consider survey sites, because a questionnaire survey will not be undertaken. Further, there are no special data analysis requirements, such as the use of computer services.

Preparing the Task List. Task statements for both the full WPSS procedures and the shortcut procedures are derived in the same way, mainly by extracting task information from job documentation, by interviewing job incumbents and supervisors, and by observing job incumbents perform their work. A job analyst, however, should derive the task statements and develop the task list for the target job(s) prior to the shortcut SME conference; SMEs will review and modify the task list brought to the conference for their consideration.

Developing a Questionnaire. A questionnaire is needed for both the full approach and the shortcut procedure. The preparation of a WPSS questionnaire for the full approach must wait until a task list is completely developed because hundreds of copies of the questionnaire will be printed. Only a small number of copies are needed for the shortcut procedure, however, and they can be prepared in advance of the conference on the basis of the task list developed by a job analyst. Modifications of the task list, presented in questionnaire form, can easily be made during the SME conference as the task list is reviewed; hence, space should be left in the questionnaire for the addition of task statements identified during the conference. In theory, a decision will have to be reached during project planning regarding the questionnaire rating scales. In practice, however, 3-point scales (High, Medium, Low) rather than the 7-point scales previously discussed will almost always be applied since the number of respondents contemplated is not sufficient to warrant statistical treatment of the task data and the data will be used to make broad rather than fine distinctions between task statements.

Distributing and Collecting Questionnaires. None of the concerns and issues associated with the distribution and collection of WPSS questionnaires, such as identifying survey sites and field coordinators and establishing sample sizes, need be addressed for the shortcut procedure. Target job incumbents are too few in number and work at too few sites to make questionnaire distribution and sampling a matter of concern. SMEs will complete questionnaires in a conference setting, while the few target job incumbents who complete questionnaires will be administered those questionnaires by their supervisors at their work sites, as is the case for the full WPSS procedure. The questionnaires can be hand delivered to the supervisors, who are given a brief, verbal explanation of what is expected.

Analyzing Data. Computer analysis is not needed for the shortcut procedure, although the task statements and the data collected can be computerized if there is reason to do so. What is recommended instead is a simple categorization analysis (described later in this chapter) that can be applied directly to SME responses during the conference to identify those tasks that are sufficiently significant parts of the job to warrant their use in additional data collection procedures.

Collecting Follow-Up Data. Follow-up data should be collected for both the full WPSS approach and the shortcut procedure as a means of advancing the human resource programs that job analyses are supposed to serve. Such data can be used to determine the skills and abilities required to perform jobs and select job candidates accordingly. For the shortcut procedure, follow-up data should be collected during the initial SME conference and can also be obtained from other SMEs (supervisors) at a later date. A 3-point rating scale can be used to establish the degree to which various factors are involved in the accomplishment of job tasks. In the full WPSS approach, follow-up data collection must await computerized data analysis, task selection, form preparation, and arrangements for follow-up meetings.

Interpreting Results and Preparing a Job Analysis Report. These are relatively simple steps because very little interpretation is required for the shortcut procedure and the job analysis report can be quite brief. The shortcut procedure yields a list of job tasks in which the tasks can be ordered on the basis of the categorization analysis. Inasmuch as the job analysis is a means toward other ends, the purpose of the initial analysis of task data conducted during the SME conference is to identify tasks that should be used in the follow-up data collections. After the initial SME conference is completed, additional task data can be obtained from other SMEs and job incumbents, and those data can be consolidated with the data obtained during the initial SME conference. To the extent that additional job data are obtained and analyzed, those results should be included in the report.

Shortcut Job Analysis Conference

A small group of three to six SMEs should be selected to participate in the shortcut job analysis conference. The main prerequisite for serving as an SME is current, detailed knowledge of the activities performed in the target job. SMEs should be selected from among those who either (1) presently perform or recently have performed the target job, (2) supervise employees in the target job and are very familiar with the job activities, or (3) are in a staff position that requires familiarity with the target job. Inasmuch as SMEs may have to write task statements and supply information about various job characteristics, it would be helpful to select SMEs who can write clearly and are likely to be cooperative in a conference setting. The shortcut procedure is recommended for small organizations so SMEs (supervisors and other staff employees) will be in short supply.

SMEs should be instructed to prepare for the job analysis conference by reviewing appropriate job documents and the materials used by target job incumbents in the accomplishment of their work. The decision as to whether SMEs should bring job materials to the conference depends on what has to be accomplished during the conference. Mainly, though, conference results will depend on the SMEs' familiarity with the target job(s).

The way that the shortcut SME conference is conducted will depend to a large extent on the effort devoted to preconference preparation. It is strongly recommended that, as part of this preparation, a job analyst develop a preliminary or "straw man" task list. As a last resort, if a task list cannot be worked out prior to the conference, the SMEs will have to develop it during the conference. The latter approach is not recommended because the complexity of the conference would thereby increase considerably; SMEs would have to be trained to write task statements in accordance with the principles and guidelines established earlier in this guide, and they would then have to write numerous task statements for the target job or set of jobs. It is, of course, possible to conduct a conference in which SMEs derive job task statements, but that kind of conference would be very difficult to manage. To make the SME conference more manageable, as much task statement derivation and writing as possible should be accomplished by a job analyst prior to the conference. Even so, SMEs will need some instruction regarding task statement structure, composition, and writing because they must be able to distinguish between well-written and poorly written task statements—they may even have to write a few task statements.

During the course of the conference, SMEs will (1) review a list of task statements brought to the conference by the conference leader and modify, add, and delete statements as deemed necessary, (2) develop a WPSS questionnaire following the steps provided in this guide, (3) provide task data by completing the WPSS questionnaire they developed, and (4) prepare and complete other rating tables and forms that will yield additional information about significant tasks and the job as a whole—for example, a skill and ability rating table, such as the one discussed in conjunction with the WPSS follow-up procedure.

An SME conference could be conducted without providing any special instruction or training for the SMEs, but the results would leave much to be desired. It is better to devote some time and effort to preparing SMEs thoroughly and systematically for the task at hand and thus to increase the chance of achieving satisfactory results.

The conference leader should provide SMEs with an agenda and schedule and begin by discussing the procedure and objectives of the conference. The agenda and schedule might be as follows:

First Day

- Introduction   8:30 A.M.
- Conference overview   8:45
- Discussion of purpose, objectives,   9:00
  and uses for information developed
- Discussion of target job(s)   9:15
- Task statement instruction and exercise   9:30
- Break   10:30
- Critique exercise results   10:45
- Introduce and discuss target job task list   11:45
- Lunch   12:00 P.M.
- Review and modify task list   1:00
- Revise/prepare questionnaire (if on word   4:30
  processor can have available for evening work)

Second Day

- Complete WPSS questionnaire (omit if assigned   8:30 A.M.
  previous evening)
- Break   10:30
- Analyze questionnaire data   10:45
- Lunch   12:30 P.M.
- Select task statements for follow-up rating table   1:30
- Prepare follow-up rating table   2:00
- Complete follow-up rating table   2:30
- Analyze follow-up ratings   5:00

The times listed in this schedule are not meant to be definitive. Follow-up ratings can be analyzed after the conference is completed. If the follow-up ratings are analyzed during the conference, a simplified procedure will have to be worked out and approximately two more hours added to the conference.

After the first few preliminary steps on the agenda have been accomplished, the conference leader should begin training SMEs to recognize and/or to write well-constructed task statements. Once SMEs have received this training, the review of the task list can start. As this review proceeds, the conference leader should attempt to elicit task statements from the SMEs to round out the preliminary task list, as well as to identify those task statements that should be modified or deleted. When the task statement list has been refined to the point where the SMEs believe that it completely and accurately portrays the target job(s), the group can turn its attention to the WPSS questionnaire. Since the questionnaire will be used mainly in a conference setting, it does not have to be as elaborate as the WPSS questionnaire described earlier. The toned-down version, however, should still contain a personal information sheet, completion directions, scale definitions appropriate for the task attribute questions selected when the project was planned, a task statement list, and spaces to record responses.

Questionnaire copies should be reproduced as inexpensively as possible, and enough copies should be made to survey all anticipated respondents — SMEs participating in the WPSS shortcut conference, other SMEs, supervisors, and job incumbents. One point to keep in mind is that as sample size and the number of subsamples increase, manual analysis of questionnaire data becomes more difficult.

The roles that the SME conference leader plays are essentially those of an instructor and interviewer. It seems natural, therefore, to select SME conference leaders who have experience as trainers or interviewers and to train them in the details of the WPSS topics needed to conduct an SME conference. The leader should come to the conference with all the materials and forms that will be needed to obtain the desired information. A WPSS questionnaire, for instance, can be prepared in advance, and modifications and fill-ins can be made directly on the questionnaire. Or, the questionnaire may be complete except for the task statements, which can be entered in blank rows once the task list has been reviewed and modified. The same is true for other forms that require task statements; that is, task statements can be typed in appropriate blank rows on the forms. Names of skills and abilities, for instance, can be entered in the column headings; and once task data have been analyzed, the rows can be filled in with the task statements that met the criteria specified for considering tasks further. The point is that an SME conference leader can take a number of steps prior to the conference to make it run as smoothly as possible.

Examples of materials that may be needed to conduct an SME job analysis conference, such as the one described here, are:

1. An agenda and schedule.
2. Brief job descriptions and an organizational chart that locates the job(s) in the organization.
3. Visual aids for task statement instruction (definition of task, structure of a task statement, examples of well-written and poorly written task statements, guidelines for writing task statements, and list of action verbs typically used in task statements).
4. Brief task list for a task statement exercise.
5. Copies of the conference questionnaire with blank rows where task statements can be inserted.
6. Easel sheets prepared for recording and analyzing task data.
7. Follow-up rating sheets for insertion of task statements that meet the criteria established.

Shortcut Task Data Analysis

To move into the follow-up data collection stage during the conference in which SMEs not only helped develop but also completed a WPSS questionnaire requires that questionnaire data be analyzed in a way not covered previously. Task attribute data provided by the SMEs should be analyzed in order to single out tasks for inclusion in a follow-up rating table because there is no need to obtain follow-up data about all the task statements included in the questionnaire. When there are only three to six SMEs, it is a simple matter to calculate a group average per task attribute for each task so that the most important and time-consuming tasks can be identified quickly and considered further. After SMEs have completed the WPSS questionnaires, their responses to task attribute questions can be processed rather quickly by having each SME call out his or her task ratings, which the conference leader then writes on an easel sheet prepared in advance of the meeting. The conference leader can calculate averages as the data are recorded, assuming averages are desired, or designate an SME to do so.

Task attribute averages can also be calculated by entering the questionnaire responses into an electronic calculator as they are called out; this allows task attribute averages to be obtained at the touch of a key. If the responses are placed on an easel, however, widely discrepant responses can be discussed. When there are a very large number of tasks, the calculations may be handled by dividing the questionnaire into parts, say about seventy-five task statements per part, and distributing the parts among the SMEs, who is turn calculate average responses for the task statements in the part they received. Task attribute statistics, of course, can be calculated by clerks during a break in the conference, and tasks that meet the criteria established for further consideration can be typed into the rows of a follow-up rating table. The rating tables can be reproduced and distributed to the SMEs when the conference resumes. Follow-up data can also be obtained from other SMEs should additional data be desired to corroborate the information obtained in the initial SME conference or for some other purpose.

A special task-rating technique may be used for the SME shortcut conference that eliminates the need to calculate task attribute statistics and considerably simplifies the selection of task statements for further consideration. A 3-point scale — High (H), Moderate (M), and Low (L) — can be used to rate each task statement on the attributes of interest. If task importance and task time are rated by the SMEs, for example, then tasks can be categorized into one of the nine boxes in a three-by-three matrix on the basis of the ratings received on both attributes. A task that received an H,H rating on both attributes would be categorized in the cell at the intersection of the column and row headed by an H. A task that received an L importance rating and an M task time rating would be categorized in the cell at the intersection of the column and row headed by an L and an M for importance and time, respectively. A selection criterion or cutoff can be established by having a particular cell or cells representing a combination of ratings that form the cutoff point; for example, a task will be selected for use in a follow-up rating table to obtain additional information about a job only if it falls in a cell labeled at least, H,M. Decision criteria might be established as follows:

Task Importance

		L	M	H
	H		**	**
Task	M			**
Time	L			

The "**" indicates that tasks categorized in that cell would be selected for further consideration; that is, the selection criterion represented by the matrix is that the classification for a task must be at least an H,M combination. More stringent standards can be set by requiring that a task receive an H,H classification or an H in importance and either an H or an M in time to be considered further. The simplified rating system provides a little less information than would be obtained if the 7-point scales recommended for the full WPSS approach were employed, but the amount of information lost, given the small number of SMEs, is negligible.

Shortcut SME Conference Process

An SME conference, assuming that appropriate set-up arrangements have been made might proceed as follows:

Introduction and Purpose. The conference leader and the SMEs should introduce themselves, and the leader should cover the purpose of the conference — to develop a complete and accurate list of task statements pertaining to a particular job or set of jobs and to obtain information about those tasks statements in a systematic way so that a detailed job description results. The conference leader should describe the job of concern to prevent any confusion over job titles from arising and to make certain that all SMEs are starting from the same point. Even though a task statement list that will pinpoint the target jobs will be given to the SMEs later, it is worth the effort to begin by describing and locating it at the appropriate place in the organization. In other words, it is important to establish a job's reporting relationships, especially if the job is located in more than one group in an organization and is at different pay grades. SMEs should be assured that their individual responses will be treated confidentially, and they should be informed how the results obtained during the conference will be used—for example, to develop an employment selection procedure, to establish training requirements, and so on.

Introduction to Task Statements. SMEs should receive instruction about the preparation of well-written task statements. Material about task statements appearing earlier in this guide can be used to develop training materials for use in an SME conference. After the basic points have been covered, SMEs can either be asked to express several task statements that the conference leader then writes on an easel or blackboard or be given a very brief list of task statements prepared specifically for training purposes. The purpose, in either case, is for the SMEs to critique the task statements in accordance with the principles and guidelines for preparing well-written task statements to which they were just exposed. When SMEs have demonstrated that they are familiar with the structure and content of task statements, they can try their hand at writing a few. A brief review of the task statements they write will point up any problems that need correction before they start reviewing and writing task statements in earnest.

Distribute Task Statement List. A list of the job task statements prepared prior to the shortcut conference should be distributed to the SMEs. The SMEs should be told, of course, how the task statements on the list were developed. They should also be told that the statements are based on the work performed by target job incumbents. Not that every incumbent performs every task, but that most of the incumbents perform most of the tasks. The work at hand for the SMEs is to review each task statement on the list and to determine whether the task statements represent actual work performed by job incumbents. Several methods can be used to review the task statements. One is for the conference leader to read each statement aloud as the SMEs follow along silently. After a statement has been read, the leader can ask for modifications (the same procedure is recommended for the follow-up interview). Another method is to have the SMEs work on their own, reviewing the list and correcting statements as they go along. After all SMEs in the group have reviewed and modified the list, the group can discuss each task statement, examine all modifications, additions, and deletions, and arrive at a consensus regarding each task statement and the task list.

Generate Task Statements. In the unusual case that only a very brief task statement list could be generated prior to the SME shortcut meeting, SMEs will have to be relied upon more heavily to develop task statements, as well as to provide the data desired. It is under this circumstance that SMEs should bring to the conference as many of the materials as used by target job incumbents in the performance of their work as possible. The conference leader should be responsible for determining the availability of training materials, job descriptions, and other documents written about the target job that the group may find useful for developing a complete and accurate task list. (To the extent that such job information is available, it should be used to prepare a task list in advance of the SME conference.)

Writing task statements is usually a solo activity, but some SMEs have found it beneficial to work in pairs. A job can be subdivided with each SME or pair of SMEs writing task statements about a different part (function) of the work. Task lists prepared by SME subgroups should be reproduced and distributed to the other subgroups for review. After the review period, the subgroups can reassemble and critique the task statements. Task statements can be revised as necessary, a tentative consolidated task list can be developed, and the entire list can be reviewed for accuracy, completeness, wording, and overlapping tasks. The follow-up interview procedure described in Chapter Five can be followed to conduct the review of the entire task list, and the task list can be finalized on the basis of the group's comments. Keep in mind that the previously described method should only be brought into play as a last resort, when a job has to be analyzed and it

simply has not been possible to generate a task list of any conse-
quence in advance of the SME conference.

Develop a WPSS Questionnaire. Even though the questionnaire
will be completed in a group setting, face to face with a conference
leader, the directions should be as detailed as those presented earlier, because the questionnaire may be completed by a few SMEs
and job incumbents who did not participate in questionnaire
development. The questionnaire should also contain the same
sections as those already described. In fact, as mentioned earlier,
most of the questionnaire can be prepared prior to the conference,
with blank rows left where task statements are to be inserted as
soon as they are finalized. Each task statement should be numbered for identification purposes and grouped in the questionnaire by function.

Questions about task attributes — for example, task significance — should be preselected to maximize the chance that information pertinent to the immediate goals of the job analysis will be
obtained; response scales can be copied from those presented
earlier in this guide, or 3-point scales can be used. Definitions for
a 3-point scale, say, for task importance, could be presented simply
as Extremely Important, Moderately Important, and Not Important, with the interpretation of "extremely," "moderately," and "not
important" left up to the respondent. Definitions, of course, could
be presented in more detail as follows: Extremely Important — an
absolutely essential and necessary part of the job; Moderately
Important — of some importance to the job but not critical; and
Not Important — of little importance to the job and not necessary
for its performance.

Complete a WPSS Questionnaire. Copies of the questionnaire
should be distributed to the SMEs, and completion instructions
should be reviewed briefly so that it will be reasonably certain that
the SMEs understand how to complete the questionnaire. Of
course, it will be necessary to review completion instructions in
greater detail for respondents who did not participate in questionnaire development.

Analyze Task Data. The purpose for analyzing task data
at this point is to identify those tasks that should be considered
further to obtain information about job or worker requirements.

As already mentioned, any of several approaches can be adopted to analyze task data obtained from SMEs during the conference. The idea is to produce results very quickly so that the SMEs can go on to provide additional data about the target job.

Obtain Follow-Up Information. After task statements that meet the criteria for further consideration have been identified, a follow-up rating table can be prepared (actually finalized), and the follow-up procedure can be initiated. As was the case for the questionnaire, the follow-up rating table can be developed, for the most part, prior to the conference, with rows left blank for the insertion of task statements that meet the selection standards.

It is easy to see that SME conference leaders should be (1) well versed in the WPSS approach, (2) trained to lead a WPSS shortcut SME conference, and (3) provided with a specially prepared guide that covers the conference procedure in step-by-step detail. One of the worst turns that can occur is for the participants to think that the conference leader is not fully prepared and that their time is being wasted. The leader should be equipped not only with a detailed schedule for the conference that can be shared with the conferees but also with visual aids and other materials that will help put points across and smooth out the flow of the conference. He or she should also practice leading a conference while using the visual aids and other materials. The procedure is deceptively simple and should not be attempted without thorough preparation, indeed, the key to avoiding problems and conducting a smooth, productive SME conference is preparation. Given the information about developing WPSS questionnaires contained in this guide and the fact that most of the questionnaire can be developed prior to the shortcut meeting, developing a WPSS questionnaire for use in the shortcut procedure should be a simple matter.

Part Two

User Manual
for Computerizing
WPSS Data

Processing and analyzing WPSS questionnaire data should be a relatively easy task, one that can be accomplished even by someone who does not have prior computer experience. WPSS computer programs were designed and developed with the inexperienced user in mind—WPSS interactive computer programs are "user friendly" and prompt the user at every step of the way. By following the procedures described in this manual, a user should be able to process and analyze WPSS computerized questionnaire data.

Inasmuch as WPSS computer programs were developed specifically for use by AT&T managers, you may find that some of the procedures described here are not useful for your purposes. One procedure, for instance, enables a user to list all other WPSS users in his or her organization, along with the names of the jobs they analyzed. In organizations where only one group analyzes jobs, that particular procedure may not have much meaning. But in an organization where a number of groups analyze jobs, the possession of such information could possibly prevent duplication and promote information exchange. Even in the former case, a

173

record of previous job analyses may be useful for future reference, especially if the job analysis group experiences significant turnover.

As is usually the case with computer programs that have been in use for several years, WPSS computer programs have been enhanced, improved, and modified periodically. In fact, the present version hardly resembles the first version and is even somewhat different from the version in use last year; from here on, though, WPSS computer programs and procedures can be considered fixed. If by chance some minor simplification or improvement is introduced after this guide is published, the modifications will be duly noted and explained in the computer message printed at the start of the interactive terminal session, so that users will not become confused by terminal sessions that do not exactly match those presented in this guide.

WPSS computer programs are available to the general public under a license agreement with AT&T. Those interested in acquiring WPSS computer programs can do so by contacting: AT&T Technology Licensing, P.O. Box 25000, Guilford Center, Greensboro, North Carolina 27420.

A few administrative steps that will probably differ from organization to organization will have to be completed before data entry and processing can be initiated. At AT&T, a user must first establish a computer account through a coordinator in the Information Systems Department or arrange to use an existing AT&T computer account. A computer that has a Conversational Monitor System (CMS) and EXEC facilities plus a Fortran compiler is needed to process WPSS data. A user at AT&T must arrange for a Virtual Machine (VM) account with at least fifteen cylinders of on-line storage. When an account is obtained, a user ID and password are established. Now, data entry can be accomplished by forwarding keypunched data to the data systems coordinator who actually enters the data into the computer. Next, the user should obtain a computer terminal, preferably one with a wide carriage— for example, 120 characters. To access and process the data, the terminal must be connected to a host computer. Generally, the hookup is accomplished by telephone, that is, by dialing a telephone number that "contacts" the computer. Since computer access can be accomplished in a variety of ways with different kinds of connecting devices, it is best that the user determine in advance exactly what has to be done to gain computer access.

If the host computer has been accessed properly, a connection message will be printed at the terminal, such as:

VM/CMS ON LINE SYS K LINE 81C

In this guide, computer output will always be in upper-case letters and user input will be in lower case, even though user input can be in either upper or lower case; the purpose, of course, is to make it easier to distinguish user input from computer output.

Logon/Logoff

After the computer has been accessed, it is a simple matter to "logon," a step that must be accomplished before WPSS procedures can be applied. Logon usually is accomplished by typing the user ID and password, for example:

l eax005 avanti hwg

The user ID (eax005) and password (avanti) are those that were established when the computer account was opened. This step protects the user's data and ensures that computer charges are made to the appropriate account. Accounting information, the last three characters in the logon statement, is strictly for the user, but it must be entered. Some users enter their initials, as in the case above.

The logon procedure must be accomplished exactly as specified or the computer session will terminate. If logon is correct, the terminal will print a logon message composed of the date, time of day, and other computer-related information. A WPSS terminal session is ended by entering "logoff" and pressing Return. The computer will then print a message and disconnect the terminal from the computer system.

Material typed at the terminal is not entered in the computer until a Return key is pressed. Prior to pressing the Return key, typing errors can be corrected by entering @ or [. Entering @

causes the last typed character to be deleted. Each @ typed will cause one previous character to be deleted. Entering [causes the entire typed line to be deleted.

WPSS Procedures

There are fourteen different WPSS computer procedures, and, as you will see, each one can be initiated simply by entering a four-character procedure name. Three of the WPSS computer procedures are essential to process WPSS data; the remaining ten are optional. It is through the essential procedures, marked with an asterisk in the list given below, that a user tells the computer what the questionnaire is like, accomplishes data entry and analysis, and obtains the results of the analysis in a series of computer reports or printouts. The remaining ten procedures either enhance the basic data analyses, help produce printouts that are easier to read and understand, or allow the user to obtain information about other WPSS users and surveys and standard WPSS items, as well as to save and retrieve WPSS survey data.

Each WPSS computer procedure is presented step by step in this guide, and sample terminal sessions that should be referred to as each procedure is discussed in the text are included in exhibits. The fourteen WPSS computer procedures, each of which has a four-character name beginning with a "Q," are as follows:

QADD—change a user address.
QALL—obtain an inventory of all WPSS surveys.
QSTD—display the names of WPSS standard items.
*QSUR—describe WPSS questionnaire content and format to the computer when a standard questionnaire is applied.
*QDEF—use instead of QSUR when a standard questionnaire is applied.
*QBLD—build a survey response data base.
QGRP—group task and item responses into categories.
QTEX—supply text for response codes.
QSUB—categorize a sample into subsamples.

*QRPT — produce reports containing the results of statistical analyses.

QSAV — save data associated with a particular survey.

QTAP — list tape identification numbers for a survey or account.

QYRS — save survey data on tape for five years from the date executed.

QGET — retrieve survey data and place them online, ready for processing.

Attach WPSS

To gain access or to attach WPSS programs, the user must specify that WPSS programs are desired, as shown in Exhibits 1a and 1b, by entering:

.att sg1079 wpss

The first time that WPSS is attached for a particular user ID the computer will respond:

B (192) R/O
B DISK ACCESSED (192).
ENTER NAME

At this point the user should enter a user name, and the computer will ask for the user's address as follows:

ENTER LINE 1 OF ADDRESS

After the first line of address has been entered, the computer will continue to ask for address information until just a Return is entered in response to a prompt for a line of address. The subsequent attaches for the particular user ID will not request a user address. Instead, after the attach request, the computer will print the user's address and provide an opportunity to change or correct the user's address — for example:

.att sg1079 wpss
B (192) R/O
B DISK ACCESSED (192).
SIDNEY GAEL
AT&T
1776 ON THE GREEN
MORRISTOWN, NEW JERSEY 07960
-------TO CHANGE THE ABOVE EXECUTE, QADD

Should the user wish to change or correct the name and address information, the QADD procedure should be executed.

To fully appreciate the capability of WPSS computer programs, you should follow the sample terminal sessions provided in the exhibits that accompany this narrative.

Exhibit 1a.

```
.att sg1079 wpss
B (192) R/O
B DISK ACCESSED (192).
ENTER NAME
.sidney gael
ENTER LINE 1 OF ADDRESS
.at&t
ENTER LINE 2 OF ADDRESS - OR JUST A RETURN
.1776 on the green
ENTER LINE 3 OF ADDRESS - OR JUST A RETURN
.morristown, nj 07960
ENTER LINE 4 OF ADDRESS - OR JUST A RETURN
.

PUN FILE 4498  TO  SG1079    CPU K    COPY  01 NOHOLD

SIDNEY GAEL
AT&T
1776 ON THE GREEN
MORRISTOWN, NJ 07960

-------- TO CHANGE THE ABOVE, EXECUTE: QADD

R;
```

Exhibit 1b.

```
.att sg1079 wpss
B (192) R/O
B DISK ACCESSED (192).

SIDNEY GAEL
AT&T
1776 ON THE GREEN
MORRISTOWN, NJ 07960

-------- TO CHANGE THE ABOVE, EXECUTE: QADD

R;
```

QADD Procedure

The first step in executing QADD is to enter "qadd," as shown in the terminal session in Exhibit 2. The terminal session will continue as follows:

Prompt: ENTER NAME:
Response: Enter the user name.
Prompt: ENTER LINE 1 OF ADDRESS
Response: Enter the first line of the user address.
Prompt: ENTER LINE 2 OF ADDRESS – OR
             JUST A RETURN
Response: Enter the second line of the user address.

A maximum of six lines of address information can be entered. When the address is complete, simply press the Return key in response to a prompt for another line of address, and the computer will print out the user name and address information. If a change or correction is desired, simply execute QADD again. In the QADD sample terminal session, a room number was added to the user address, as shown in Exhibit 2.

Exhibit 2.

```
.qadd
ENTER NAME
.sidney gael
ENTER LINE 1 OF ADDRESS
.at&t
ENTER LINE 2 OF ADDRESS - OR JUST A RETURN
.room 48-4all
ENTER LINE 3 OF ADDRESS - OR JUST A RETURN
.1776 on the green
ENTER LINE 4 OF ADDRESS - OR JUST A RETURN
.morristown, nj 07960
ENTER LINE 5 OF ADDRESS - OR JUST A RETURN
.

PUN FILE 4512  TO  SG1079   CPU K   COPY  01 NOHOLD

SIDNEY GAEL
AT&T
ROOM 48-4All
1776 ON THE GREEN
MORRISTOWN, NJ 07960

-------- TO CHANGE THE ABOVE, EXECUTE; QADD

R;
```

QALL Procedure

The QALL procedure is executed to obtain a list of surveys that you or anyone else may have conducted using the same computer system. To obtain the list, simply enter "qall," and the computer will respond first with all the surveys you have defined, including the survey name, the target job, the number of task statements in the WPSS questionnaire, and the number of survey respondents. The computer will then ask if a record layout is desired for any of the surveys listed. In the QALL sample terminal session shown in Exhibit 3, none was desired so just a Return was entered instead of a survey name. Had a record layout been requested, one would have been printed that looks like the record layout contained in Exhibit 6. The computer then proceeds to ask if a list of subsets (subsamples) constructed for any of the surveys is desired. In the sample terminal session, subsamples for Survey 1000 were requested, and the subsample names, LAKE-MICH and WESTERN, are listed. The computer will continue to ask whether subset information is desired until just a Return is entered in response to the prompt. At that point, the terminal session will continue:

Prompt: LIST WPSS SURVEYS ON OTHER USERIDS (Y OR N)?

Response: If additional user and survey information is desired, enter a "y"; otherwise, enter an "n."

In the sample terminal session a "y" is entered, and another user name and address and two surveys are listed.

Exhibit 3.

```
.qall

SURVEY       JOB                        TASKS     SURVEYS

1000         DISTRICT MANAGER            246        456

2000         UNIT MANAGER/SUPERVISOR     378        617

3000         SERVICE REPRESENTATIVE      280        617

4000         SUPPORT CLERKS              178        519

ENTER SURVEY NAME - IF RECORD LAYOUT DESIRED
   OTHERWISE - ENTER JUST A RETURN:
.

ENTER SURVEY NAME - IF SUBSET LIST DESIRED
   OTHERWISE - ENTER JUST A RETURN:
.1000

SUBSET NAMES FOR - 1000

 LAKEMICH
 WESTERN

ENTER SURVEY NAME - IF SUBSET LIST DESIRED
   OTHERWISE - ENTER JUST A RETURN:
.
LIST WPSS SURVEYS ON OTHER USERIDS (Y OR N)?
.y

-------------------------------------
USERID: JDHS7

J.D.H. SIDLEY & ASSOCIATES
7210 PARK TERRACE DRIVE
ALEXANDRIA, VA  22307

SURVEY       JOB                        TASKS     SURVEYS

DAOPER       DA OPERATOR                 378        217

RSA          REPAIR SERVICE ATTENDANT    251        159

;R
```

QSTD Procedure

Standard definitions have been established for several items that conventionally appear in WPSS questionnaires used in the Bell System. The standard items and their definitions can be printed (displayed) at the terminal by entering "qstd," as in Exhibit 4. The system can also be directed to display the codes and text assigned to any standard item. The same information is also available through the QDEF procedure to be described later.

The standard items displayed in response to the entry "qstd" are Bell Tenure, Company, Education, Sex, State, Title Tenure, and Titles Held. The definitions are as follows:

- Name. This is the name of the survey item — for example, Company.
- Codes. These are minimum and maximum numerical values for responses. The Company codes, for example, are 1 to 20.
- Default codes. These codes are assigned to responses that are not within the established range. If Company is not coded between 1 to 20, for example, the entry for Company for that particular questionnaire is a nonresponse.
- Text. Four of the seven standard items, as can be seen in Exhibit 4, are noted as having text. The text will appear in WPSS reports instead of codes.
- Grouping. Three WPSS standard items — Bell Tenure, Title Tenure, and Titles Held — are noted to have groupings. Summary statistics can be obtained in WPSS printouts for selected groupings or for each code individually. The grouping for Bell Tenure is presented in the sample terminal session.

Although the standard items were developed specifically for Bell System applications, they can be modified rather easily to suit your needs. The names and content of the standard items can be changed by using your system Edit program, a procedure that, of course, requires some computer expertise. Once you have changed the standard items and text so that they are appropriate for your organization, the new text will appear in your computer printouts. For instance, Bell Tenure can be changed to Years of

Exhibit 4.

```
.qstd

STANDARD WPSS DEFINITIONS MAY BE USED FOR:

                    CODES      DEFAULT CODES
    NAME          MIN  MAX    <MIN >MAX  INV

    BELL TENURE     0   40      0   40   -1          GROUPING
    COMPANY         1   20     -1   -1   -1   TEXT
    EDUCATION      11   17     11   -1   -1   TEXT
    SEX          **** ****     -1   -1   -1   TEXT
    STATE        **** ****     -1   -1   -1   TEXT
    TITLE TENURE    0  360      0  360   -1          GROUPING
    TITLES HELD     0   15      0   15   -1          GROUPING

    **** = ALPHA CODES      -1 DEFAULT = NONRESPONSE


IF CODES AND TEXT DESIRED, ENTER THE NAME - OTHERWISE ENTER N
.company

CODE  TEXT

    1   AT&T
    2   C&P
    3   CINCINNATI
    4   ILLINOIS
    5   INDIANA
    6   MICHIGAN
    7   MOUNTAIN
    8   NEW ENGLAND
    9   NEW JERSEY
   10   NEW YORK
   11   NORTHWESTERN
   12   OHIO
   13   PACIFIC
   14   PACIFIC NW
   15   PENNSYLVANIA
   16   SOUTHERN
   17   SO CENTRAL
   18   SO NEW ENG
   19   SOUTHWESTERN
   20   WISCONSIN
```

cont'd. on p. 187

QSTD Procedure, cont'd.

Service, along with a change in the range of service, and Company, which presently pertains to Bell System telephone companies, can be changed to Region or Division with associated region or division names. The WPSS procedures as they presently stand, however, will be used for illustrative purposes.

As a result of the prompt "IF CODES AND TEXT DESIRED, ENTER THE NAME—OTHERWISE ENTER N:" and the response "company," Company codes and text are displayed in the QSTD sample terminal session shown in Exhibit 4. This prompt will continue to appear after each code and text display. The item Bell Tenure is entered next (incorrectly at first), and Bell Tenure codes and text are displayed. (Text can also be supplied for other codes with the QTEX procedure to be described later.) When code and text displays are no longer desired, enter an "n," as in the sample terminal session, and the QSTD procedure will end.

Exhibit 4, cont'd.

```
IF CODES AND TEXT DESIRED, ENTER THE NAME - OTHERWISE ENTER N
.belltenure
 BELLTENURE        DOES NOT EXIST

IF CODES AND TEXT DESIRED, ENTER THE NAME - OTHERWISE ENTER N
.bell tenure

BELL TENURE        CONSISTS OF ALL CODES FROM    0 TO    40
A DEFINED GROUPING IS:

 LOW HIGH    CODE   TEXT

    1-   1     1    1 YEAR
    2-   2     2    2 YEARS
    3-   3     3    3 YEARS
    4-   4     4    4 YEARS
    5-   5     5    5 YEARS
    6-  10     6    10 YEARS
   11-  40     7    MORE THAN 10

IF CODES AND TEXT DESIRED, ENTER THE NAME - OTHERWISE ENTER N
.n
R;
```

QSUR Procedure

If a questionnaire corresponds to a standard WPSS questionnaire, that is, one with the same Parts A, B, and C already described (Part D is optional), the QSUR procedure should be used to define the survey data base; otherwise, the more lengthy and difficult QDEF procedure described in the next section must be used. As can be seen in the QSUR terminal session shown in Exhibit 5, the procedure is initiated by entering "qsur." The terminal session will continue as follows:

Prompt: ENTER SURVEY NAME (MAX 8
CHARACTERS — NO INTERMEDIATE
BLANKS)
Response: Enter the survey name.
Prompt: ENTER JOB SURVEYED (MAX 24
CHARACTERS — INTERNAL BLANKS
ALLOWED)
Response: Enter the name of the job surveyed.
Prompt: ENTER NUMBER OF TASK STATEMENTS
Response: Enter the number of task statements included in the
WPSS questionnaire.
Prompt: ENTER NAME OF PART B QUESTION
(MAX 16 CHARACTERS)
Response: Enter the name that will be used as a reference for
the Part B task attribute question, such as
"significance," "importance," or "difficulty."
Prompt: ENTER NAME OF PART C QUESTION
(MAX 16 CHARACTERS)
Response: Enter the name that will be used as the reference for
the Part C task attribute question. (If the task
attribute question pertains to task time, percent task
time will be available in addition to task time
statistics. A more detailed description of percent time
appears in the discussion of the QDEF procedure.)
Prompt: ENTER NUMBER OF FUNCTIONS IN PART D
Response: Enter the number of functions listed in Part D of the
WPSS questionnaire. (If the survey does not have a
Part D, enter a zero.)

Prompt: DISPLAY RECORD LAYOUT (Y OR N)
Response: Enter a "y" if the record layout is desired; otherwise, enter an "n."

In the QSUR terminal session shown in Exhibit 5, the responses to each prompt are "1000" for survey name, "district manager" for job surveyed, "246" for number of task statements, "significance" for the name of the Part B questions, "time" for the name of the Part C question, "11" for number of functions in Part D, and "n" for displaying the record layout. If a "y" had been entered in response to the last prompt, a record layout would have been typed at the terminal.

Exhibit 5.

```
.qsur
ENTER SURVEY NAME (MAX 8 CHARACTERS - NO INTERMEDIATE BLANKS)
.1000
ENTER JOB SURVEYED (MAX 24 CHARACTERS - INTERNAL BLANKS ALLOWED)
.district manager
ENTER NUMBER OF TASK STATEMENTS
.246
ENTER NAME OF PART B QUESTION (MAX 16 CHARACTERS)
.significance
ENTER NAME OF PART C QUESTION (MAX 16 CHARACTERS)
.time
ENTER NUMBER OF FUNCTIONS IN PART D
.11
DISPLAY RECORD LAYOUT (Y OR N)
.n
PUN FILE 7896  TO  SG1079   CPU K   COPY  01 NOHOLD
R;
```

QDEF Procedure

The QDEF procedure can be used to describe either a standard or a nonstandard questionnaire. Survey 1000, which was used to illustrate the QSUR procedure, will also serve to illustrate the QDEF procedure. If the questionnaire is a nonstandard questionnaire, QDEF must be used and QSUR cannot be used. The result of using QDEF is the same as using QSUR—the contents of the WPSS questionnaire are described for the computer so that data can be entered appropriately.

Names and allowable response ranges are provided through QDEF for each survey item or question contained in a WPSS questionnaire. Items in a WPSS questionnaire are classified for data-processing purposes as:

- Type A—personal information such as company, location, education, job title, and so on.
- Type T—task attribute responses that, for instance, answer task significance and task time questions.
- Type B—responses other than Types A and T—for example, answers to general questions about work, such as estimates of percentages of time devoted to functions.

Type A items must be defined first, Type T items next, and then Type B items, if any. The computer will provide prompts to indicate when it is appropriate to begin defining a particular type of information.

As can be seen in the QDEF sample terminal session contained in Exhibit 6, the QDEF procedure is initiated by entering "qdef." The computer will display WPSS standard item definitions along with the prompt:

IF CODES AND TEXT DESIRED, ENTER
THE NAME—OTHERWISE ENTER N

As was the case with QSTD, if codes and text for a WPSS standard item are desired, simply enter the item name. If information about standard items is not needed, enter "n." The computer session will continue:

Exhibit 6.

```
.qdef

STANDARD WPSS DEFINITIONS MAY BE USED FOR:

                   CODES      DEFAULT CODES
   NAME           MIN  MAX   <MIN >MAX  INV

   BELL TENURE      0   40      0   40   -1        GROUPING
   COMPANY          1   20     -1   -1   -1   TEXT
   EDUCATION       11   17     11   -1   -1   TEXT
   SEX           **** ****     -1   -1   -1   TEXT
   STATE         **** ****     -1   -1   -1   TEXT
   TITLE TENURE     0  360      0  360   -1        GROUPING
   TITLES HELD      0   15      0   15   -1        GROUPING

   **** = ALPHA CODES      -1 DEFAULT = NONRESPONSE


IF CODES AND TEXT DESIRED, ENTER THE  NAME - OTHERWISE ENTER N
.education

CODE   TEXT

   11    LESS THAN HS
   12    HS GRAD
   13    1 YR COLLEGE
   14    2 YR COLLEGE
   15    3 YR COLLEGE
   16    COLLEGE GRAD
   17    POST GRAD
   18    COL & TECH




IF CODES AND TEXT DESIRED, ENTER THE NAME - OTHERWISE ENTER N
.n
```

cont'd. on p. 193

QDEF Procedure, cont'd.

Prompt: ENTER NAME OF SURVEY (MAX 8
         CHARACTERS – NO INTERMEDIATE
         BLANKS)
Response: Enter the survey name. The maximum survey name
         is eight characters: if a longer name is entered, the
         prompt will be repeated.

In the sample terminal session, the survey name entered is "1000."
If the name entered is one of an already defined survey, the computer session will continue:

Prompt: SURVEY ALREADY DEFINED. REDEFINE
         (Y OR N)
Response: Enter a "y" to redefine the survey or an "n" to
         terminate QDEF.

After the survey name has been entered, the computer
session will continue:

Prompt: ENTER JOB SURVEYED (MAX 24
         CHARACTERS – INTERNAL BLANKS
         ALLOWED)
Response: Enter the job name or title.
Prompt: RECORD TYPE A
         ENTER ITEM NAME
Response: Enter the name of the first questionnaire item to be
         defined.

In the sample terminal session, the first item entered is
"company." Should the name contain more than sixteen characters, the prompt will be repeated until the name entered has sixteen or fewer characters. If the item name is one of the WPSS standard items, no further information will be requested about the item.

If the entry is not a standard item, the response definition sequence shown in the sample terminal session should be followed. The response definition cycle simply sets the minimum and maximum values for responses and establishes the default value that

Exhibit 6, cont'd.

```
ENTER NAME OF SURVEY (MAX 8 CHARACTERS-NO INTERMEDIATE BLANKS)
.1000

ENTER JOB SURVEYED (MAX 24 CHARACTERS-INTERNAL BLANKS ALLOWED)
.district manager

RECORD TYPE- A


ENTER ITEM NAME
.company

ENTER ITEM NAME
.state
```

cont'd. on p. 195

QDEF Procedure, cont'd.

the computer will assign a response that does not fall within the acceptable range. The sequence is as follows:

Prompt: ENTER MIN CODE FOR RESPONSE

Response: Enter the minimum numerical value for the survey response to the item.

Prompt: ENTER DEFAULT CODE IF RESPONSE < MIN

Response: Enter the value that should be assigned to inputs that are less than the specified minimum value. The value entered must be greater than or equal to the defined minimum. If an "n" is entered, survey-responses below the defined minimum will be considered. A blank is considered less than any number, including zero.

Prompt: ENTER MAX CODE FOR RESPONSE

Response: Enter the maximum numerical value for the response to the survey item. The value must be greater than the defined minimum and less than or equal to 999.

Prompt: ENTER DEFAULT CODE IF
RESPONSE > MAX

Response: Enter the value that should be assigned inputs that exceed the defined maximum response. If "n" is entered, the default code will be a nonresponse. If the default value entered is outside the defined minimum-maximum range, the prompt will be repeated.

Prompt: ENTER DEFAULT CODE IF RESPONSE
CONTAINS INVALID CHARACTERS

Response: Enter the code that the data should be assigned when the input contains nonnumerical (other than blank) characters. If "n" is entered, the default value will be a nonresponse. If the default value entered falls outside the defined minimum-maximum range, the prompt will be repeated.

In the sample terminal session, the first item for which a definition cycle appears is "city." The values entered are:

Exhibit 6, cont'd

```
ENTER ITEM NAME
.city
ENTER MIN CODE FOR RESPONSE
.1
ENTER DEFAULT CODE IF RESPONSE < MIN
.n
ENTER MAX CODE FOR RESPONSE
999
ENTER DEFUALT CODE IF RESPONSE > MAX
.n
ENTER DEFAULT CODE IF RESPONSE CONTAINS INVALID CHARACTERS
.n

ENTER ITEM NAME
.district
ENTER MIN CODE FOR RESPONSE
.1
ENTER DEFAULT CODE IF RESPONSE < MIN
.999
ENTER MAX CODE FOR RESPONSE
.999
ENTER DEFAULT CODE IF RESPONSE > MAX
.999
ENTER DEFAULT CODE IF RESPONSE CONTAINS INVALID CHARACTERS
.999

ENTER ITEM NAME
.title tenure

ENTER ITEM NAME
.bell tenure

ENTER ITEM NAME
.bell tenure
BELL TENURE        *** ALREADY USED

ENTER ITEM NAME
.titles held

ENTER ITEM NAME
.title
ENTER MIN CODE FOR RESPONSE
.10
ENTER DEFAULT CODE IF RESPONSE < MIN
.13
ENTER MAX CODE FOR RESPONSE
.13
ENTER DEFAULT CODE IF RESPONSE > MAX
.13
ENTER DEFAULT CODE IF RESPONSE CONTAINS INVALID CHARACTERS
.13
```

cont'd. on p. 197

QDEF Procedures, cont'd.

Minimum Code Value — 1
Default Minimum Value — n
Maximum Code Value — 999
Default Maximum Value — n
Default Invalid Value — n

In essence, the system has been informed to accept City code
values ranging from 1 to 999 and to treat all other values as nonresponses. Leading zeros are unnecessary — 0001, 001, and 01 are
all treated as 1.

At this point the response cycle will repeat to define another
item. If the name entered has been used already, as in the case of
Bell Tenure in the sample terminal session, the computer will
indicate that the item name was "ALREADY USED."

After all Type A items have been defined, just press Return
and QDEF will continue:

Prompt: RECORD TYPE T
ENTER TOTAL NUMBER OF TASKS
Response: Enter the total number of task statements contained
in the questionnaire. The maximum number of task
statements that can be entered is 999.
Prompt: ENTER NUMBER OF TASKS PER
INPUT RECORD
Response: Enter the number of sets of task attribute responses
that should be keypunched in one record. The value
should range from 10 to 30 and be less than or
equal to the total number of task statements.
Prompt: ENTER ATTR NAME
Response: Enter the name of a task attribute about which a
question has been asked.

In the QDEF sample terminal session, the entries to the
above three prompts are "246," "10," and "significance," indicating
that the questionnaire contains 246 task statements, that 10 sets of
task attribute responses should be contained in one input record,
and that the task attribute named first is task significance. (Note

Exhibit 6, cont'd.

```
ENTER ITEM NAME
.last title
ENTER MIN CODE FOR RESPONSE
.0
ENTER DEFAULT CODE IF RESPONSE < MIN
.1
ENTER MAX CODE FOR RESPONSE
./
*** CORRECTION

ENTER DEFAULT CODE IF RESPONSE < MIN
.0
ENTER MAX CODE FOR RESPONSE
.1
ENTER DEFAULT CODE IF RESPONSE > MAX
.1
ENTER DEFAULT CODE IF RESPONSE CONTAINS INVALID CHARACTERS
.n

ENTER ITEM NAME
.education

ENTER ITEM NAME
.

RECORD TYPE T

ENTER TOTAL NUMBER OF TASKS
.246
ENTER NUMBER OF TASKS PER INPUT RECORD
.ten
TEN    *** INVALID ENTRY
ENTER NUMBER OF TASKS PER INPUT RECORD
.10

ENTER ATTR NAME
.significance
ENTER MIN CODE FOR RESPONSE
.0
ENTER DEFAULT CODE IF RESPONSE < MIN
.7@0
ENTER MAX CODE FOR RESPONSE
.7
ENTER DEFAULT CODE IF RESPONSE > MAX
.7
ENTER DEFAULT CODE IF RESPONSE CONTAINS INVALID CHARACTERS
.n
```

cont'd. on p. 199

QDEF Procedures, cont'd.

that "ten" is an invalid entry and "10" is a valid entry.) The system will then sequence a response definition cycle the same as for Type A items. In the sample terminal session, the information entered indicates that the response range is zero to seven, the default values are zero and seven, and an invalid character should be treated as a nonresponse. Note the @ correction for a default code where a seven was deleted and a zero entered.

The attribute definition cycle will repeat until all desired attribute responses have been defined and just a Return is pressed in response to a prompt for an attribute name. At this point, a prompt will be printed at the terminal as follows:

IF A %TOTAL CALCULATION IS DESIRED, ENTER
THE ATTR. NAME (IF NOT, ENTER JUST A RETURN)

When an attribute name is entered, a percentage can be computed for each task response per respondent for that attribute; for example, to determine the percentage of a total job that a particular task or combination of tasks (function) represents, enter the attribute name Time, and the result will be %Time calculations. The percentages computed can be displayed in WPSS reports as long as the calculations are requested when the survey data are defined. Should an attribute name be entered that does not exist, the prompt will be repeated. For Survey 1000, as can be seen in the sample terminal session, percent computations were requested for the Time attribute.

If %Total calculations are not desired, press Return in response to the above prompt. The computer will respond with a prompt to define Type B information:

Prompt: RECORD TYPE B
        ENTER ITEM NAME
Response: Press Return if there are no Type B items;
          otherwise enter the name of the first Type B item.

Prompts for allowed value ranges and default codes will be displayed just as with Types A and T items. There is, however, an additional prompt for Type B items:

Exhibit 6, cont'd.

```
ENTER ATTR NAME
.time
ENTER MIN CODE FOR RESPONSE
.0
ENTER DEFAULT CODE IF RESPONSE < MIN
.0
ENTER MAX CODE FOR RESPONSE
.7
ENTER DEFAULT CODE IF RESPONSE > MAX
.7
ENTER DEFAULT CODE IF RESPONSE CONTAINS INVALID CHARACTERS
.n

ENTER ATTR NAME

.

IF A %TOTAL CALCULATION IS DESIRED,
ENTER THE ATTR. NAME (IF NOT ENTER JUST A RETURN)
.time

RECORD TYPE- B

ENTER ITEM NAME
.part d
ENTER MIN CODE FOR RESPONSE
.0
ENTER DEFAULT CODE IF RESPONSE < MIN
.0
ENTER MAX CODE FOR RESPONSE
.100
ENTER DEFAULT CODE IF RESPONSE > MAX
.n
ENTER DEFAULT CODE IF RESPONSE CONTAINS INVALID CHARACTERS
.n
ENTER NUMBER OF TIMES RESPONSE IS REPEATED
.11

ENTER ITEM NAME

.
```

cont'd. on p. 201

QDEF Procedures, cont'd

Prompt: ENTER NUMBER OF TIMES RESPONSE
         IS REPEATED
Response: Enter the number of parts for the item.

In the sample terminal session, responses to the above two prompts are "part d" and "11," indicating that the name Part D was given to a set of eleven responses. QDEF will repeat the definition cycle until all Type B items have been defined and a Return is pressed in response to a prompt for a Type B item name.

Errors in a preceding entry can be corrected by entering a slash (/). If a slash is entered in response to a prompt for an item name, all definitions for the preceding item are re-requested — all entries will replace preceding entries. To move back several items, enter a slash and Return in response to the prompt for an item name as many times as needed to move back to the item to be corrected. If a slash is entered in response to a prompt for one of the item codes, the preceding item code is requested again. As can be seen on page 197, a slash is entered in response to the PROMPT "ENTER MAX CODE FOR RESPONSE," and the prompt "ENTER DEFAULT CODE IF RESPONSE IS < MIN" reappears. The default code "1" entered incorrectly is replaced with a "0."

When QDEF is terminated by entering just a Return in response to the prompt ENTER ITEM NAME, a record layout will automatically be typed at the terminal.

Exhibit 6, cont'd.

```
RECORD LAYOUT
----------------------------------------------------------------------------------
```

NAME	1ST RESP. START END	NUM. OF RESPONSES	LAST RESP. START END	CODES MIN MAX	DEFAULT CODES <MIN >MAX INV

NAME	1ST RESP.		NUM. OF	LAST RESP.		CODES		DEFAULT CODES		
	START	END	RESPONSES	START	END	MIN	MAX	<MIN	>MAX	INV
(RECORD TYPE- A)										
RESPONDENT ID	1	8								
RECORD TYPE- A	9	9								
COMPANY	10	11	1			1	20	-1	-1	-1
STATE	12	13	1			***	***	-1	-1	-1
CITY	14	16	1			1	999	-1	-1	-1
DISTRICT	17	19	1			1	999	999	999	999
TITLE TENURE	20	22	1			0	360	0	360	-1
BELL TENURE	23	24	1			0	40	0	40	-1
TITLES HELD	25	26	1			0	15	0	15	-1
TITLE	27	28	1			10	13	13	13	13
LAST TITLE	29	29	1			0	1	0	1	-1
EDUCATION	30	31	1			11	18	11	-1	-1
SKIP	32	42	1							
(RECORD TYPE -T)										
RESPONDENT ID	1	8								
RECORD TYPE- T	9	9								
SIGNIFICANCE	13	13	10	31	31	0	7	0	7	-1
TIME	14	14	10	32	32	0	7	0	7	-1
SKIP	33	42	1							
(RECORD TYPE -B)										
RESPONDENT ID	1	8								
RECORD TYPE- B	9	9								
PART D	10	12	11	40	42	0	100	0	-1	-1

*** = ALPHA CODES,   -1 DEFAULT = NONRESPONSE

--- LENGTH FOR EACH RECORD SHOULD BE 42

R:

QBLD Procedure

The QBLD procedure builds the survey data base from the keypunched data tape. To execute the procedure, enter "qbld," as in the sample terminal session in Exhibit 7 (see page 205). The terminal session will continue:

Prompt: SURVEY NAME
Response: Enter the same survey name used in the QDEF procedure.

In the sample terminal session, the survey name entered is "1000." If QBLD should not be executed, the procedure will end with the message:

SURVEY (NAME) ALREADY BUILT!
or
SURVEY (NAME) NOT DEFINED.

The terminal session will continue:

Prompt: ENTER TAPE NUMBER
Response: Enter the tape number of the keypunched survey data.
Prompt: DOES TAPE HAVE INTERNAL LABEL?
(Y OR N)
Response: Enter "y" if tape has an internal (standard) label or "n" if it does not.
Prompt: IS TAPE DENSITY 6250 BPI? (Y OR N)
Response: Ener "y" if density is 6250 BPI (bytes per inch) or "n" if it is 1600 bpi.
Prompt: ENTER RECORD PHYSICAL LENGTH
Response: Enter the actual length of each keypunched record.
Prompt: ENTER BLOCK SIZE
Response: Enter the block size.

All the information needed for the above responses should be supplied by the keypunch organization. The responses in the sample terminal sessions are:

QBLD Procedure, cont'd.

Tape Number   — v10881
Internal Label   — n
Tape Density 6250 BPI   — n
Record Physical Length   — 42
Block Size   — 4200

At this point the computer will search for and mount the appropriate tape and print the message shown in the sample terminal session. Then the QBLD procedure will continue as follows:

Prompt: CONTINUE BUILDING THE SURVEY DATA
           BASE NOW (Y OR N)?
Response: Enter a "y" to continue or an "n" to stop. If "n" is
           entered, the keypunched tape specifications will not
           be requested again the next time that QBLD is
           executed.

The QBLD procedure will end if, instead of the above message, an error message is displayed as follows:

TAPE NUMBER/DENSITY/LABEL STATUS INCORRECT
or
RECORD LENGTH/BLOCK SIZE INCORRECT

At this point, QBLD should be re-executed and the corrections made.
       The final QBLD prompt is:

Prompt: DISPLAY ALL DATA ERRORS OR ONLY
           THOSE MADE A NONRESPONSE (A OR N)
Response: Enter an "a" to display all invalid responses in every
           questionnaire or an "n" to display only invalid
           responses converted to nonresponses.

       In the sample terminal session an "n" is entered, and the displayed information shows that Survey 1000 has 113 questionnaires; there were no data errors resulting in a nonresponse and

QBLD Procedure, cont'd.

no errors in the expected number of each of the record types. (Data treated as nonresponses are not entered into any calculations.) If an "a" had been entered and there were some invalid responses, they would have been printed with a respondent ID. The computer would have specified the types of records involved (A, T, or B), where in the records the errors are located, and what the errors are, for instance:

4 A RECORD LOCATIONS 27–28 CONTAINED = AA
67 A RECORD LOCATIONS 30–31 CONTAINED = 00

In both cases above, an A record is involved. In the first case, an invalid "AA" has been punched in columns 27–28 where the codes for job title (10 through 13) should appear: in the second case, an invalid "00" has been punched where an educational level code ranging from 11 through 18 should appear. After QBLD is completed, any procedure except QBLD and QDEF can be executed with the questionnaire data.

Exhibit 7.

```
.qbld
SURVEY NAME
.1000
ENTER TAPE NUMBER
.v10881
DOES TAPE HAVE INTERNAL LABEL? ( Y OR N )
.n
IS TAPE DENSITY 6250 BPI? ( Y OR N )
.n
ENTER RECORD PHYSICAL LENGTH
.42
ENTER BLOCK SIZE
.4200
..... WAITING FOR TAPE MOUNT .....
TAPE 181 ATTACHED

CONTINUE BUILDING THE SURVEY DATA BASE NOW ( Y OR N )?
.y

DISPLAY ALL DATA ERRORS OR ONLY THOSE MADE A NONRESPONSE (A OR N)
.n

SURVEY 1000      HAS    113 QUESTIONNAIRES
R;
```

QGRP Procedure

The QGRP procedure enables numerical response codes for questionnaire items or task statements to be grouped into broader categories and the associated data to be analyzed. The groupings are accomplished solely for WPSS analyses and reports, and the stored data are not affected; they remain intact and available for further analyses. It is also possible to respecify different groupings of the same data by executing QGRP again.

To execute QGRP, simply enter "qgrp," as in the terminal session shown in Exhibit 8a. The terminal session will continue as follows:

Prompt: ENTER NAME OF SURVEY
Response: Enter the survey name, such as "1000" in the sample terminal session.

If the survey name entered is incorrect, QGRP will terminate with the message that the survey for the name entered has not been defined. If a correct survey name has been entered, the terminal session will continue as follows:

Prompt: GROUPING FOR TASKS (Y OR N)
Response: Enter "y" if tasks are to be grouped into broader work categories for analytical purposes or "n" if item responses are to be grouped. If an "n" is entered, a list of the standard items, each with an associated number, will be displayed.
Prompt: ENTER NUMBER OF ITEM TO BE GROUPED
Response: Enter the number that appears to the left of the item name, such as "10" (Education).
Prompt: ENTER GROUP NUMBER
Response: Enter any number other than zero—usually "1" for the first group.
Prompt: ENTER LOW CODE FOR GROUP #1
Response: Enter the lowest response code for an item or the lowest number for a task to be contained in the first grouping—for example, "11," as in the sample terminal session.

Exhibit 8a.

```
.qgrp

ENTER NAME OF SURVEY
.1000
GROUPING FOR TASKS (Y OR N)
.n

NUM  NAME            PARTS

  1  COMPANY           1  TEXT
  2  STATE             1  TEXT
  3  CITY              1
  4  DISTRICT          1
  5  TITLE TENURE      1         GROUPING
  6  BELL TENURE       1         GROUPING
  7  TITLES HELD       1         GROUPING
  8  TITLE             1
  9  LAST TITLE        1
 10  EDUCATION         1  TEXT   GROUPING
 14  PART D           11

ENTER NUMBER OF ITEM TO BE GROUPED
.10
CODES RANGE FROM  10 TO  18

ENTER GROUP NUMBER
.1
ENTER LOW CODE FOR GROUP #   1
.11
ENTER HIGH CODE FOR GROUP #   1
.12

ENTER GROUP NUMBER
.2
ENTER LOW CODE FOR GROUP #   2
.13
ENTER HIGH CODE FOR GROUP #   2
.15

ENTER GROUP NUMBER
.2
ENTER LOW CODE FOR GROUP #   2
.18
ENTER HIGH CODE FOR GROUP #   2
.20
ENTER HIGH CODE FOR GROUP #   2
.18

ENTER GROUP NUMBER
.3
ENTER LOW CODE FOR GROUP #   3
.16
ENTER HIGH CODE FOR GROUP #   3
.17

ENTER GROUP NUMBER
.0

GROUPING GENERATED FOR: EDUCATION
R;
```

QGRP Procedure, cont'd.

Prompt: ENTER HIGH CODE FOR GROUP #1

Response: Enter the highest consecutive response code for an
item or the highest consecutive number for a task to
be included in the first grouping, such as "12" in the
sample terminal session. The value must be greater
than, or equal to, the low value for group 1, and it
will include all intervening values—for example,
from 11 through 12. (If the group consists of more
than one range of codes or task numbers, the other
ranges should be specified later in the QGRP
execution.)

Prompt: ENTER GROUP NUMBER

Response: Enter "1" again if there are code values that should
be part of the group already formed; otherwise,
enter another number—for example, "2."

Group numbers do not have to be entered in any particular
sequence. For each group number entered, low and high code
values will be prompted. In the sample terminal session, three
education groups are formed. The low and high codes for Group 1
are 11 and 12 (no college), for Group 2 they are 13 through 15 and
18 (some college), and for Group 3 they are 16 and 17 (college
graduate). The second time that "2" is entered as a group number,
both the low and high code values entered are 18.

In the second QGRP sample terminal session, shown in
Exhibit 8b, the 246 task statements are grouped according to the
functions contained in the Survey 1000 questionnaire—the sixth
group was intentionally omitted because tasks were not assigned
to the sixth function in the questionnaire. The first grouping
(function) contains the tasks numbered 1 to 24 in the questionnaire, the second grouping contains tasks numbered 25 to 62, and
so on.

QGRP entries can be corrected by entering a slash (/) and
making the desired correction. The correction procedure is the
same as the one discussed for QDEF. QGRP is terminated by
entering a zero in response to a prompt for a group number.

Exhibit 8b.

```
.qgrp

ENTER NAME OF SURVEY
.1000
GROUPING FOR TASKS (Y OR N)
.y
TASKS RANGE FROM   1 TO 246

ENTER GROUP NUMBER
.1
ENTER LOW TASK FOR GROUP #   1
.1
ENTER HIGH TASK FOR GROUP #   1
.24

ENTER GROUP NUMBER
.2
ENTER LOW TASK FOR GROUP #   2
.25!
25! *** INVALID ENTRY
ENTER LOW TASK FOR GROUP #   2
.25
ENTER HIGH TASK FOR GROUP #   2
.62

ENTER GROUP NUMBER
.3
ENTER LOW TASK FOR GROUP #   3
.63
ENTER HIGH TASK FOR GROUP #   3
.90

ENTER GROUP NUMBER
.4
ENTER LOW TASK FOR GROUP #   4
.91
ENTER HIGH TASK FOR GROUP #   4
.105

ENTER GROUP NUMBER
.5
ENTER LOW TASK FOR GROUP #   5
.106
ENTER HIGH TASK FOR GROUP #   5
.127

ENTER GROUP NUMBER
.7
ENTER LOW TASK FOR GROUP #   7
.128
ENTER HIGH TASK FOR GROUP #   7
.172
```

```
ENTER GROUP NUMBER
.8
ENTER LOW TASK FOR GROUP #   8
.173
ENTER HIGH TASK FOR GROUP #   8
.184

ENTER GROUP NUMBER
.9
ENTER LOW TASK FOR GROUP #   9
.185
ENTER HIGH TASK FOR GROUP #   9
.199

ENTER GROUP NUMBER
.10
ENTER LOW TASK FOR GROUP #   10
.200
ENTER HIGH TASK FOR GROUP #   10
.223

ENTER GROUP NUMBER
.11
ENTER LOW TASK FOR GROUP #   11
.224
ENTER HIGH TASK FOR GROUP #   11

ENTER GROUP NUMBER
.246

GROUPING GENERATED FOR: TASKS
R;
```

QTEX Procedure

The QTEX procedure is used to provide text for each survey item code, each task identification number, and each group number so that WPSS computer printouts will be easier to read and understand. If text is not provided, column and row headings in WPSS computer reports will contain item codes, task identification numbers, and group numbers.

QTEX can be executed anytime after a survey has been defined with QDEF or QSUR. As can be seen in the three sample terminal sessions shown in Exhibits 9a, 9b, and 9c, QTEX is initiated by entering "qtex." Exhibit 9a pertains to supplying text suitable for either row or column headings, Exhibit 9b pertains to supplying text suitable for row headings only, and Exhibit 9c shows how QTEX can be used with an existing text file. The reasons for executing QTEX for an existing text file are to:

1. Determine whether text for items, task statements, and groupings has been supplied and is accurate.
2. Correct earlier mistakes in text, including omissions and duplications.
3. Continue text input that was stopped prior to completion.

QTEX entries can be corrected by entering a slash (/), as previously described for QBLD and QGRP. QTEX can be terminated at any time by entering a period (.) for the first line of text in response to a prompt for text. Any remaining text can be furnished by executing QTEX again.

After "qtex" is entered, the terminal session will continue:

Prompt: ENTER NAME OF SURVEY
Response: Enter the survey name

A mistake at this point will terminate QTEX, and a message will be printed at the terminal informing the user that the survey has not been defined. If the survey name entered is correct, the terminal session will continue:

QTEX Procedure, cont'd.

Prompt: TEXT FOR TASKS (Y OR N)
Response: Enter a "y" if text for tasks will be supplied or an "n"
if text for items will be supplied.

At this point the computer will provide a display and a prompt that accord with the response to the above prompt. In response to a "y," the computer will expect task statement text and, in response to an "n," item text. In each sample terminal session, the survey name entered is "1000." In the QTEX sample session shown in Exhibit 9a, the "n" response to the above prompt indicates that item text will be supplied. When the focus of the terminal session is item text, the computer will display a list of items and associated numbers. The QTEX terminal session will continue:

Prompt: ENTER NUMBER OF ITEM FOR WHICH
TEXT IS TO BE SUPPLIED
Response: Enter the number associated with the item for which
text will be supplied.
Prompt: CODES RANGE FROM [low code to high code]*
WILL THE TEXT BE USED ONLY IN ROW
NAMES (Y OR N)?
Response: Enter a "y" if the text desired is three lines of up to
twenty characters per line or enter an "n" if the text
input desired is one line of up to twelve characters.

WPSS computer reports contain column and row headings. Column headings are limited to one line of twelve characters (numbers, letter, and spaces), whereas row headings may contain three lines of up to twenty characters each. Text for items, groups, and task statements can appear in either row or column headings, but only the first twelve characters of the first line of text will appear in a column heading. It is the user's option to supply three lines of up to twenty characters each or one line of up

---

*Variable information will be shown in brackets for the purpose of illustration only; brackets do not appear in computer terminal sessions.

QTEX Procedure, cont'd.

to twelve characters to describe the text that will appear in WPSS reports. If a "y" is entered in response to the above prompt, the computer will accept three lines of up to twenty characters per line of text; whereas if an "n" is entered, the computer will accept only one line of up to twelve characters of text. In either case, the text can be used as a row or column heading, but the computer will print only the first twelve characters of the first line of text in a column heading.

In the first QTEX sample terminal session, an "8" (representing job title) and an "n" are entered in response to the above two prompts, indicating that one line of up to twelve characters will be used to head each column. The job title codes, as can be seen in the terminal session prompt, range from 10 to 13. The sample terminal session continues:

Prompt: ENTER TEXT FOR CODE 10
Response: Enter one line of text with a twelve-character
maximum.

In the sample session "district mgr ba" is entered, and the computer prints the message:

TOO LONG! RE-ENTER

The computer will continue to prompt for text until all valid codes have been processed. Then a final message, TEXT GENERATED FOR: [ITEM], will appear, and the QTEX session will terminate.

Exhibit 9a.

```
.qtex

ENTER NAME OF SURVEY
.1000
TEXT FOR TASKS (Y OR N)
.n

NUM  NAME              PARTS

  1  COMPANY            1  TEXT
  2  STATE              1  TEXT
  3  CITY               1
  4  DISTRICT           1
  5  TITLE TENURE       1           GROUPING
  6  BELL TENURE        1           GROUPING
  7  TITLES HELD        1           GROUPING
  8  TITLE              1
  9  LAST TITLE         1
 10  EDUCATION          1  TEXT   GROUPING
 14  PART D            11

ENTER NUMBER OF ITEM FOR WHICH TEXT IS TO BE SUPPLIED

.8
CODES RANGE FROM 10 TO  13
WILL THE TEXT BE USED ONLY IN ROW NAMES (Y OR N)?
.n
ENTER TEXT FOR CODE  10
.district mgr ba
             ++++++++TOO LONG!  RE-ENTER
.DIST MGR BA
ENTER TEXT FOR CODE  11
.dist mgr br
ENTER TEXT FOR CODE  12
.d mgr aim
ENTER TEXT FOR CODE  13
.other

TEXT GENERATED FOR: TITLE
R;
```

QTEX Procedure, cont'd.

In the sample terminal session shown in Exhibit 9b, a "y" is entered in response to the second prompt; this indicates that text for task statements will be supplied. After the "y" entry, the computer displayed the number, the task attribute names, and the grouping status for each attribute. The number of task statements (PARTS) per attribute is also shown — 246 per attribute.

Prompt: TEXT FOR GROUPING OF TASKS (Y OR N)
Response: Enter a "y" if text for task groupings (functions) will be supplied or an "n" if text will not be supplied.

Prompt: WILL THE TEXT BE USED ONLY IN ROW NAMES (Y OR N)?
Response: Enter "y" if text input desired is three lines of up to twenty characters per line or enter an "n" if the text input desired in one line of up to twelve characters.

In the sample session, a "y" is entered in response to both prompts above to indicate that task-grouping text will be supplied for row headings.

The QTEX terminal session will continue:

Prompt: ENTER TEXT FOR [lowest code/task/group number]
Response: Enter up to three lines of text with a twenty-character maximum per line if a "y" was entered in response to the previous prompt; a Return can be entered for the second or third line if there is only enough text for one or two lines. Enter one line of text with up to twelve characters if the response to the previous prompt was an "n."

Since all valid codes for the task grouping were defined, Group Zero does not exist. Group Zero becomes an entity only when a grouping has been defined with the QGRP procedure and all valid codes have not been included in a defined grouping. In

Exhibit 9b.

```
.qtex

ENTER NAME OF SURVEY:
.1000
TEXT FOR TASKS (Y OR N)
.y

NUM  NAME           PARTS

 11  SIGNIFICANCE    246        GROUPING
 11  TIME            246        GROUPING
 12  %TIME           246        GROUPING

TEXT FOR GROUPING OF TASKS          (Y OR N)
.y
GRP. 0 CONSISTS OF ANY ITEMS NOT COVERED IN A GROUP
WILL THE TEXT BE USED ONLY IN ROW NAMES (Y OR N)?
.y
ENTER TEXT FOR GRP.   0
.???

ENTER TEXT FOR GRP.   1
.administrative planning
                 ++++++++TOO LONG!  RE-ENTER
.administrative
.planning

.
ENTER TEXT FOR GRP.   2
.gather &
.analyze data
.
ENTER TEXT FOR GRP.   3
.traing &[training &
.development
.
ENTER TEXT FOR GRP.   4
.customer
.contacts
.
ENTER TEXT FOR GRP.   5
.interdept.
.relations
.
ENTER TEXT FOR GRP.   7
.administering
.office records & personnel
                 ++++++++TOO LONG!  RE-ENTER
.office records &
.personnel
```

cont'd. on p. 217

QTEX Procedure, cont'd.

other words, it is a catchall or miscellaneous category for those valid codes that have not been included in a grouping—for example, task statements not included in any of the defined functions. At least one character, however, must be entered in the first row and then just a Return. Whatever is entered, such as the three question marks that appear in the sample terminal session, will not appear in WPSS reports when all valid codes are included in the grouping.

The first function name entered in the same terminal session exceeds the twenty-character maximum, so the computer prompted for a reentry. Note that function six does not appear in the terminal session. As long as the character maximum row or column length has not been exceeded, the system will continue prompting, ENTER TEXT FOR [Next Code/Task/Group Number], until the highest valid code/task/group number has been processed. Text is supplied in this manner for every task statement included in the questionnaire. For Survey 1000, the system will prompt for text for 246 task statements.

The sample terminal session shown in Exhibit 9c, developed solely for illustrative purposes, is an example of how QTEX can be used to modify an existing text file. The session is the same as the first QTEX session up to the point where a "3" is entered in response to a prompt for the number of the item for which text is to be supplied. The session continues:

Exhibit 9b, cont'd.

```
ENTER TEXT FOR GRP.   8
.community &
.public relations
.
ENTER TEXT FOR GRP.   9
.personnel
.evaluation
.
ENTER TEXT FOR GRP.  10
.inter-level
.communication
.
ENTER TEXT FOR GRP.  11
.problem handling
                    ++++++++TOO LONG!  RE-ENTER
.problem
.handling
.

TEXT GENERATED FOR: TASKS          GROUPING
R;
```

QTEX Procedure, cont'd.

Prompt: LIST TEXT FOR: [ITEM NAME] (Y OR N)
Response: Enter a "y" to display a list of code numbers and
text for the item or an "n" if the list is not desired.
Prompt: TEXT OK (Y OR N)
Response: Enter a "y" if text is correct or an "n" if some
modification is desired.

If a "y" is entered in response to the above prompt, QTEX terminates; if an "n" is entered, however, the session continues:

Prompt: ELIMINATE TEXT FOR [ITEM NAME]
(Y OR N)
Response: Enter a "y" only if it would be better to reassign text
entirely with another QTEX run than to attempt to
salvage the text; otherwise, enter an "n."

If an "n" is entered, the text can be corrected as follows:

Prompt: ENTER CODE NUMBER OF TEXT TO BE
MODIFIED—OR AN A IF ALL COMPLETED
Response: Enter the code number as it appears in the above
listing for the first modification.

Codes must be entered in ascending order. If they are not in ascending order, the computer will display the message

**CANNOT BE PROCESSED (NUMBER ENTERED) IN
THIS PASS

and QTEX will terminate (with all previous corrections included).
Additional modifications can be made by executing QTEX again.
If a valid code number is entered, the session will continue:

Prompt: ENTER E—TO ELIMINATE, I—TO INSERT,
C—TO CHANGE TEXT
Response: Enter an "e," "i," or "c."

Exhibit 9c.

```
.qtex

ENTER NAME OF SURVEY
.1000
TEXT FOR TASKS (Y OR N)


.n

NUM  NAME            PARTS

  1  COMPANY           1  TEXT
  2  STATE             1  TEXT
  3  CITY              1  TEXT
  4  DISTRICT          1
  5  TITLE TENURE      1        GROUPING
  6  BELL TENURE       1        GROUPING
  7  TITLES HELD       1        GROUPING
  8  TITLE             1  TEXT
  9  LAST TITLE        1
 10  EDUCATION         1  TEXT  GROUPING
 14  PART D           11

ENTER NUMBER OF ITEM FOR WHICH TEXT IS TO BE SUPPLIED
.3
LIST TEXT FOR: CITY              (Y OR N)
.y
---
  1 ACCOTINK

  2 ADEN

  3 AGNEVILLE

  4 ALDIE

  5 ALEXANDRIA

  6 ANNANDALE

  7 ARCOLA

  8 ARCTURUS

  9 ARLINGTON

 10 ASHBURN
```

cont'd. on p. 221

QTEX Procedure, cont'd.

If "e" is entered, the following prompts and responses are omitted. If "i" is entered, the user is requested to enter the text that should be inserted above displayed text. When text is inserted, the numbers for all items that follow the inserted text are increased by one. If text is deleted, the numbers for all items following the deleted text are decreased by one. Both the old and new numbers where modified are displayed by the computer. If "c" is entered, the following appears:

Prompt: ENTER TEXT FOR CODE [CODE NUMBER]
Response: Enter text that should replace text already in the file.
Prompt: ENTER CODE NUMBER OF TEXT TO BE
        MODIFIED—OR AN A IF ALL COMPLETED

The above response will be repeated until there are no more modifications, at which point a period (.) can be entered to terminate QTEX.

In the sample terminal session shown in Exhibit 9c, the text for cities will be modified as indicated by the "3" entered. According to the terminal session entries, a city name, Allison, will be inserted above the city name Annandale. In response to the next series of prompts, the city name Ashburn is changed to Ashbourne, and additional city names are added to the list until a period (.) is entered to terminate the QTEX session. The computer then responds with the message "TEXT REGENERATED FOR: CITY" and terminates the session.

Exhibit 9c, cont'd.

```
   11 ASH GROVE

   12 BEL AIR

   13 BELEHAVEN

   14 BELVEDERE

   15 BRISTOW

TEXT OK (Y OR N)
.n
ELIMINATE TEXT FOR: CITY                    (Y OR N)
.n
ENTER CODE NUMBER OF TEXT TO BE MODIFIED
- OR AN A IF ALL COMPLETED


.6
    ANNANDALE
ENTER E -TO ELIMINATE, I -TO INSERT, C -TO CHANGE TEXT
.i
ENTER TEXT FOR CODE  6
.allison
ENTER CODE NUMBER OF TEXT TO BE MODIFIED
- OR AN A IF ALL COMPLETED
.10
    ASHBURN
ENTER E -TO ELIMINATE, I -TO INSERT, C -TO CHANGE TEXT
.c
ENTER TEXT FOR CODE 10
.ashbourne
ENTER CODE NUMBER OF TEXT TO BE MODIFIED
- OR AN A IF ALL COMPLETED
.a
ENTER TEXT FOR CODE 17
.buchanan
ENTER TEXT FOR CODE 18
.buckhall
ENTER TEXT FOR CODE 19
.bull run
ENTER TEXT FOR CODE 20
..

TEXT REGENERATED FOR: CITY
R;
```

QSUB Procedure

The QSUB procedure is used to define subsamples. The user specifies criteria by which questionnaire responses provided by members of the desired subsample will be chosen for special analyses. The criteria will be codes or ranges of codes used for Type A survey items; for example, a subsample of all respondents with four years of college *and* more than ten years of Bell System experience may be desired. The subsample, in other words, must satisfy two conditions — four years of college and more than ten years of Bell System service. The defined codes for the subsample are 16 and 11 to 40, respectively. In another situation, a subsample may be desired for only one condition.

To execute the QSUB procedure, simply enter "qsub," as in the sample terminal session in Exhibit 10, and the terminal session will continue:

Prompt: ENTER SURVEY NAME
Response: Enter the survey name.

If a data base does not exist for the specific survey, the QSUB procedure will terminate with the message:

SURVEY [name] NOT BUILT!

If the survey name is correct, the QSUB terminal session will continue:

Prompt: ENTER SUBSAMPLE NAME (MAX 8
        CHARACTERS)
Response: Enter any meaningful name that does not begin
          with Q.

If an invalid or duplicate subsample name is entered, the above prompt will be repeated. A survey can have an unlimited number of subsamples. In the QSUB sample terminal session, the subsample name entered is "lakemich."

In response to the subsample name entered, the computer

QSUB Procedure, cont'd.

will display the list of standard items, and the terminal session will continue:

Prompt: ENTER ITEM NUMBER FOR SUBSAMPLE
CRITERION

Response: Enter the number associated with the survey item that is the basis of the first subsample criterion.

In the sample terminal session, the number "1" is entered, indicating that the subsample will pertain to Company. At the user's option, the code range for the criterion item can be described as a range to be either selected or rejected.

The computer will display the code range for the selected item, and the terminal session will continue:

Prompt: IF SELECTION RANGE WILL BE INPUT,
ENTER S
IF REJECTION RANGE WILL BE INPUT,
ENTER R

Response: Enter "s" if a range will be described within which the criterion item in a questionnaire must fall to be selected for the subsample; enter an "r" if questionnaire responses will *not* be selected for the subsample because the criterion item falls within a specified range.

Prompt: ENTER MIN CODE FOR
SELECTION/REJECTION RANGE

Response: Enter the minimum code for the item response to be in the selection/rejection range.

Prompt: ENTER MAX CODE FOR
SELECTION/REJECTION RANGE

Response: Enter the maximum code for the item response to be in the selection/rejection range.

In an invalid code is entered in response to either prompt given above, the prompt will be repeated. If the codes are valid,

QSUB Procedure, cont'd.

the computer will display a message specifying the number of
questionnaires in the subsample and will continue:

Prompt: IF SUBSAMPLE IS FULLY DEFINED,
          ENTER FULL
          TO COMBINE WITH A NEW CONDITION,
          ENTER AND/OR

Response: Enter "full" if all entries for the subsample have
been described.
Enter "or" if the full subsample is to consist of
questionnaire responses that *either* are in the
existing subsample *or* will satisfy the criterion
to be entered next.
Enter "and" if the full subsample is to consist of
questionnaire responses that are in *both* the existing
subsample *and* will satisfy the criterion to be entered
next.

In the event that "and" or "or" is entered, the criterion-defining
procedure described above will be repeated until the subsample is
fully defined.

Exhibit 10.

```
.qsub
ENTER SURVEY NAME
.1000
ENTER SUBSAMPLE NAME (MAX 8 CHARACTERS)
.lakemich

NUM  NAME            PARTS

  1  COMPANY          1  TEXT
  2  STATE            1  TEXT
  3  CITY             1
  4  DISTRICT         1
  5  TITLE TENURE     1          GROUPING
  6  BELL TENURE      1          GROUPING
  7  TITLES HELD      1          GROUPING
  8  TITLE            1  TEXT
  9  LAST TITLE       1
 10  EDUCATION        1  TEXT  GROUPING

ENTER ITEM NUMBER FOR SUBSAMPLE CRITERION


.1
   THE DEFINED CODES RANGE FROM   1 TO  20 FOR COMPANY
IF SELECTION RANGE WILL BE INPUT, ENTER S
IF REJECTION RANGE WILL BE INPUT, ENTER R
.s
ENTER MIN CODE FOR SELECTION RANGE
.4
ENTER MAX CODE FOR SELECTION RANGE
.6
SUBSAMPLE CONTAINS   13 QUESTIONNAIRES

IF SUBSAMPLE IS FULLY DEFINED, ENTER FULL
TO COMBINE WITH A NEW CONDITION, ENTER AND / OR
.or


NUM  NAME            PARTS

  1  COMPANY          1  TEXT
  2  STATE            1  TEXT
  3  CITY             1
  4  DISTRICT         1
  5  TITLE TENURE     1          GROUPING
  6  BELL TENURE      1          GROUPING
  7  TITLES HELD      1          GROUPING
  8  TITLE            1  TEXT
  9  LAST TITLE       1
 10  EDUCATION        1  TEXT  GROUPING
```

cont'd. on p. 227

QSUB Procedure, cont'd.

In the sample terminal session, the entries to form a subsample are as follows:

Select company codes 4 to 6 and 20
Reject job title (8) with the code 13.

The subsample created consists of fourteen Business Service Center district managers in four companies with codes 4, 5, 6, and 20 that border Lake Michigan; the managers did not select "other" (code 13) in response to a question about a job title that best fits their jobs. The entry "full," in response to the last QSUB prompt, indicates that the subsample is fully defined.

Exhibit 10, cont'd.

```
ENTER ITEM NUMBER FOR SUBSAMPLE CRITERION
.1
    THE DEFINED CODES RANGE FROM    1 TO   20 FOR COMPANY
IF SELECTION RANGE WILL BE INPUT, ENTER S
IF REJECTION RANGE WILL BE INPUT, ENTER R
.s
ENTER MIN CODE FOR SELECTION RANGE
.20
ENTER MAX CODE FOR SELECTION RANGE
.20
SUBSAMPLE CONTAINS    15 QUESTIONNAIRES

IF SUBSAMPLE IS FULLY DEFINED, ENTER FULL
TO COMBINE WITH A NEW CONDITION, ENTER AND / OR
.and

NUM  NAME            PARTS

  1  COMPANY           1  TEXT
  2  STATE             1  TEXT
  3  CITY              1
  4  DISTRICT          1
  5  TITLE TENURE      1        GROUPING
  6  BELL TENURE       1        GROUPING
  7  TITLES HELD       1        GROUPING
  8  TITLE             1  TEXT
  9  LAST TITLE        1
 10  EDUCATION         1  TEXT  GROUPING


ENTER ITEM NUM FOR SUBSAMPLE CRITERION
.8
    THE DEFINED CODES RANGE FROM   10 TO   13 FOR TITLE
IF SELECTION RANGE WILL BE INPUT, ENTER S
IF REJECTION RANGE WILL BE INPUT, ENTER R
.r
ENTER MIN CODE FOR SELECTION RANGE
.13
ENTER MAX CODE FOR SELECTION RANGE
.13
SUBSAMPLE CONTAINS    14 QUESTIONNAIRES

IF SUBSAMPLE IS FULLY DEFINED, ENTER FULL
TO COMBINE WITH A NEW CONDITION, ENTER AND / OR
.full

SUBSAMPLE LAKEMICH OF SURVEY 1000      COMPLETED
R;
```

QRPT Procedure

A variety of indices can be obtained for any survey item or task attribute, but basically only two types of reports are generated. One type is a statistical analysis of questionnaire data, and the other is a cross tabulation of the data. Two sample terminal sessions, one for each type of report, are shown in Exhibits 11a and 11b.

To execute QRPT, simply enter "qrpt," and the terminal session will continue:

Prompt: MAIL COPY TO YOU (Y OR N)
Response: Enter a "y" if you desire a copy of the printout or an "n" if you do not.

If another copy is desired, it can be sent to yourself or to the person whose name and address are entered in response to the next series of prompts. Name and address prompts will continue until an "n" is entered. The terminal session will then continue:

Prompt: ENTER SURVEY NAME
Response: Enter the survey name.

Entry of an invalid system name will terminate the QRPT procedure, and the computer will print the message:

SURVEY [name] NOT BUILT!

If a valid survey name is entered and subsamples have been specified through the QSUB procedure, the computer will continue:

Prompt: SUBSAMPLE NAME OR JUST A RETURN
Response: Enter a subsample name to obtain reports about the subsample or press Return to obtain reports about the entire sample.

If just a Return is pressed, the computer will print all item and task attribute names and associated numbers and continue as follows:

QRPT Procedure, cont'd.

Prompt: ENTER ITEM NUMBER FOR ROW OUTPUT
Response: Enter the number for the item that will appear in the row headings.

If there is a grouping for the item, the next prompt will be:

Prompt: GROUPING FOR ITEM [name] (Y OR N)
Response: Enter a "y" if the grouping is desired or an "n" if it is not.

    The above prompt will appear only if there is a grouping for the item number entered. If there is no grouping, the terminal session will continue:

Prompt: ENTER ITEM NUMBER FOR LEVEL 1
        COLUMN OUTPUT
Response: Enter the number for the item that will appear in the column headings.

Again, if there is a grouping for the item, the next prompt will ask whether or not the grouping is to be used. If there is no grouping, the terminal session will continue:

Prompt: ENTER ITEM NUMBER FOR LEVEL 2
        COLUMN – OR ENTER 0 IF LEVEL 2 NOT
        DESIRED
Response: Enter the item number for the item that will appear in the second level column headings, or enter a zero if there is no second level.

    The computer will continue to request column-heading levels until a zero response is entered or until level 4 is reached. In either case, the terminal session will continue:

Prompt: ENTER ITEM NUMBER FOR STATISTICS OR
        ENTER 0 IF STATISTICS NOT DESIRED

QRPT Procedure, cont'd.

Response: Enter the item number for which statistics (means and standard deviations) are desired or enter a zero to obtain a cross tabulation with row and column frequencies and percentages instead of means and standard deviations.

If statistics are requested, the next prompt will be:

Prompt: INCLUDE ZERO RESPONSE IN STATISTICS? (Y OR N)

Response: Enter a "y" if zero responses should be included in statistical calculations or an "n" if zeros should not be included.

If zero has been defined as a valid response, the user must decide whether or not to include zero responses in statistical calculations. The next prompt will be:

Prompt: DISPLAY COPY ON TERMINAL (Y OR N)

Response: Enter a "y" if a copy of the report should be printed at the terminal or an "n" if the report should not be printed at the terminal.

Exhibit 11a.

```
.qrpt
MAIL COPY TO YOU ( Y OR N )
.y
MAIL ANOTHER COPY ( Y OR N )
.n

ENTER SURVEY NAME
.1000
SUBSAMPLE NAME OR JUST A -RETURN-
.

NUM  NAME            PARTS

  1  COMPANY            1   TEXT
  2  STATE              1   TEXT
  3  CITY               1
  4  DISTRICT           1
  5  TITLE TENURE       1             GROUPING
  6  BELL TENURE        1             GROUPING
  7  TITLES HELD        1             GROUPING
  8  TITLE              1   TEXT
  9  LAST TITLE         1
 10  EDUCATION          1   TEXT   GROUPING
 11  SIGNIFICANCE     246   TEXT   GROUPING
 12  TIME             246   TEXT   GROUPING
 13  %TIME            246   TEXT   GROUPING
 14  PART D            11

ENTER ITEM NUMBER FOR ROW OUTPUT
.10
GROUPING FOR EDUCATION
.n
ENTER ITEM NUMBER FOR LEVEL 1 COLUMN OUTPUT
.8
ENTER ITEM NUMBER FOR LEVEL 2 COLUMN -OR ENTER 0 IF LEVEL 2 NOT DESIRED
.0
ENTER ITEM NUMBER FOR STATISTICS -OR ENTER 0 IF STATISTICS NOT DESIRED
.0

DISPLAY COPY ON TERMINAL ( Y OR N )
.y
```

cont'd. on p. 233

QRPT Procedure, cont'd.

Since task statement reports usually are too long to be printed at the terminal, they are directed to a high-speed printer and forwarded to the addresses listed at the beginning of the QRPT terminal session. For illustrative purposes, Exhibits 11a and 11b contain a sample of the report specified in the QRPT sample terminal session. The QRPT prompt, which appears beneath the printouts, asks if the reports yet to be defined should be mailed to the addresses listed at the start of the QRPT terminal session.

In Exhibit 11a, the seven responses to the prompts and their intent are as follows:

10 — Educational levels should be the row headings.

n — The educational grouping is not desired.

8 — Job titles should appear in the column headings.

0 — There is no second-level column heading.

0 — A cross tabulation is desired.

y — A copy of the report should be displayed at the terminal.

n — Additional reports will not be generated in this QRPT session, and QRPT terminates. Had a "y" been entered, QRPT simply would continue with the prompt "ENTER SURVEY NAME," and another report would be defined; copies of the report would be sent to the same addresses specified at the start of the QRPT session.

The report printed at the terminal is an educational level by job title cross tabulation. The labels for the information presented in each cell of the printout are defined as follows:

FREQ. — The number of respondents categorized in a cell.

COL. % — The percentage of the particular column that the number of respondents in the cell represents.

ROW % — The percentage of the particular row that the number of repondents in the cell represents.

The first data cell, for example, contains the information that the total sample is composed of 113 respondents who represent

Exhibit 11a, cont'd.

EDUCATION	: TITLE : :	TOTAL	:DIST MGR BA	:DIST MGR BR	:D MGR AIM	:OTHER	:
	: N= :	113	101	1	1	10	
HS GRAD	:FREQ:	9	6	0	1	2	
	:COL%:	7.9646%	5.9406%	0.0 %	100.0000%	20.0000%	
	:ROW%:	100.0000%	66.6667%	0.0 %	11.1111%	22.2222%	
1 YR COLLEGE	:FREQ:	6	6	0	0	0	
	:COL%:	5.3097%	5.9406%	0.0 % :	0.0 % :	0.0 % :	
	:ROW%:	100.0000%	100.0000%	0.0 % :	0.0 % :	0.0 % :	
2 YR COLLEGE	:FREQ:	16	16	0	0	0	
	:COL%:	14.1593%	15.8416%	0.0 % :	0.0 % :	0.0 % :	
	:ROW%:	100.0000%	100.0000%	0.0 % :	0.0 % :	0.0 % :	
3 YR COLLEGE	:FREQ:	13	12	0	0	1	
	:COL%:	11.5044%	11.8812%	0.0 % :	0.0 % :	10.0000%	
	:ROW%:	100.0000%	92.3077%	0.0 % :	0.0 % :	7.6923%	
COLLEGE GRAD	:FREQ:	44	39	1	0	4	
	:COL%:	38.9381%	38.6139%	100.0000% :	0.0 % :	40.0000%	
	:ROW%:	100.0000%	88.6364%	2.2727% :	0.0 % :	9.0909%	
POST GRAD	:FREQ:	25	22	0	0	3	
	:COL%:	22.1239%	21.7822%	0.0 % :	0.0 % :	30.0000%	
	:ROW%:	100.0000%	88.0000%	0.0 % :	0.0 % :	12.0000%	

SURVEY: 1000 (header)

---------MORE REPORTS FOR ABOVE MAILING (Y OR N)
.n
R;

100 percent of the respondents in the TOTAL column. A glance at the second cell in the row indicates that the classification District Manager—Business Accounts (DIST MGR BA) contains 101 respondents who represent 100 percent of the column total and 89.4 percent of the row total. The HS GRAD row indicates that six respondents, or 5.9 percent of the DIST MGR BA classification, graduated from high school and did not go on to college. The 1 YR COLLEGE row shows that the six managers who completed one year of college are all in the DIST MGR BA column. Inasmuch as 101 district managers, or 89 percent of the sample, selected the DIST MGR BA alternative to describe their job title, the TOTAL and DIST MGR BA columns contain similar values. The other columns cover the few district managers who chose other job title alternatives listed in the questionnaire.

QRPT Procedure, cont'd.

The terminal session shown in Exhibit 11b differs from the previous session in that task significance statistics by compnay are requested. The eight responses to the prompts and their intent in this case are as follows:

11 — Task statements will be listed as row headings, and the report will pertain to task significance.

n — There is a grouping for task statements, but it will not be used.

1 — Column headings will be company names.

0 — There is no second-level column heading.

11 — Task significance statistics are desired.

n — Zero responses should not be included in statistical calculations.

y — A copy of the report will be printed at the terminal (as previously explained, for this lengthy printout the response would have been "n").

n — Additional reports will not be defined during this QRPT session, and QRPT terminates.

Exhibit 11b.

```
.qrpt
MAIL COPY TO YOU ( Y OR N )
.y
MAIL ANOTHER COPY ( Y OR N )
.n

ENTER SURVEY NAME
.1000
SUBSAMPLE NAME OR JUST A -RETURN-
.

NUM  NAME          PARTS

  1  COMPANY         1   TEXT
  2  STATE           1   TEXT
  3  CITY            1
  4  DISTRICT        1
  5  TITLE TENURE    1        GROUPING
  6  BELL TENURE     1        GROUPING
  7  TITLES HELD     1        GROUPING
  8  TITLE           1   TEXT
  9  LAST TITLE      1
 10  EDUCATION       1   TEXT GROUPING
 11  SIGNIFICANCE  246   TEXT GROUPING
 12  TIME          246   TEXT GROUPING
 13  %TIME         246   TEXT GROUPING
 14  PART D         11

ENTER ITEM NUMBER FOR ROW OUTPUT
.11
GROUPING FOR SIGNIFICANCE
.n
ENTER ITEM NUMBER FOR LEVEL 1 COLUMN OUTPUT
.1
ENTER ITEM NUMBER FOR LEVEL 2 COLUMN -OR ENTER 0 IF LEVEL 2 NOT DESIRED
.0
ENTER ITEM NUMBER FOR STATISTICS -OR ENTER 0 IF STATISTICS NOT DESIRED
.11
INCLUDE 0 RESPONSES IN STATISTICS? ( Y OR N )
.n

DISPLAY COPY ON TERMINAL ( Y OR N )
.y
```

cont'd. on p. 237

QRPT Procedures, cont'd.

The report obtained summarizes the responses to the task significance question for the entire sample and for each company subsample. Report headings show the survey name — Survey 1000 — and the report topic — task significance statistics. Column headings are TOTAL (total sample), and company names are arranged alphabetically; row headings are task statements. The three numbers that appear in each cell are the proportion of sample responses used in the calculations, the mean value calculated from the responses, and the standard deviation.

The information in the first cell in the TOTAL column shows that the task statement Analyze Office Costs/Expenses for Budgeting Purposes is performed by .97 of the district manager sample, that the mean significance value is 3.7 (on a 1 to 7 scale), and that the standard deviation is 1.7. The second cell in the C&P column shows that the task statement Assign Development of Long-Range Force/Training Requirements is performed by .80 of the C&P district manager sample, that the mean significance value is 4.0, and that the standard deviation is 1.2. The higher the mean and number responding, the more significant the task. The remaining cells are interpreted similarly.

Exhibit 11b, cont'd.

```
                              SURVEY: 1000
STATISTICS FOR SIGNIFICANCE
--------------------------:----:-------------:-------------:-------------:-------------:-------------
                          :    COMPANY
SIGNIFICANCE              :    :  TOTAL  :C&P        :ILLINOIS  :INDIANA   :MICHIGAN
--------------------------:----:-------------:-------------:-------------:-------------:-------------
                          : N= :  113    :   5     :   6      :   2      :   5
--------------------------:----:-------------:-------------:-------------:-------------:-------------
  1. ANALYZE OFFICE  :PROP:    0.97  :    1.00  :    0.83  :    1.00  :    1.00
COSTS/EXPENSES FOR   :MEAN:    3.673 :    3.400 :    2.800 :    5.000 :    4.400
BUDGETING PURPOSE    :STD :    1.714 :    0.894 :    1.789 :    1.414 :    2.302
--------------------------:----:-------------:-------------:-------------:-------------:-------------
  2. ASSIGN DEVELOP- :PROP:    0.92  :    0.80  :    0.83  :    1.00  :    1.00
MENT OF LONG RANGE   :MEAN:    4.048 :    4.000 :    4.000 :    6.500 :    3.000
FORCE/TRNG REQRMNT   :STD :    1.787 :    1.155 :    1.414 :    0.707 :    2.000
--------------------------:----:-------------:-------------:-------------:-------------:-------------
  3. DETERMINE       :PROP:    0.90  :    1.00  :    0.83  :    1.00  :    0.80
PERSONNEL NEEDS FOR  :MEAN:    3.578 :    5.000 :    2.800 :    3.500 :    3.000
A NEW PROJECT        :STD :    1.714 :    2.000 :    2.049 :    2.121 :    1.414
--------------------------:----:-------------:-------------:-------------:-------------:-------------
  4. DETERMINE       :PROP:    0.92  :    0.60  :    0.83  :    1.00  :    0.80
WORK FLOW &          :MEAN:    3.375 :    4.333 :    3.000 :    2.500 :    3.250
OFFICE DESIGN LAYO   :STD :    1.769 :    1.528 :    2.121 :    2.121 :    1.258
--------------------------:----:-------------:-------------:-------------:-------------:-------------
  5. DEVELOP         :PROP:    0.79  :    0.80  :    1.00  :    1.00  :    0.40
ABSENCE & TARDINESS  :MEAN:    3.382 :    3.750 :    3.000 :    4.500 :    2.000
POLICY               :STD :    1.655 :    0.500 :    2.000 :    2.121 :    1.414
```

```
----------MORE REPORTS FOR ABOVE MAILING (Y OR N)
.n
R;
```

QSAV Procedure

Through the QSAV procedure, a survey data base is copied so that it can be stored off line; survey data must be on line to be processed. When WPSS survey data are to be processed, it is advisable to remove a previous WPSS data base from on-line storage and save it for future use. Data stored off line can be retrieved on demand. Normally after QSAV is executed, the on-line data base is erased. QSAV will save data for ten days, but data can be saved for a longer time by executing the QYRS procedure to be described later.

To execute QSAV, simply enter "qsav," as in Exhibit 12, and the computer system will continue:

Prompt: ENTER SURVEY NAME
Response: Enter the name of the survey to be saved.

The computer system then will display a message regarding a volume serial (VOLSER) number and a dumping operation, and continue:

Prompt: OK TO ERASE [survey name] — ENTER Y OR N
Response: Enter an "n" to maintain the survey data on line or a "y" to erase the on-line data.

In the sample terminal session, the QSAV procedure is employed to save all files associated with Survey 1000, but the files were not erased from on-line storage. Only two user entries are contained in the sample terminal session: "1000" and "n."

Exhibit 12.

```
.qsav
ENTER SURVEY NAME
.1000
PLEASE ENTER MEMO INFORMATION
..... WAITING FOR TAPE MOUNT .....
TAPE 181 ATTACHED VOLSER=V10882
DUMPING ......
1000      QRAW        A1
1000      QUNS        A1
1000      QTTSK       A1
1000      QGTSK       A1
1000      QTXAB008    A1
1000      QGRAB010    A1
1000      QGRAB014    A1
1000      QATA        A1
1000      QATD        A1
1000      QAT1        A1
1000      QAT2        A1
1000      QATP        A1
1000      LAKEMICH    A1
OK TO ERASE 1000- ENTER Y OR N
.n
TAPE 181 DETACHED
R;
```

QTAP Procedure

The QTAP procedure is executed to obtain the list of tape identification numbers that will be needed to execute the QYRS and QGET procedures. When the QTAP procedure is executed, as shown in Exhibit 13, information will be displayed about tapes saved for a user identification or for a particular survey. To obtain a display of all tapes saved, enter "qtap'; to obtain a display of tapes saved for a particular survey, enter "qtap [survey name]." If no tapes were saved or an incorrect survey name is entered, the computer will respond:

NO VOLUMES FOUND

Otherwise, the following will be displayed for each tape:

VOLSER — tape id number
USERID — user account number
ALLOCATION DATE — date the tape was created
EXPIRATION DATE — current retention date
MEMO — survey name, if created by QSAV;
for tapes not created within WPSS,
information supplied by an analyst
when the tape was created appears
under MEMO
STATUS — the current location of the tape
(such as onsite in the tape library)

In the QTAP sample terminal session, the only user entry is "qtap." The computer response shows that there are two VOLSERS (tape ids) on the same USERID. One VOLSER is for Survey 1000, the other is for the original keypunch data used in QBLD and is called 1000 INPUT. Both tapes are onsite.

Exhibit 13.

```
.qtap
VOLSER   USERID   ALLOCATION EXPIRATION  MEMO         STATUS
                  DATE       DATE
V10881   EAX002   10/17/80   10/16/82    1000INPUT    ONSITE
V10882   EAX002   10/17/80   10/27/80    1000         ONSITE
- R;
```

QYRS Procedure

Execution of the QYRS procedure increases the expiration date of any tape to five years from the date QYRS is executed. The procedure requires only two entries—"qyrs" and the tape VOLSER, which can be obtained through the QTAP procedure. If an incorrect VOLSER is entered, the procedure will terminate with the message:

VOLSER DOES NOT EXIST

In the QYRS sample terminal session shown in Exhibit 13, the VOLSER entry is "v10882," indicating that Survey 1000 files are to be retained for five years from the date of execution.

Exhibit 14.

```
.qyrs
ENTER VOLSER NUMBER FOR SURVEY TAPE TO BE SAVED
(FOR FIVE YEARS FROM TODAY)
.v10882
R;
```

QGET Procedure

The QGET procedure is used to retrieve survey files previously saved. The files will be retrieved and placed online, where they can be processed by other WPSS procedures.

To execute QGET, simply enter "qget," as in Exhibit 15. The computer system will display the same tape status shown when executing QTAP. The only other entry required is the VOLSER number for the particular survey. In the sample terminal session, the VOLSER number entered is "v10882," and a series of loading messages are displayed to show that Survey 1000 files have been restored online and are ready for processing. If an incorrect VOLSER is entered, the QGET procedure will terminate with the message:

MOUNT FOR DEVICE 181 CANCELLED

Exhibit 15.

```
.qget
VOLSER   USERID   ALLOCATION EXPIRATION MEMO       STATUS
                  DATE       DATE
V10881   EAX002   10/17/80   10/16/82   1000INPUT  ONSITE
V10882   EAX002   10/17/80   10/13/85   1000       ONSITE
ENTER VOLSER NUMBER FOR SURVEY
.v10882
..... WAITING FOR TAPE MOUNT .....
TAPE 181 ATTACHED
LOADING ......
1000      QRAW        A1
1000      QUNS        A1
1000      QTTSK       A1
1000      QGTSK       A1
1000      QTXAB008    A1
1000      QGRAB010    A1
1000      QGRAB014    A1
1000      QATA        A1
1000      QATD        A1
1000      QAT1        A1
1000      QAT2        A1
1000      QATP        A1
1000      LAKEMICH    A1
TAPE 181 DETACHED
R;
```

Appendix: Coordinating Correspondence

Letter Requesting Survey Coordinators

Response to Request
for Survey Coordinators

Instructions to Survey
Coordinators

Attachment to Letter:
Guidance for Local Administration
of Accounting Office Job Survey

Sample of Survey
Distribution Schedule
(Attached to Instructions)

Instructions to Field Managers
Participating in the AO Job Survey
(from Survey Coordinators)

247

LETTER REQUESTING SURVEY COORDINATORS

October 10, 1981

To: All Region Managers

Your assistance is needed to ensure effective administration of the
forthcoming job analysis survey being conducted by our department in
cooperation with the Human Resources Department. A survey coordinator is needed to distribute and keep track of survey questionnaires
in your Region. Specific distribution instructions will be enclosed
with the package of questionnaires to be shipped within the next few
weeks to your Region coordinator.

The purpose of the job survey is to update information about Accounting
Office management and nonmanagement jobs. Survey responses will be used
to gain a better understanding of AO jobs performed under different
operating conditions. Survey results will be used in several ways,
for example, to determine the need of job redesign and to provide data
for job evaluation purposes. Responses will not be used to evaluate
individuals or AO organizations.

The survey coordinator you appoint will distribute survey questionnaires
directly to AO district managers, who, in turn, will distribute them
further in accordance with instructions. Specific numbers of respondents for each job type will be contained in the distribution instructions. Each AO manager should forward completed questionnaires
to the data-processing company named in the instructions and inform
the coordinator of the status of questionnaire completion by job type.

Respondents will require about two hours to complete questionnaires,
and force scheduling should reflect the time needed for questionnaire
completion. We anticipate that about 400 clerks and 150 managers
throughout the company will complete questionnaires, so each AO will
not be overburdened by the time required for questionnaire completion.
Please let me know if you anticipate any problems about the time that
will be needed for questionnaire completion.

Please provide the name, address, and telephone number of your survey
coordinator to Ron Smith, Room 6211, 701 Washington Street, Morristown,
New Jersey, 07960. Questions regarding the survey and its administration may be referred to Ron at (201) 251-6260 or to Jim Mitchell at
(201) 251-6258.

A. B. Charles

A. B. Charles
AO Division Manager - Operations

RESPONSE TO REQUEST FOR SURVEY COORDINATORS

October 15, 1981

Mr. Ron Smith
Room 6211
701 Washington Street
Morristown, New Jersey 07960

Mr. Smith:

This is in response to Al Charles' October 10, 1981 letter
concerning the need to appoint a survey coordinator who
will be responsible for distributing and keeping track of
survey questionnaires for our Region.

For the Eastern Region, the coordinator is:

              Ms. Robert Emile
              Room 401
              211 James Street
              Silver Spring, Maryland 20910

Should you have any questions on this matter, please call
Ms. Emile on (301) 555-8614.

Wes Gribben

Copy to: Mr. J. L. Walker

INSTRUCTIONS TO SURVEY COORDINATORS

November 7, 1981

To: All Job Survey Coordinators

Your assistance is needed to ensure effective administration of the job analysis survey being conducted by our department in cooperation with the Human Resources Department. As survey coordinator, you will be responsible for distributing and keeping track of survey questionnaires in your Region.

The package you received contains survey materials including copies of four different questionnaires developed specifically for the following jobs:

1. AO District Manager
2. AO Manager (Account and Support), Account Supervisor, and Support Supervisor
3. Processing Clerk
4. Service Order Clerk and Service Order Completion Clerk

Attached is a copy of guidance for local administration of the AO job survey and a survey distribution schedule for your Region that contains the number of respondents required in each job category. It is imperative that the selection of respondents reflect a geographic and functional mix. The AO Organization and Administrative Guidelines provide definitions of the AO job functions and can be used to help in selecting survey respondents. Another factor to consider is that survey respondents should be selected so that the mix of operational conditions in your Region, as defined in the Guidelines, are represented.

Respondents will require about two hours to complete their questionnaires. Force scheduling should reflect the time required for prompt completion of questionnaires at a location away from the work area.

If you have any questions about the survey and its administration, please do not hesitate to call me at (201) 251-6260 or Jim Mitchell at (201) 251-6258.

R. A. Smith

R. A. Smith
AO District Staff Manager

attachments - 2

ATTACHMENT TO LETTER:
GUIDANCE FOR LOCAL ADMINISTRATION OF
ACCOUNTING OFFICE JOB SURVEY

ATTACHMENT

For the types of AO jobs to be surveyed at any one particular location, survey respondents should be selected so that they represent
a mix of experience and of work assignments. It is not desired,
for instance, that all respondents be selected from one unit or
section within an AO. Instead, employees selected should represent
a cross section of office activities.

Supervisors should be informed of the survey purpose so that they
may be able to respond to employee questions. In particular, it
may be necessary for supervisors to assist employees in completing
the personal information section of the questionnaire (Part A),
which asks for names of the particular unit and district in which
the employee works.

Each survey respondent should turn in his or her completed survey
booklet, sealed in its accompanying envelope, to his or her supervisor, who, in turn, will forward it to the AO manager. The AO
manager will:

1. Follow up to ensure that all questionnaires are completed
    and returned.

2. Pack and send completed questionnaires in the envelopes
    directly to:

    Old Town Business Center

    600 Main Street

    Alexandria, VA 22314

3. Immediately inform the AO Job Survey Coordinator at
    Region Headquarters of the number of surveys completed
    and when they were sent to the above address in Virginia.

The coordinator at Region Headquarters will periodically inform his
or her contacts at Corporate of the status of the survey within the
Region.

Sincere thanks are expressed to all AO managers and supervisors for
their valued assistance in accomplishing a complete and prompt
administration of this job survey.

SAMPLE OF SURVEY DISTRIBUTION SCHEDULE
(ATTACHED TO INSTRUCTIONS)

                                                    ATTACHMENT

                        WESTERN REGION

AO District Manager   4

AO Manager   16

AO Supervisor   40

AO Support Supervisor   15

Processing Clerk   70

Service Order Clerk   30

Service Order Completion Clerk   19

INSTRUCTIONS TO FIELD MANAGERS PARTICIPATING
IN THE AO JOB SURVEY
(FROM SURVEY COORDINATORS)

November 10, 1981

To: AO Managers Participating in the Job Survey

AO employees are being asked to participate in a job survey by completing one of the questionnaires contained in the package you received. The purpose of the survey is to update information on the
way AO jobs are being performed. The information can be used in a
number of ways, for instance, to identify training requirements and
to improve employee selection procedures.

Two different questionnaires plus instructions for administering
them are contained in the material you received. Instructions
should be distributed to managers and supervisors along with the
questionnaires. Those with the blue covers are to be completed by
AO managers and supervisors, and those with the green covers are
designated for clerical employees. Explicit instructions are contained in each questionnaire, and they should be read carefully before questionnaires are completed. Supervisors also should
familiarize themselves with the questionnaire clerks will complete,
so that they will be able to answer questions that may arise. Questionnaires should be completed as soon as possible and returned.

Each respondent will require about two hours to complete his or her
questionnaire. Instructions provided for supervisors emphasize the
point that respondents should complete each questionnaire item.
Please mention that point again in your transmittal letter as well,
because we would like to avoid having to contact employees again to
fill in omitted responses.

Questionnaire instructions ensure respondents that their responses
will be treated confidentially. The envelopes provided should be
given to them with the questionnaire so that they can seal completed
questionnaires before turning them in. Your district manager is
familiar with the survey requirements, and the union has been informed of and supports the job survey.

Returned envelopes containing completed questionnaires should be
placed in the large, addressed envelopes and mailed for keypunching.
We realize that filling out the questionnaires will take valuable
time, but AO managers, supervisors, and clerical employees are the
only ones that can provide the vitally needed job information.

Please call Evelyn Tovy at (415) 628-1144 if questions arise that
cannot be answered locally. Thank you for your cooperation.

R. L. Foster

R. L. Foster
AO District Staff Manager
Western Region

Annotated
Bibliography

The articles annotated here were selected from among about 350 reports pertaining to job inventories that I discovered by searching several computerized literature data bases, as well as some reports in my personal library that did not show up in the computer searches. This bibliography covers work designed to improve the job inventory approach to job analysis or work that represents a somewhat unique application of the job inventory approach. Job inventory analyses of jobs are not included in the bibliography because the volume of material is simply too great to annotate here. In U.S. Air Force work alone, according to a recent (November 1981) memorandum from the Occupational Analysis Branch, Occupational Measurement Center, Randolph Air Force Base, Texas, over 300 job titles were covered by occupational surveys during the years 1973 to 1981, and many more surveys were conducted in prior years.

Abstracts are arranged alphabetically by the primary author's name. In cases where more than one volume was prepared under the same title, I took the liberty of including all authors' names even though they did not coauthor every volume. The annotations almost always are abbreviations of abstracts. I hope that the condensed versions catch the primary purpose and flavor of the works and do not omit too much useful information.

Adde, E. N. *A Methodological Strategy for Identifying Similarities Among Jobs.* No. PRR-80-25. Washington, D.C.: U.S. Office of Personnel Management, 1980. A quantitative methodology for identifying similarities among federal occupations is described. The methodology is particularly suitable for evaluating the efficiency of occupational classification systems that are characterized by measures of duty and task performance. Interrelated jobs are identified from a single-linkage cluster solution and a complete-linkage cluster solution applied to the same data base. An "index or average similarity" is used to relate cluster solutions to job family constructions.

Ammerman, H. L., and Pratzner, F. C. *Performance Content for Job Training.* 5 Vols. Columbus: Center for Vocational Education, Ohio State University, 1977. This series is devoted to describing the job task inventory survey methodology and how it can be used to develop curricula and instructional materials that are required for effective job performance.

Archer, W. B. *Computation of Group Job Descriptions from Occupational Survey Data.* No. PRL-TR-66-12. Lackland Air Force Base, Tex.: Personnel Research Laboratory, 1966. The analysis of occupational survey data is demonstrated in detail through use of miniature examples. Beginning with the responses of ten incumbents to a job inventory consisting of ten task statements, composite job descriptions are derived for (1) special groups of incumbents, selected on the basis of background information data; and (2) job type members, identified by an automated job-clustering program. Computer outputs from both types of analyses are illustrated and explained.

Archer, W. B., and Fruchter, D. A. *The Construction, Review, and Administration of Air Force Job Inventories.* No. PRL-TDR-63-21.

Lackland Air Force Base, Tex.: Personnel Research Laboratory, 1963. This project was directed toward improving procedures for constructing and administering USAF job inventories through use of methods described in the current Occupational Analysis Manual. In constructing inventories for twenty airman career ladders, the authors evaluated source materials for duty and task statements. Review procedures were compared with respect to yield of information from technical advisers (specialty experts), both from field review and from direct interview. Results of the administration of ten inventories to large samples of incumbents showed that efficient use of source materials and technical advisers yielded practically complete inventories, since incumbents produced only a negligible number of task write-ins.

Carpenter, J. B. *Sensitivity of Group Job Descriptions to Possible Inaccuracies in Individual Job Descriptions.* No. AFHRL-TR-74-6. Brooks Air Force Base, Tex.: Air Force Human Resources Laboratory, 1974. A study was conducted to determine the relative impact of dichotomized task performance data compared to estimates of percent of time spent for those members performing each task in the group job descriptions. The percent members performing vector and the percent time spent by the total group vector or group job description were significantly correlated. These findings suggest that with groups of five or more individuals, dichotomized task performance data, which have previously been shown to have high reliability and validity, are critical components in the resultant group job description.

Carpenter, J. B., and Christal, R. E. *Predicting Civilian Position Grades from Occupational and Background Data.* No. AFHRL-TR-72-24. Brooks Air Force Base, Tex.: Air Force Human Resources Laboratory, 1972. A job inventory was administered to civilian USAF employees in the accounting and finance career field; and task performance data, analyzed through multiple-regression techniques, were found to be highly predictive of the GS grade authorized for the position. Knowledge of specific tasks performed, it seems, can be used as a stable predictor of appropriate grade. Factors unrelated to job requirements, such as the incumbent's sex, age, or marital status, and unique job characteristics, such as geographical location and command to which assigned, do not act as significant sources of bias in grade determinations. In general, both the stability and the objectivity of existing civil service grade classifications are strongly supported.

Carpenter, J. B., Giorgia, M. J., and McFarland, B. P. *Comparative Analysis of the Relative Validity for Subjective Time Rating Scales.* No. AFHRL-TR-75-63, Brooks Air Force Base, Tex.: Air Force Human Resources Laboratory, 1975. The results of two separate investigations aimed at determining the inherent accuracy of job descriptions derived from job inventories are summarized. In general, five-point relative scales were found to be inferior to the other scales used in this study. It was further established that job incumbents can use scales of greater complexity (for example, a wider range of response options) than had previously been indicated in the literature. The discrepancies in estimates of absolute time or percentage values previously reported were confirmed, but the inaccuracies within this approach were found to relate only to the absolute raw values. When these absolute values were treated as relative indices, no significant differences in the validity of the derived job descriptions were universally obtained.

Carr, M. J. *The SAMOA Method of Determining Technical, Organizational, and Communicational Dimensions of Task Clusters.* No. NPRA-STB-68-5. San Diego: Naval Personnel Research Activity, 1967. This describes a pilot study of a research method, Systematic Approach to Multidimensional Occupational Analysis (SAMOA), for collecting and analyzing occupational information that will be used as a major input for the development of an occupational classification structure. The pilot study demonstrates the technical feasibility of SAMOA for determining current work requirements. SAMOA consists of two major phases: (1) specification of specialty areas by means of a computerized clustering program that identified relatively homogeneous work groups on the basis of similarity of task patterns; and (2) stratification of such groups (clusters) on the basis of technical, organizational, and communicational variables by means of a set of computerized procedures.

Indices of these variables form the basis for cluster profiles that constitute the primary input for an occupational classification structure.

Center for Vocational Education. *Directory of Task Inventories.* Vol. 1. Columbus: Center for Vocational Education, Ohio State University, 1974. This directory was compiled from a review of documents produced by a variety of organizations. In all, 77 task inventories covering about 300 job titles and/or occupational areas are listed, and instructions for obtaining copies of inventories are included.

Christal, R. E. *Stability of Consolidated Job Descriptions Based on Task Inventory Survey Information.* No. AFHRL-TR-71-48. Lackland Air Force Base, Tex.: Air Force Human Resources Laboratory, 1971. This study was designed to determine the stability of data reported in consolidated job descriptions computed from task inventory survey returns. It was found that the vectors "percent performing" and "percent time spent by total group" are highly stable, even for relatively small samples.

Christal, R. E. *The United States Air Force Occupational Research Project.* No. AFHRL--TR-73-75. Brooks Air Force Base, Tex.: Air Force Human Resources Laboratory, 1974. The first part of the paper describes how and why the USAF uses the job inventory approach for collecting, analyzing, and reporting information that describes the work performed by its personnel. This is followed by a brief description of the Comprehensive Occupational data Analysis Programs (CODAP). The last section describes applications of job survey information to problems in managing the personnel system.

Clary, J. N. *Naval Occupational Task Analysis Program Data Bank Information: Its Use in the Development/Updating or Qualifications for Advancement.* No. WTR-73-32. Washington, D.C.: Naval Personnel Research and Development Laboratory, 1973. This study is concerned with the analysis of data bank information and with demonstrating the feasibility of using such information to develop and/or update the qualifications for advancement of U.S. Navy enlisted personnel. Methodologies for determining the validity of tasks for inclusion in the qualifications for advancement are described. It appears that the use of data bank information may preclude the necessity for the separate rating surveys currently conducted.

Cragun, J. R., and McCormick, E. J. *Job Inventory Information: Task and Scale Reliabilities and Scale Interrelationships.* No. PRL-TR-67-15. Lackland Air Force Base, Tex.: Personnel Research Laboratory, 1967. Officer job incumbents were surveyed with job inventories to determine the reliability of task information, the reliability of five different scales used to rate tasks performed, the relationships between the five rating scales, and the reactions of incumbents to the inventories and scales.

Drauden, G. M., and Peterson, N. G. "Domain-Sampling Approach to Job Analysis." JSAS *Catalog of Selected Documents in Psychology,* 1977, 7, 27–28. A step-by-step guide for obtaining job analysis information that meets Equal Employment Opportunity Coordinating Council (EEOCC) guidelines is provided. The manual details the development of a job analysis questionnaire through group brainstorming sessions, the collection of questionnaire results from samples of job incumbents, and the analysis of the questionnaire results by means of computer programs. The most important elements of the method are as follows: (1) an emphasis on task checklists that describe a job in terms of the behaviors that constitute that job; (2) a reliance on relative percentage of time spent on tasks as the major indicator of task criticalness; and (3) a matrix-rating technique with which job incumbents identify the knowledges, skills, and abilities that are necessary to perform each of the job tasks.

Farrell, W. T., Stone, C. H., and Yoder, D. *Guidelines for Sampling in Marine Corps Task Analysis.* No. TR-11. Los Angeles: California State University, 1976. The specific objective of the research described in this report was to develop guidelines for the selection of occupational field samples sizes to which task inventories will be administered. A summary of requirements for a sampling design is given. Research findings are reported that suggest a uniform optimum sample size, and a recommended sampling strategy is outlined for guidance in data collection.

Fugill, J. W. K. *Task Difficulty and Task Aptitude Benchmark Scales for the Mechanical and Electronics Career Feilds.* No. AFHRL-TR-7240. Brooks Air Force Base, Tex.: Air Force Human Resources Laboratory, 1972. The feasibility of constructing benchmark scales on the dimensions of task difficulty and task aptitude for tasks in USAF mechanical and electronics job areas was examined. It was determined that small numbers of work supervisors and behavioral scientists can achieve high interrater agreement on the dimensions of task difficulty and task aptitude, respectively.

Fugill, J. W. K. *Task Difficulty and Task Aptitude Benchmark Scales for the Administrative and General Career Fields.* No. AFHRL-73-13. Brooks Air Force Base, Tex.: Air Force Human Resources Laboratory, 1973. A high positive relationship was found between relative task difficulty values and corresponding relative task aptitude requirements. For 3,200 tasks not used in the original scaling procedure, relative task difficulty values could be inferred at a high level of confidence, and relative task aptitude requirements could be inferred at a moderately high level of confidence.

Gael, S. "Development of Job Task Inventories and Their Use in Job Analysis Research." JSAS *Catalog of Selected Documents in Psychology,* 1977, *7,* 25. An approach to developing job inventory questionnaires by interviewing supervisors of job incumbents is described. Applications of job inventory questionnaires in studies of engineering, sales, and clerical jobs are described, and summaries of study results are presented.

Gilbert, A. C. F. *Dimensions of Certain Army Officer Positions Derived By Factor Analysis.* No. ARI-TP-269. Arlington, Va.: Army Research Institute for the Behavioral and Social Sciences, 1975. Task analysis data were collected from 403 infantry officers and 74 quartermaster officers in representative duty positions described by 93 duty modules. These data were factor analyzed, and results indicate that army officer duty positions can be divided into six factors that describe the functions of unit command, operations and training, manpower and personnel, logistics, intelligence, and troop welfare.

Gilpatrick, E., and Gullion, C. *The Health Service Mobility Study Method of Task Analysis and Curriculum Design.* Research Report No. 11. 4 Vols. Washington, C.D.: Office of Research and Development, 1977. The Health Service Mobility Study (HSMS) task analysis and curriculum design method is presented. Volume 1 includes an introduction to the method and to the basic HSMS task analysis instruments and gives an overview of the HSMS system and concepts. Volume 2, a manual for directors of task analysis work and for job analysts, covers the use of HSMS instruments. Vol 3 is a manual for using HSMS computer-based statistical procedures to design job structures and ladders (the HSMS computer programs are listed in appendixes). Volume 4 presents the HSMS curriculum design method.

Gott, S. P., and Alley, W. E. "Physical Demands of Air Force Occupations: A Task Analysis Approach." Paper presented at 22nd annual conference of the Military Testing Association, Toronto, Oct., 1980. The use of the Physical Demand Survey to assess physical demands for eighty-seven USAF specialties is described. The purpose was to establish specialty-specific minimum entry-level standards based on empirically derived job requirements. Of the eighty-seven specialties studied, twenty-eight (32 percent) have the highest physical demand designation, forty-five (52 percent) have the middle designation, and fourteen (16 percent) the lowest designation. There is a disproportionate number of high-demand specialties. A means for calculating an Average Physical Load Index for a specialty is presented.

Hollenbeck, G. P., and Borman, W. C. "Two Analyses in Search of a Job—The Implications of Different Job Analysis Approaches." Paper presented at 84th annual meeting of the American Psychological Association, Washington, D.C., Sept., 1976. A job activity questionnaire and a performance behavior approach were used to analyze the job of stockbroker. The two approaches yielded different types of information and different results. The advantages and disadvantages of each approach are discussed, along with the implications for validation strategies of the types of information obtained.

Johns, B., Kern, J., and Koch, C. *Military Occupational Information Data Bank.* No. ORI-TR-508. 5 Vols. Silver Spring: Operations Research, 1968. The Military Occupational Information Data Bank (MOIDB) is described. MOIDB is a total operating system with the capability of providing military job information on an army-wide basis. The system provides computerized processing and storage of data collected in the field through questionnaires and permits retrieval of information on military jobs in the army.

Kishi, A., and Stone, C. H. *Task Inventory Construction.* No. TR-14. Los Angeles: California State University, 1976. This report was designed to aid in the construction of effective task analysis inventories. An experimental design is given for dividing a lengthy task inventory into a series of shorter inventories with sufficient overlap of task statements in each small questionnaire booklet to provide adequate samples of responses to each item. Major attention is given to the wording of task statements and task inventory instructions. Data are presented from the application of six measures of readability to nine task inventories.

Koym, K. G. *Familiarity Effects on Task Difficulty Ratings.* No. AFHRL-TR-77-25. Brooks Air Force Base, Tex.: Air Force Human Resources Laboratory, 1977a. Interrater reliability estimates for task difficulty ratings provided by raters having differing levels of familiarity with rated tasks were examined. Interrater reliability estimates decreased from .930 to .802 for six task difficulty rating-scale conditions in which ratings were eliminated due to levels of familiarity. This finding suggests that little is to be gained from eliminating task difficulty ratings that are based upon an experienced judge's level of familiarity with tasks.

Koym, K. G. *Predicting Job Difficulty in High-Aptitude Career Ladders with Standard Score Regression Equations.* No. AFHRL-TR-77-26. Brooks Air Force Base, Tex.: Air Force Human Resources Laboratory, 1977b. This research was designed to study a method for evaluating the difficulty levels of USAF enlisted jobs. Multiple-regression equations that captured the job difficulty evaluation policy of supervisors in two electronics and two general career ladders were produced. The equations yielded predicted difficulty values for 250 jobs from each career ladder. These values correlated above .81 with supervisory rankings of job difficulty and thus confirmed the findings of previous job difficulty studies conducted in twelve USAF career ladders.

McCormick, E. J. *Effect of Amount of Information Required on Reliability of Incumbents' Checklist Reports.* No. WADD-TN-60-142. Lackland Air Force Base, Tex.: Personnel Laboratory, Wright Air Development Division, 1960. This examines the effect of the number of questions asked about each task on the consistency and amount of information provided by USAF personnel when completing task inventories. Incumbents who were required to report more types of information about their tasks provided more reliable information. There was considerable stability from group to group in the proportion who reported that they performed a particular task.

McCormick, E. J., and Ammerman, H. L. *Development of Worker Activity Checklists for Use in Occupational Analysis.* No. WADD-TR-60-77. Lackland Air Force Base, Tex.: Personnel Laboratory, Wright Air Development Division, 1960. Several forms of task activity checklists were completed by job incumbents in three USAF positions to determine the consistency of job incumbents' responses. Consistency in reporting frequency of task performance and length of task time was fairly satisfactory, with mean reliabilities around .70. Reliability coefficients for relative proportion of total time per task and for general task difficulty were considerably lower (.53 and .52). Analyses showed that (1) consistency in reporting task occurrence is not generally related to consistency in reporting other types of task information; (2) a recall period of six months elicits more reliable task occurrence information than a one-month period, but the one-month recall yields greater consistency of time and difficulty judgments than the six-month period; and (3) interactions among experimental factors (scales, recall periods, position and equipment types, methods of response) were generally negligible. The degree of reliability obtained and the absence of important interactions were taken as evidence that the checklist may prove a useful procedure for gathering information over a large variety of conditions and jobs.

McCormick, E. J., and Tombrink, K. B. *A Comparison of Three Types of Work Activity Statements in Terms of the Consistency of Job Information Reported by Incumbents.* No. WADD-TR-60-80. Lackland Air Force Base, Tex.: Personnel Laboratory, Wright Air Development Division, 1960. The consistency of job information collected with three types of work activity statements (tasks, elements, and work actions) was compared. Checklists of activities for two maintenance positions were administered to incumbents and supervisors and provided job information on seven scales. For the quantitative scales, tasks and elements yielded more consistent information than work actions; with the qualitative scales, however, work actions were more consistent that tasks, with elements falling between them and not differing significantly from either. Patterns of differences were found between the two jobs, but there were no systematic differences between incumbents and supervisors in reporting information about incumbents' jobs.

Madden, J. M., Hazel, J. T., and Christal, R. E. *Worker and Supervisor Agreement Concerning the Worker's Job Description.* No. PRL-TDR-64-10. Lackland Air Force Base, Tex.: Aerospace Medical Division, 1964. To compare worker and supervisor descriptions of what constitutes the worker's job, an inventory of 579 tasks, listed under 15 duties, was completed independently by 94 airmen and their immediate supervisors. When compared to supervisors, subordinates did not tend to exaggerate the number or the difficulty of tasks they perform. Supervisors showed higher agreement with subordinates on a broad (duty) work level than on a more specific (task) work level. Since supervisors and subordinates generally agree about the nature of the subordinates' job and there was no tendency for the subordinates to exaggerate the nature of their jobs, it is preferable to collect job information directly from incumbents.

Marshall, C. T. *Occupational Analysis: Transition of the Navy Occupational Task Analysis Program (NOTAP) from Research to Operational Status — Evaluation of Program and Summation of Results.* No. WTR-73-37. Washington, D.C.: Navy Personnel Research and Development Center, 1973. A comprehensive review of the exploratory and advanced development research that led to operational status of the Navy Occupational Task Analysis Program (NOTAP) is presented. Collection, processing, analysis, and application of NOTAP data are covered in detail. A brief review of the history of military occupational analysis is included. Task analysis methodology and application of techniques in the other military services and the U.S. Coast Guard are summarized.

Mayo, C. C. *Three Studies of Job Inventory Procedures: Selecting Duty Categories, Interviewing, and Sampling.* No. AFHRL-TR-69-32. Brooks Air Force Base, Tex.: Air Force Human Resources Laboratory, 1969. Three USAF job inventory procedures were studied in depth: categorizing task statements by duties, interviewing technical advisers for job information, and detecting bias in survey samples. Criteria are suggested for determining the point at which interviews become more productive than publications research.

Mayo, C. C., Nance, D. M., and Shigekawa, L. *Evaluation of the Job Inventory Approach Analyzing USAF Officer Utilization Fields.* No. AFHRL-TR-75-22. Brooks Air Force Base, Tex.: Air Force Human Resources Laboratory, 1975. The purpose of this study was to evaluate and improve the job inventory method of job analysis as applied to officer positions. The basic finding was that the inventory method can be used operationally in the analysis of officer jobs if job analysts use specific approaches to task statement construction and if more front-end research than is usually needed to construct airman job inventories is performed prior to the finalization of job inventories for officer positions.

Mead, D. F. *Development of an Equation for Evaluating Job Difficulty.* No. AFHRL-TR-70-42. Lackland Air Force Base, Tex.: Air Force Human Resources Laboratory, 1970a. This is the first in a series of studies designed to produce a method for evaluating the difficulty levels of USAF enlisted jobs. Regression analyses identified three variables that predicted the job difficulty rankings with an R of .95 — number of tasks performed, difficulty of tasks performed per unit time, and number of tasks performed, squared. Results of the study indicate that the difficulty level of jobs within the medical materiel career ladder can be adequately determined using the three-variable regression equation.

Mead, D. F. *Continuation Study on Development of a Method for Evaluating Job Difficulty.* No. AFHRL-TR-70-43. Lackland Air Force Base, Tex.: Air Force Human Resources Laboratory, 1970b. The development of a multiple-regression equation that satisfactorily predicted the difficulty level of 250 jobs from the vehicle maintenance career ladder is described. The primary factors reflected in the job difficulty evaluation policy were number of tasks in the job description, difficulty level of tasks performed, and time spent performing the tasks. These findings provide support for the hypothesis that there are common factors that influence supervisors' judgments of job difficulty in all USAF career ladders.

Mead, D. F., and Christal, R. E. *Development of a Constant Standard Weight Equation for Evaluating Job Difficulty.* No. AFHRL-TR-70-44. Lackland Air Force Base, Tex.: Air Force Human Resources Laboratory, 1970. The development of a multiple-regression equation that captured the job difficulty evaluation policy of accounting and finance supervisors is described. These results validated the findings of two previous job difficulty studies that used jobs from the vehicle maintenance and medical materiel career ladders. A constant standard weight equation was developed that reflected the job evaluation policy of supervisors from the three diverse career fields. Applying this equation to the appropriate predictor data from the three studies yielded valid difficulty measures for 750 jobs within the three career ladders tested.

Melching, W. H., and Borcher, S. D. *Procedures for Constructing and Using Task Inventories.* Columbus: Center for Vocational and Technical Education, Ohio State University, 1973. This manual is designed to teach procedures for constructing task inventories and for analyzing occupational performance. Methods, procedures, and forms are provided for using the USAF job inventory concept to acquire useful information concerning occupational performance.

Morsh, J. E., Madden, J. M., and Christal, R. E. *Job Analysis in the United States Air Force.* No. WADD-TR-61-113. Lackland Air Force Base, Tex.: Personnel Laboratory, Wright Air Development Division, 1961. The USAF's revised method of job analysis, including the research and development that led to its present form, is described. The method centers on the use of the task inventory, while also including many of the more desirable features of traditional methods. The uses of job analysis data, statistical treatment, and special problems for future research are discussed.

Nelson, E. C., Jacobs, A. R., and Breer, P. E. "Study of the Validity of Task Inventory Method of Job Analysis." *Medical Care,* 1975, *13,* 104–113. Trained observers studied thirteen primary care physicians practicing in New England for a one-week period. A task inventory and an observer checklist, both containing the same set of task statements, were used to gather data to evaluate the task inventory method of job analysis. The degree of correlation between the data supplied by the observers and the physicians was insufficient to conclude that reporting by one group could substitute for reporting by the other. Serious questions as to the validity of the task inventory method were raised.

Pass, J. J., and Robertson, D. W. *Methods to Evaluate Scales and Sample Size for Stable Task Inventory Information.* No. NPRDC-TR-80-28. San Diego: Navy Personnel Research and Development

Center, 1980. Methods were developed to determine (1) the stability and redundancy of responses to two job scales — the continuous Relative Time Spent Scale and the dichotomous Task-Performed Scale; (2) the stability of "job types" (that is, clusters of job incumbents) derived from scale responses; and (3) the change in stability when sample size is reduced. Results indicated that the Task-Performed Scale yields stable, meaningful task information (that is, percentages of personnel who perform tasks) but that no practical gain in information is achieved from the Relative Time Spent Scale. A better way to collect time spent data is proposed. Findings also demonstrate that highly stable scale data and cluster solutions are obtainable from samples substantially smaller than those presently obtained.

Schroeder, P. E. (Ed.). *Proceedings of a Symposium on Task Analyses/ Task Inventories.* Columbus: Center for Vocational Education, Ohio State University, 1975. To promote interchange of information about task analysis and task inventories, a national symposium was sponsored by the Task Inventory Exchange (TIE) project at the Center for Vocational Education. Representatives of industrial, military, business, governmental, and educational organizations attended and shared their experiences with job and task analysis.

Siegel, A. I., Bartter, W. D., and Kopstein, F. F. *Job Analysis for Maintenance Mechanics in Nuclear Power Plants.* Wayne, Pa.: Applied Psychological Services, 1981. A job inventory was administered to maintenance mechanics working in nuclear power plants to obtain information about the safety implications of improper task performance. Tasks with high-risk implications were isolated, and recommendations were made for performance standards and regulations, quality control and assurance programs, and periodic proficiency testing for those tasks.

Stacy, W. J., and Hazel, J. T. *A Method of Determining Desirable Task Experiences for First-Line Supervisors.* No. AFHRL-TR-75-23. Brooks Air Force Base, Tex.: Air Force Human Resources Laboratory, 1975. Accounting and finance supervisors rated journeyman-level tasks on the importance of a supervisor knowing how to perform those tasks to be a satisfactory supervisor. Job analyses indicated that many supervisors had limited career experience in the desirable journeyman-level tasks and that the present accounting and finance work management unit may be too broad for the required work activities. Interviews with accounting and finance personnel supported the findings of this study with regard to the problem of supervisory work experience, and separation of the accounting and disbursement career ladders through the seven-skill level appears advisable.

Stone, C. H. *Evaluation of the Marine Corps Task Analysis Program.* No. TR-16, Los Angeles: California State University, 1976. The basic objective of this research project was to determine the effectiveness of the U.S. Marine Corps Task Analysis (TA) Program. Overall, the program was found to be highly effective in improving utilization of the Marine Corps human resources.

Swann, J. H. *Interpretation and Training Uses of Computer Printout Data of Naval Occupational Task Analysis Program (NOTAP).* No. WTR-73-34. Washington, D.C.: Naval Personnel Research and Development Laboratory, 1973. NOTAP computer printouts are interpreted in terms of their use in the design and development of Navy training programs, courses, and curricula. The study shows how NOTAP data may be used most effectively in the design and development of training programs. Examples of a training program design and a format for a curriculum based on job and task analysis are presented along with some recommendations.

Terry, D. R., and Evans, R. N. *Methodological Study for Determining the Task Content of Dental Auxiliary Education Programs.* No. HRP 000-4628. Bethesda, Md.: Bureau of Health Manpower Education, National Institutes of Health, 1973. The purpose of this study was to develop a method for collecting data on dental tasks taught and the responsibility levels to which they are taught in programs for dental auxiliary personnel, that is, dental assistant, dental hygienist, and dental laboratory technician; to evaluate the method for its potential usefulness in studying dental auxiliary education nationwide; and to determine differences among educational institutions and their educators that may account for the varying numbers and kinds of tasks taught. A dental task inventory was developed and completed by 107 faculty and 113 preceptors at nineteen accredited dental auxiliary education programs. The inventory was sufficiently sensitive to identify gross and subtle differences in the task content of auxiliary education progress.

Trattner, M. H. "Task Analysis in the Design of Three Concurrent Validity Studies of the Professional and Administrative Career Examination." *Personnel Psychology,* 1979, *32,* 109–119. Task inventory data were used to develop supervisory rating forms, job information tests, and work samples that served as criteria in three criterion-related validity studies.

References

Aldag, R. J., and Brief, A. P. *Task Design and Employee Motivation.* Glenview, Ill.: Scott, Foresman, 1979.

American Telephone and Telegraph Company. *Survey of Business Service Center Jobs: Technical Supplement.* Basking Ridge, N.J.: American Telephone and Telegraph Company, 1980.

Cascio, W. F. *Applied Psychology in Personnel Management.* Reston, Va.: Reston Publishing, 1978.

Cornelius, E. T. III, and Lyness, K. S. "A Comparison of Holistic and Decomposed Judgment Strategies in Job Analyses by Job Incumbents." *Journal of Applied Psychology, 65* (2), 1980, 155–163.

Drauden, G. M., and Peterson, N. G. *A Domain-Sampling Approach to Job Analysis.* St. Paul, Minn.: Test Validation Center, 1974.

Driskill, W. E. "Occupational Analysis in the United States Air Force." In P. E. Schroeder (Ed.), *Proceedings of a Symposium on Task Analysis/Task Inventories.* Columbus: Center for Vocational Education, Ohio State University, 1975.

Employment Research and Systems Group. *Analysis of Three Outside Craft Jobs.* Morristown, N.J.: American Telephone and Telegraph Company, 1980.

273

Employment Research and Systems Group. *Analysis of Four Inside Craft Jobs.* Morristown, N. J.: American Telephone and Telegraph Company, 1981.

Gael, S. "Development of Job Task Inventories and Their Use in Job Analysis Research." JSAS *Catalog of Selected Documents in Psychology,* 1977, *7,* 25.

Hackman, J. R., and Oldham, G. R. *Work Redesign.* Reading, Mass.: Addison-Wesley, 1980.

Hemphill, J. K. *Dimensions of Executive Positions.* Columbus: Bureau of Business Research, Ohio State University, 1960.

Human Resources Laboratory. *Bell System Ability Requirement Scales.* New York: American Telephone and Telegraph Company, 1975.

Jones, J. J., Jr., and DeCoths, T. A. "Job Analysis: National Survey Findings." *Personnel Journal,* 1969, *49,* 805–812.

Kershner, A. M. *A Report on Job Analysis.* No. ONR Report ACR-5. Washington, D. C.: Office of Naval Research, Department of the Navy, 1955.

McCormick, E. J. "Job and Task Analysis." In M. D. Dunnette (Ed.), *Handbook of Industrial and Organizational Psychology,* Chicago: Rand McNally, 1976.

McCormick, E. J. *Job Analysis Methods and Applications.* New York: AMACOM, 1979.

Meister, D. *Human Factors: Theory and Practice.* New York: Wiley, 1971.

Moore, B. E. *Occupational Analysis for Human Resource Development: A Review of Utility of the Task Inventory.* No. OCMM-RR-25. Washington, D.C.: Office of Civilian Manpower Management, Navy Department, 1976.

Rupe, J. C. *Research into Basic Methods and Techniques of Air Force Job Analysis – I.* No. TR-52-16. Chenute Air Force Base, Ill.: Human Resources Research Center, 1952.

Rupe, J. C. *Research into Basic Methods and Techniques of Air Force Job Analysis – IV.* No. AFPTRC-TN-56-51. Lackland Air Force Base, Tex.: Air Force Personnel and Training Research Center, 1956.

Rupe, J. C., and Westen, R. J. *Research into Basic Methods and Techniques of Air Force Job Analysis – II.* No. AFPTRC-TN-555-51. Lackland Air Force Base, Tex.: Air Force Personnel and Training Research Center, 1955a.

Rupe, J. C., and Westen, R. J. *Research into Basic Methods and Techniques of Air Force Job Analysis — III.* No. AFPTRC-TN-55-53. Lackland Air Force Base, Tex.: Air Force Personnel and Training Research Center, 1955b.

U.S. Air Force Occupational Measurement Center. *Ground Radio Operator Career Ladder AFSC 293X3.* No. AFPT90-293-415. Randolph Air Force Base, Tex.: U.S. Air Force Occupational Measurement Center, 1981a.

U.S. Air Force Occupational Measurement Center. *Reprographics Career Ladder AFSC 703X0.* No. AFPT90-703-444. Randolph Air Force Base, Tex.: U.S. Air Force Occupational Measurement Center, 1981b.

U.S. Department of Labor. *Dictionary of Occupational Titles.* (4th ed.) Washington, D.C.: U.S. Government Printing Office, 1977.

Index

A

Action verbs: list of, 60; in task statements, 55-60
Adams, J. D., xii
Adde, E. N., 256
Address, in computer program, 176, 180-181
Aldag, R. J., 153, 273
Allen's pioneering work, 20
Alley, W. E., 32-33, 262
American Telephone and Telegraph Company (AT&T): Business Service Centers (BSCs) of, 26, 31, 128-132, 273; computer program of, 173-245; job inventory approach of, x, xii-xiii, 12, 13, 22; license agreement by, 16, 174; Residence Service Centers (RSCs) of, 31
Ammerman, H. L., 24, 256, 264-265
Applied Psychological Services, xiii
Archer, W. B., 256-257

B

Bartter, W. D., 32, 269
Beach, Paolucci, and Milano's equipment-oriented task inventory, 21
Bell System: job analysis approach and, xii, xiii, 13, 28-29; standard definitions by, 184
Borcher, S. D., 9, 268
Borman, W. C., 262-263
Breer, P. E., 268
Brief, A. P., 153, 273

C

Campbell, R. J., xiii
Carpenter, J. B., 27, 257-258
Carr, M. J., 258-259
Cascio, W. F., 145, 273
Center for Vocational Education, 259; Task Inventory System (TIS) of, 22
Christal, R. E., 20, 25-26, 27, 257-258, 259, 265-266, 267-268
Clary, J. N., 259-260

119–121; response directions for, 97–99, 105–106; returning, 120–121; and sample size, 115–119; and shortcut procedures, 159–160, 164, 170; survey sites for, 119; task attribute questions for, 94–97; as technique, 16; tracking progress of, 121
QYRS: defined, 177; procedure of, 242–243

R

Rating scale: range of, 96–97; in shortcut procedures, 160, 166–167, 170; task-oriented, 134–136
Reliability, and job inventories, 23–26
Reports, in computer program, 177, 228–237
Resources, for job inventories, 38–41
Response code text, in computer program, 176, 210–221
Response directions, for questionnaires, 97–99, 105–106
Response grouping, in computer program, 176, 206–209
Results: computer reports of, 123–132; conclusions on, 136–137; decision criteria for, 133; direct uses for, 133–137; follow-up uses for, 138–156; for future analysis, 136; interpretation and use of, 122–156; samples of computer reports of, 128–132; in shortcut procedure, 161; for standards compared with practices, 135–136; for task-oriented rating (TOR), 134–136; for training requirements, 133–134
Retrieval of data, in computer program, 177, 244–245
Robertson, D. W., 27–28, 30–31, 115, 268–269
Rupe, J. C., 20, 274–275

S

Sample size: in each organization, 118; and factors to be studied, 116–118; and field coordinators, 114; in job inventories, 46; and questionnaires, 115–119

Schroeder, P. E., 269
Shigekawa, L., 266
Shortcut procedures: analysis of, 157–171; applicability of, 157; compared with full-scale WPSS, 159–161; conference process in, 167–171; data analysis in, 160, 165–167, 170–171; follow-up procedures in, 160–161, 171; job analysis shortcut in, 161–165; materials and forms in, 164–165; for planning, 159; for questionnaires, 159–160, 164, 170; rating scales in, 160, 166–167, 170; results in, 161; and task lists, 159, 162, 164; for time economies, 42–43
Sidley, J. D. H., xiii
Siegel, A. I., 32, 269
Snyder, M. T., xii
Stackfleth, E. D., xii
Stacy, W. J., 269–270
Standard deviation, in statistical summary reports, 125
Standard items, in computer program, 176, 184–187
Statistical summary reports: described, 123; indices in, 124–127; samples of, 129, 130
Stone, C. H., 260–261, 263, 270
Subject-matter experts (SMEs): conference process for, 167–171; for follow-up procedures, 143–146, 148, 150, 151, 152; and shortcut procedures, 157–171; training and preparation of, 162–164
Subsamples, in computer program, 176, 222–227
Subtask, task distinct from, 62
Survey data base, in computer program, 176, 202–205
Swann, J. H., 270

T

Tape identification, in computer program, 177, 240–241
Task, concept of, 8–9, 54, 62
Task attribute questions: averaging for, 165–166; for questionnaires, 94–97; rating scale for, 96–97; selection guide for, 95